BOOKS BY KARL E. MEYER

THE
PLUNDERED
PAST

KARL E. MEYER

THE
PLUNDERED
PAST

ATHENEUM

New York

1973

The poem "The Collector" by Ogden Nash, from The Old Dog Barks Backward is reprinted by permission of Little, Brown and Company. Copyright © 1972 by Frances Nash as the Executrix of the Estate of Ogden Nash. The poem "Ode to a Grecian Urn" by Felicia Lamport, which appeared in the New York Times Magazine, is reprinted by permission.

Portions of this book appeared originally in The New Yorker in somewhat different form.

For
TIBEL
and the memory of
DAN

ACKNOWLEDGMENTS

My first debt is to Simon Michael Bessie of Atheneum, and to William Shawn of *The New Yorker*, both of whom at an early stage in an extended project gave moral and financial support; I am grateful also to Gillon Aitken of Hamish Hamilton. I benefited from the counsel of my agent, Julian S. Bach. William D. Rogers of Arnold & Porter was instrumental in helping obtain for me a grant from the Center for Inter-American Relations, which enabled me to visit Guatemala. A score of people helped arrange appointments, delved in archives, and mailed the precious newspaper clippings. I am especially obliged to Bonnie Bonham Flam, in Paris; Gillian Darley, in London; Alice Marie Galassi, in Rome; Sermin Emre, in Ankara; Maria Bearns, in Mexico City; James McC. Truitt, in San Miguel de Allende; Robert C. Dorion, in Guatemala City; Judith Martin, in Washington, D.C.; Melinda Custer and Robert Meyers, in Los Angeles. In New York, I was assisted by Alexandra Anderson and Georgina d'Angelo. Gabriella and Andrew Hale gave special help in Rome, as did Sidney Alexander in Florence. Florence Norton and Bonnie Shalin aided in the thankless chore of typing, and much of my correspondence was cheerfully transcribed

vii

by Jean Reid. Finally, the photographs were gathered with the inestimable assistance of Laurie Winfrey.

Several hundred persons contributed information to this book. In the partial list that follows, I have omitted the names of thirty-seven dealers in nine countries in order to protect the identity of informants. It goes without saying that no one but the author is responsible for views expressed in these pages.

Anderson, Adrian D., Iowa City, Iowa
Andrews, Mrs. E. Willys, Mérida
Asher, Frederick K., Minneapolis
Ayala, Armando, Mexico City

Bareis, Charles J., Urbana, Illinois
Bass, George, Philadelphia
Bastian, Tyler, Baltimore
Bator, Paul, Cambridge, Massachusetts
Berman, Eugene (dec.), Rome
Bernal, Ignacio, Mexico City
Bernoulli, Christophe, Basel
Bonfil Batalla, Guillermo, Mexico City
von Bothmer, Dietrich, New York
Brantley, Robin
Brenner, Edgar H., Washington
Bronson, Bennet, Chicago
Bruhns, Karen Olsen, San Jose, California
Burnham, Sophy, New York
Butler, B. Robert, Pocatello, Idaho

Cadorin, Paulo, Basel
Canaday, John, New York
Canfield, Gabriella, New York
Carettoni, Tullia, Rome
Cartwright, Aubrey (dec.), Paris
Chagall-Meyer, Ida, Basel
Chapman, Carl H., Columbia, Missouri
Charbonnier, Georges, Paris
Coe, Michael D., New Haven
Coggins, Clemency, Cambridge, Massachusetts
Cole, David L., Eugene, Oregon

Colombo, Furio, Rome
Colombo, Alice, Rome
Connor, Patricia, London
Cooney, John D., Cleveland
Corbett, John, Washington
Coughlin, Frances, Lima, Peru
Cummer, W. Willson, Ankara

Davis, Hester A., Fayetteville, Arkansas
DeJarnette, David L., Moundville, Alabama
Dyson, Robert, Philadelphia

Easby, Dudley T. (dec.), New York
Ekholm, Gordon, New York
Eckman, Fern Marja, New York
Elon, Amos, Jerusalem
Elon, Beth, Jerusalem
Erim, Kenan T., New York
Esterow, Milton, New York
Evans, Clifford, Washington

Feldman, Mark, Washington
Fıratlı, Nizeh, Istanbul
Ford, Richard I., Ann Arbor, Michigan
Franco, José Luis, Mexico City
Freeman, Joan E., Madison, Wisconsin
French, David, Ankara
Friendly, Alfred, London
Frison, George C., Laramie, Wyoming
Funk, Robert E., Albany, New York

Gage, Nicholas, New York
de García Prendes, Laura, Guatemala City
Gendel, Milton, Rome
González, Raul, Panama
Graham, Ian, Cambridge, Massachusetts
Gray, James A., New York
Griffin, Gillett, Princeton
Griffin, James B., Ann Arbor, Michigan
Guthe, Alfred K., Knoxville, Tennessee
Guzmán de la Cruz, Amilcar, Tikal, Guatemala

Haag, William G., Baton Rouge, Louisiana
von Hagen, Victor Wolfgang, Rome
Hairs, Joya, Guatemala City
Hamblin, Dora Jane, Rome
Hanfmann, George, Cambridge, Massachusetts
Hannifin, Jerry, Washington
Haviland, William A., Burlington, Vermont
Hayes, Charles F., Rochester, New York
Heath, Dwight B., Providence, Rhode Island
Heyden, Doris, Mexico City
Hellmuth, Nicholas, St. Louis, Missouri
Herrera, Oscar, San José, Costa Rica
Hess, John, New York
Hess, Thomas B., New York
Holloway, R. Ross, Providence, Rhode Island
Hoving, Thomas P. F., New York
Hughes, Robert, New York
Hurst, Peter, Ballston Lake, New York

de Jesus, Prentiss S., Ankara
Johnson, Elden, Minneapolis
Johnson, Harmer, New York
Johnston, Roger D., New York
Jones, Julie, New York
Jordan, Douglas F., Storrs, Connecticut

Katz, Karl, New York
Kellar, James H., Bloomington, Indiana
King, Tom, Riverside, California

Ladejinsky, Wolf, New Delhi
Lehman, Edward J., Washington
Lerici, Carlo Maurilio, Rome
Lewin, Seymour Z., New York
Lilyquist, Christine, New York
Linares, Olga, Panama
Love, Iris C., New York
Luján Muñoz, Luis, Guatemala City

MacKendrick, Paul, Madison, Wisconsin
McFadden, Elizabeth, New York

Acknowledgments

McGimsey, Charles R., Fayetteville, Arkansas

Mambor, Felice, Rome
Mata Amada, Guillermo, Guatemala City
Malone, James M., Austin, Texas
Marshall, Richard A., State College, Mississippi
Matson, Frederick R., University Park, Pennsylvania
Meggers, Betty, Washington
Mellaart, James, London
Mellink, Machteld, Bryn Mawr, Pennsylvania
Melton, Jim, Houston
Melville, Richard A., New York
Meyer, Susan E., New York
Millon, René, Rochester, New York
Morales Fernández, Rafael, Guatemala City
Muscarella, Oscar, New York

Nash, David, New York
Naumann, Rudolf, Istanbul
Newton, Douglas, New York
Noble, Joseph V., New York
Nottebohm, Karl Heinz, Guatemala City

Oliver, Andrew, New York
Owen, David, Philadelphia

Parsons, Sherman, New York
Pearson, Kenneth, London
Peckham, Stewart L., Santa Fe, New Mexico
Pomerance, Leon, Great Neck, New York
Pritchard, James, Philadelphia
Proskouriakoff, Tatiana, Cambridge, Massachusetts
Puleston, Dennis E., Minneapolis

Rainey, Froelich, Philadelphia
Rathbone, Perry T., Boston
Rice, Harvey S., Pullman, Washington
Robbins, Maurice, Boston
Robertson, Merle Greene, San José, California
Ross, John, Rome
Rossides, Eugene T., Washington
Rutsch, Edward S., Madison, New Jersey

Sáenz, Josué, Mexico City
Sáenz de Tejada, Guillermo, Guatemala City
Sarceño, Edgar, Guatemala City
Schimmel, Norbert, New York
Schmidt, Peter J., Puebla, Mexico
Shearman, John, London
Shook, Edwin, Antigua, Guatemala
Sigstad, John S., Vermillion, South Dakota
Siviero, Rodolfo, Florence
Solheim, Wilhelm G., Hawaii
Stavenhagen, Kurt, Mexico City
Sterling, Claire, Rome
Sterling, Thomas, Rome
Sullivan, Lynn, Seattle

Temizer, Raci, Ankara
Thomas, Ronald A., Dover, Delaware
Thompson, Homer, Athens
Thompson, Margaret, New York
Torres de Arauz, Reina, Panama
Torrey, Margery, New York

de Varine-Bohan, Hugues, Paris
Vermeule, Cornelius, Boston

Walter, Richard, London
Wauchope, Robert, New Orleans
West, Frederick Hadleigh, Anchorage, Alaska
Williams, Stephen, Cambridge, Massachusetts
Witty, Thomas A., Topeka, Kansas
von Wuthenau, Alexander, Mexico City
Wycoff, Don G., Norman, Oklahoma

Young, Rodney, Philadelphia

Zahn, Marilyn, Worcester, Massachusetts
Zelle, Ann, Washington

INTRODUCTION

Speaking at a meeting of the College Art Association in Chicago in 1971, the Stanford art historian Albert Elsen said that, in his opinion, "there is no more explosive issue before the art world than that of the illegal international traffic in works of art." Since then, there have been scores of articles and speeches about the illicit trade, and about the related matter of museum acquisition policies. But there is no book on the subject. This, to my knowledge, is the first of its kind—an attempt at a full and documented report on one of the world's sadder problems, the destruction and theft of the remains of the human past.

Because it is the first book, the author has been aware of a special obligation. Nothing has been more lacking than a detailed description of the scope and nature of the illicit trade. There are reasons for this. The art market is a closed world whose denizens seek to keep important information strictly within it. Prices, the names of dealers and customers, the routes of supply—all these matters tend to be cloaked in the chiaroscuro language of the trade. Such secrecy was perhaps justified when the art market was a cozy club consisting of a few thousand people and when its profits were minuscule by comparison with other markets. This is no longer so. Art is big business, and the international market has an annual turnover of at least one billion dollars. Yet though works of art are increasingly regarded as a speculative commodity, there is no equivalent in the United States, where most of the money is spent, to a Securities and Exchange Commission to enforce fair dealing and to protect the public interest.

Is there a public interest in what happens to works of art? The premise of this book is that there clearly is. A collector or museum may "own" a Rembrandt, but in a larger sense the painting belongs to the world. Since the collective judgment of mankind gives any work its value, the collective conscience of mankind should rightly be concerned with its preservation. Those who profit from the rising prices of art cannot justifiably complain about public concern, since it is the public that gives their property its value—a value often realized when bequests or gifts are made to museums. A comparison may be useful. A real estate speculator can earn large profits by wisely buying lots in a developing commercial district, but the value of what he owns derives from community enterprise, and the community has an unchallenged right to impose limits—such as building codes or zoning laws—on how the owner uses his property. An extension of the same principle should apply to works of art.

This is particularly relevant in the special case of antiquities buried in archaeological sites. Though an American may "own" an Indian mound or an Italian may "own" an Etruscan tomb, there is a general interest in what either does with his property. (In Italy this interest is recognized if not enforced by law; in the case of most Indian sites in the United States, it is neither recognized nor enforced.) Every archaeological site is like a time capsule, and each contains in varying degrees unique evidence about our past. When such a time capsule is destroyed, either by a looter or a bulldozer, the loss is total. One cannot grow another Indian mound. And yet, the tempo of destruction is presently so great that by the end of the century most remaining important archaeological sites may well be plundered or paved over. We face a future in which there may be no past beyond that which is already known and excavated. Or equally sad, what is left may be so ruinously mutilated as to afford only a forlorn fragment of a vanished legacy.

To return to the writer's direct concern, since this book should have a reference value I have included in it an extensive appendix with primary information, much of it never published before. The cost in research ran into thousands of dollars. I have also appended the first comprehensive bibliography on the subject, drawn mainly from files I have accumulated. Aside from the valuable library of the International Council of Museums in Paris, there are no archives on the subject accessible to the public. This in itself is a measure of the suddenness with which the problem has arisen. We are in about the same stage in the preservation campaign as that reached in the kindred movement to safeguard the environment when its adherents were known as "conservationists" and too often dismissed as high-minded zealots. We are at Consciousness Zero.

Research was one expense; travel was another. In the course of three years, I have visited Latin America four times and Europe three times, and have traveled extensively within the United States to attend professional meetings and to interview everyone remotely involved in the problem. Their names are listed in the acknowledgments. This book could not have been written without the selfless assistance of hundreds of people, some of whom, I fear, will disagree profoundly with what I have to say. But I found that even those who benefit from the destruction of the past—either as dealers or buyers—were troubled by the implications of what was happening. Otherwise they would not have talked so freely to me.

Here I must discuss the most difficult ethical problem I have yet faced as a journalist. How much should I disclose? A word first about my own involvement. From 1956 to 1971, I was a member of the staff of the Washington *Post*, and one of the subjects I wrote about was Latin American politics. In 1959 my newspaper generously made possible an extended trip through Latin America, and I fortuitously became interested in archaeology when I saw Machu Picchu in Peru, Tikal in Guatemala, and Teotihuacán in Mexico. On my return, I pursued my curiosity and met scholars in the pre-Columbian field. During the next few years I arranged holiday trips to France, Greece, Italy, and the Middle East, where I visited major sites. These travels led to a book, *The Pleasures of Archaeology*, published in 1970, which gave me the status of a tolerated outsider in a field otherwise chary of journalists. In the process, I became aware of the international illicit traffic in art.

In 1971, I resigned from the Washington *Post* with many misgivings because I was devoted to the paper and esteemed my colleagues on it. But I wanted to write a book about the destruction of the past and knew how much time and effort the project would take. With the help of publishers' advances, and with the assistance of a modest grant—the only one I received—from the Center for Inter-American Relations, I was able to undertake my travels. I went to Guatemala with the help of the Center and saw firsthand the devastation of Maya sites. This trip resulted in a report, *The Maya Crisis*, which in turn, gratifyingly, led to a grant of $20,000 by the Tinker Foundation of New York to a Maya Rescue Fund. The money is being used in Guatemala to protect or move imperiled Maya monuments.

During my inquiries, to return to the ethical problem, I found that I had, figuratively, the lives of many people in my hands. As a journalist I had had a similar experience in Eastern Europe where I benefited from the confidence of many informants who would face jail or worse if their identity was disclosed. But in that case the dilemma was easy to resolve, and there was ample precedent to guide me. The art market is different. Though in the great majority of cases I told those whom I saw that I was writing about the illicit trade, I was nevertheless favored with indiscreet information. Why my informants spoke so freely is a question about which I thought a good deal. One reason was probably simple vanity, a wish to prove access to inside information. But beyond that there was also, I felt, a prudent calculation—an awareness that I would learn a good deal anyway and that selective disclosure might put me in my informant's debt and incline me to protect his identity. It is the kind of calculation a shrewd dealer would make. But what was I to do about it?

In the event, I compromised. Where I have learned privileged information from vulnerable sources, I have masked the identity of these sources, using, in order to avoid guessing games, the Greek alphabet as an arbitrary code. An unsatisfactory solution no doubt, but there it is. I have of course supplied my publishers and their lawyers with all the names I have suppressed, along with tape recordings of some important interviews. The purpose of this book is to illuminate a problem and not to punish anyone. Violations of the law are properly the responsibility of the police, and the author is not an informer.

Still, the reader may well ask how I came upon some of the more bizarre tales in the pages that follow. The secret is a simple one, known to any political reporter—the half-informed bluff. In the course of my inquiry, I often felt like an archaeologist unearthing the fragment of a pot, a sherd big enough to give an idea of the original design. I would come upon the fragment not in a burial tomb but in a conversation, and would grasp it in my mind, referring to it with misleading knowingness in later interviews, as if I had the whole pot. More often than not, I would be rewarded with further pieces of the same vessel. With this technique, I was able to reconstruct some of the choicer tales about the plunder of the past.

The subject is inherently sensational. I have tried to describe it without superfluous varnish. But I have also tried to retain the human element—the quirks of behavior and the absurdities of the marketplace—while avoiding the easy righteousness so at variance with the spirit of art. Whether I have succeeded the reader must judge.

June, 1973

Weston, Connecticut

AUTHOR'S NOTE: *The Metropolitan Museum released its long-promised* Report on Art Transactions, 1971–1973 *in late June, 1973, when this book was in proof. Regarding the controversial secret sales of major works, the report said in effect that the museum had done nothing wrong but would not do it again. The Metropolitan seemed to promise that all major "deaccessioned" works will be sold only at public auction and only after ample advance notice. Concerning the Euphronios vase, the museum said that on the basis of its own investigation it was certain that the krater had not been smuggled from Italy. But Douglas Dillon, President of the Metropolitan trustees, admitted at a news conference that Dikran A. Sarrafian, the vase's supposed original owner, had never been questioned by anyone at any time from the museum. The evidence on which the museum based its judgment, Mr. Dillon said, was obtained through the dealer, Robert E. Hecht, Jr. "We could be wrong," Dillon said. "If we were wrong, this is one of the most fantastic swindles that has ever been perpetrated. . . ." In Italy, meanwhile, authorities issued a warrant for the arrest of Mr. Hecht on charges of exporting the vase illegally. When he was contacted by a reporter in Switzerland, Mr. Hecht said he had no intention of returning to Italy to face trial.*

CONTENTS

Contents

CHAPTER THREE: SEE ITALY QUICKLY

CHAPTER FOUR: THE SHERD TRADE

CHAPTER FIVE: WHOSE PAST?

Contents

xxi

ILLUSTRATIONS

In the Name of Art
Courtesy of Joya Hairs

Rescue Campaign
Courtesy of Joya Hairs

Smuggled Goods
Courtesy of Joya Hairs

The Nay-Sayer: Joseph V. Noble

The Winged Temple
Courtesy of Melville Bearns

The Washington Treasure

The Boston Treasure
Copyright by Philippe Halsman

The New York Treasure

Tombaroli at Work
Courtesy of Velio Cioni

Unprotected Art
Courtesy of UPI

A Mock Attack
Courtesy of UPI

Decline and Fall
Courtesy of UPI

An Olmec Treasure

Shopper's Portfolio: I

Shopper's Portfolio: II

Shopper's Portfolio: III

In the Beginning
Courtesy of Laurie Winfrey

The Collectors: I. Norton Simon
Copyright John Bryson, *Fortune*, 1972

A Stolen Shiva
Courtesy of the New York *Post*

THE PLUNDERED PAST

CHAPTER ONE

AFTER CORTÉS

*But I came to get gold, not to till
the soil, like a peasant.*
HERNAN CORTÉS, QUOTED
BY PRESCOTT

1. The Profits of Art

The art market is not the biggest business in the world, but in the past two decades its growth has outpaced that of almost every other field for risk capital. Even those in the art market are impressed, puzzled, and sometimes a bit worried. When there is a high-money market, art prices go up; when there are recessions, political upheavals, or fiscal crises, art prices go up; and when there is a boom, art prices soar like a balloon exuberantly out of control. A bit of canvas with a few dollars' worth of paint—providing that the brush was wielded by a Cézanne or a Renoir—can bring greater capital gains than glamour stocks or a corner lot in Wall Street.

Where it will end is impossible to predict, but one can be

3

fairly precise about its beginnings. The postwar art boom started with an auction, in Paris, of the Gabriel Cognacq collection in 1952, at which record new price levels were set by Impressionist and post-Impressionist paintings—Cézanne's *Pommes et Biscuits* was knocked down for the equivalent of $94,280, impelling an American present to remark that that was "a lot of money for fourteen apples." In the next few years, more records were broken in other public sales, notably those of the Weinberg and Goldschmidt collections in London and that of the Lurcy collection in New York, landmark auctions to which those in the trade refer with awe and nostalgia. But the biggest breakthrough was the sale, in 1961, at Parke-Bernet, of Rembrandt's *Aristotle Contemplating the Bust of Homer*. The gallery's chief auctioneer, Louis Marion, had somewhat nervously predicted that *Aristotle* would fetch at least $1 million; when his ivory hammer finally closed the sale, the price was a headline sensation, $2.3 million, the most ever paid at public auction for any work of art.

Since that purchase, by the Metropolitan Museum of Art, the record figure has been more than doubled—also by the Metropolitan, with the purchase of a Velázquez in 1970. The precise increase in overall values is difficult to measure, since most sales are private; but auctions are public and a recent index of fine arts sales compiled by Sotheby's and the London *Times* shows that prices have been multiplied by ten or eleven in twenty years, with values in the more fashionable fields increasing thirty or forty times. By comparison, the average price for industrial stocks in the same period has only been multiplied by five. As early as 1955, *Fortune* magazine was able to advise its executive readership that art "can be the most lucrative investment in the world."*

That Cézanne and Rembrandt should perform more profitably

---

* Geraldine Keen, the statistician who compiled the *Times*-Sotheby index, gives these price multiplications for special fields between 1951 and 1969:

than General Motors may seem, on the face of it, an occasion for civilized celebration. Whatever the motives of those who bid up prices for pictures, they are bearing witness to the power of art, and by generating curiosity, and even serious interest, the sales doubtless augment public support for the arts. Clearly, the boom market has been good for dealers, good for auction houses, good for collectors and some museums, and good for the more successful living artists. Yet even those in the trade are troubled by the confusion of values implicit in rating some works as "gilt-edge," others as "blue-chip," and the rest as "growth" or "speculative issues" (to borrow the terminology of the *Fortune* article). Not long ago Geoffrey Agnew, chairman of the Society of London Art Dealers, protested publication in the London *Times* of the auction price index, saying that in his view "works of art should be bought primarily for their aesthetic, rather than investment values." The ensuing hilarity in the Letters column of *The Times* suggested that Mr. Agnew's customers were not so high-minded.

Yet aside from the confusion of values, the bull market in art poses more practical problems. More than any other single element, the increase in art prices has been responsible for the

Modern pictures	29
Old Master drawings	22
Impressionists	18
English pictures	10
Old Masters	7
Chinese ceramics	24½
Antiquarian books	13
English glass	9
English silver	8½
French furniture	5
English porcelain	4
Old Master prints	37

The mathematical precision of these figures has been justifiably questioned since every work of art is unique. But the index surely gives a good rough impression of rising price levels, and is used as a yardstick by those who invest in art. See Keen, 1971. (All sources are fully cited in the Bibliography.)

wholesale theft, mutilation, and destruction of art everywhere in the world, and it is this problem that I propose to examine in some detail.

First and most visibly, there is the matter of art thefts. Within the past decade, the stealing of art has been transformed from an amusing nuisance into an international plague. Every day, an important work of art is stolen somewhere, and though some of the thefts are committed by cranks or the simpleminded, most are not. In some instances, the thieves extort ransom for the stolen art, which then turns up in an abandoned car or a baggage locker. More often the missing works are sold. Paintings by lesser-known masters can be sold to unsuspecting dealers or collectors; sometimes the works are doctored by restorers so that the risk of discovery is minimal. In other cases, art is stowed in Swiss banks while the owners wait for statutes of limitation on the sale of stolen goods to expire (in Italy it is a ten-year wait).

The theft of even major works is so widespread that two lists of "most wanted" art circulated by the International Criminal Police Organization, or Interpol, comprise two dozen works that would form the nucleus of a first-rate small museum, as these examples suggest:

Masaccio, *Virgin and Child*, stolen in 1971 from the Palazzo Vecchio in Florence.

Memling, *Portrait of a Gentleman*, stolen at the same time from the same place.

Toulouse-Lautrec, *Marcelle*, stolen in 1968 in Kyoto, Japan, and owned by a museum in Albi, France.

Caravaggio, *Nativity*, stolen in 1969 from a church in Palermo.

Correggio, *The Holy Family*, stolen in 1970 from a museum in Pavia, Italy.

6

Rembrandt, *The Flight into Egypt*, stolen in 1971 from a museum in Tours, France.

Gainsborough, *Portrait of Sir Robert Fletcher*, stolen in 1972 from the Montreal Museum of Fine Arts.

Hals, *Portrait of a Young Woman*, stolen in 1972 from a museum in Düsseldorf.

What is interesting is that nearly all twenty-four works, many of which have a value of at least $1 million, were stolen since 1965 and are only a selection from an aggregate of more than one thousand works stolen within the past decade and still in the Interpol "wanted" files. By conservative estimate, $100 million worth of stolen art is still at large, and by general agreement the rate of discovery has been dismal.*

In the case of stolen paintings, there is a consolation—albeit a thin one. Very few of them are destroyed; they may vanish for years into clandestine vaults but they do survive, and so— in the most important cases at least—do photographic reproductions of them. The illicit looting of archaeological sites gets less publicity, but its consequences are more serious because they include the total loss of unrecorded information. The stimulus of the art market has made ancient sites the targets for unexampled assault by looters armed with shovels, bulldozers, and even dynamite. Objects taken from a site are often mutilated and, in any case, their context is obliterated; the looted piece becomes an orphan without a pedigree, its very legitimacy open to question.

In the looting of ancient temples and ceremonial centers, pillagers are spared the trouble of digging, and they simply wrench statuary, friezes, and tablets from their setting; this is happening wherever there are unprotected sites, from the Maya areas of Latin America to the Khmer ruins of Cambodia. An especially sad instance was the devastation of Bangla Desh,

* A table of major thefts since 1911 is included in Appendix A.

7

during that country's war for independence in 1971. After the fighting, a survey was carried out by Enamul Haque, the director of the Dacca Museum. To his surprise, he found that military action accounted for very little of the destruction of cultural properties; most of the damage was the result of deliberate plunder.

Dr. Haque reported that at least two thousand Hindu temples had been destroyed or substantially damaged, and that some six thousand pieces of sculpture had been removed or destroyed by looters. Much of the art was smuggled abroad and sold. He adds: "The situation was aggravated by the presence of eager-to-collect aid officials from abroad working with international relief agencies. The local thugs were too willing to please them by recklessly looting icons from temples." Thirty-five bronze sculptures were taken from the Archaeological Museum at Mainamati and the entire collection of the Dinajpur Museum was looted. Doubtless a good part of this art will ultimately find its way into Western museums and private collections.

Poverty and desperation are extenuating factors in Bangla Desh, but not in the United States, where pot hunting is a weekend hobby of the more affluent. The rise in price for American Indian art, while it has been good for the collector, has had disastrous consequences for scholarship. One can see the link between the art market and looting by examining the unwanted consequences of a single sale—the auction, in November, 1971, at Parke-Bernet, of the Green Collection of American Indian Art. The sale itself was thoroughly reputable, but as a result of the publicity given new record price levels for Indian art, looting, which was already epidemic, spread with fresh intensity.

Parke-Bernet, long the leading American auction house, was taken over by Sotheby's in 1964, and the merged firm is the single most potent force in the international art market. The floss and elegance of the New York gallery has been preserved

8

since the merger, but the arrival of Sotheby's English officers and experts—the ablest and most competitive in the art world —has given a new air of bustle to Parke-Bernet. The Sotheby's approach is not to wait for trends but to develop them aggressively, stimulating new fields of collector interest, such as antique cars or vintage wines. Thus, ample energy and imagination was applied to the Green Collection of Indian Art, which was the first major auction in the East of American Indian art.

The sale date, to begin with, was timed to coincide with the opening of a major exhibition at the Whitney Museum, "Two Hundred Years of American Indian Art," the first of its scope in New York since 1941. The opening assured additional attention for the auction, which was vigorously promoted in the media. Press releases described the colorful story of Colonel George Green, a splendid eccentric who served as a surgeon in the Civil War and subsequently founded a patent-medicine business and made a fortune selling Green's Dyspepsia Salt, August Flower, Ague Conqueror, and Boschee's German Syrup. A man of whim, he acquired two private railroad cars for his business trips, during one of which he visited Pasadena and found that none of the hotels was adequately fireproof; he thereupon built the fireproof Hotel Green, which stands today. While Colonel Green was investigating medicinal potions, he became interested in Indian art, and bought extensively at low prices. (He later added to his fortune by inventing a can opener small enough to be carried on a key chain, a device later used by millions of American soldiers.) After his death, in 1925, his son and grandchildren added to his collection, increasing it to 2,500 pieces by 1971, when the Green family put more than three hundred pieces up at auction.

Thanks to the growing interest in American Indians, the opening of the Whitney show, and the colorful Colonel's biography, press coverage was lavish. A richly illustrated catalogue, selling for $4, was prepared by Harmer Johnson, the Englishman who is the gallery's expert in primitive art. Mr. Johnson estimated that the sale would bring from $40,000 to $67,000. He underestimated the enthusiasm of the bidders. (One of them, a Wyoming collector, turned up in a cowboy hat, boots, and beaded jacket.) In the event, the sale realized $161,000; one item, a Navajo blanket, that had been sold at Parke-Bernet for $100 in 1963 brought $1,000 in the Green auction. The headlines the next day conveyed the message: "For Indian Artifacts, the Price Trend Is Up" (*The New York Times*) and "Indian Art: Big Money" (*The Post*).

In the month after the sale, Parke-Bernet was engulfed by Indian artifacts as tomahawks, wampum belts, and old blankets came spilling out of attics and closets. Such private enterprise is of small concern to archaeologists. Their worry is that a growing market, like a powerful magnet, draws rare and interesting objects from the soil. An example is Mimbres pottery. This beautiful ware, named for the valley in New Mexico in which it was first found, consists of painted bowls, most of them "killed" when they were buried in tombs, by having a small hole knocked in the bottom. Made a millennium ago, Mimbres pots have "a humor and liveliness unprecedented in Indian art," according to Miguel Covarrubias in his authoritative 1954 study of North American aboriginal art. The pottery constitutes a vivid catalogue of Southwestern zoology— striking depictions of deer, antelope, mountain sheep, buzzards, opossum, turtles, frogs, turkeys, quail, ducks, heron, fish, lizards, horned toads, flying and crawling insects.

One of the scholars interested in Mimbres ware is Stewart L. Peckham, chief archaeologist of the Museum of New Mexico, in Santa Fe. Peckham, who has been conducting a survey of all Indian sites in the state, was distressed to find that almost all major Mimbres sites, even those on federal or state-owned land, had been ravaged by pot hunters. He discovered that Mimbres burials on private land had been attacked with front-end loaders or bulldozers so that the sites looked like "a shell-pocked World War I battlefield." In a letter to me describing the assaults, he wrote:

> You can probably detect that I have more than just a mild contempt for the pot hunter. Although he deserves eternal damnation, he isn't the only one to blame. The affluent art collector should also be roasted in Hell. His demand for new conversation pieces to add to his collection, regardless of price, only stimulates the pot hunter to seek out and pillage major archaeological sites.

A few days after Peckham mailed this letter, the following advertisement appeared in the June 26, 1972, issue of the Deming, New Mexico, *Graphic*:

MIMBRES POTTERY WANTED
Private Collector Will Soon Be in Deming Area Buying Mimbres Pottery of All Types: Story Bowls, Picture Bowls, Geometrics.
Top Prices Paid for Single Items or Whole Collections. Please Contact: Anthony Berlant, P.O. Box 24C84, Los Angeles, Cal. 90024 . . . Also Buying Old Navajo Blankets, Anasazi and Early Historic Pueblo Pottery.

Here it should be noted that Mr. Peckham, like archaeologists elsewhere, is as much concerned with industrial and real estate development as he is with pot hunters. He reports that Indian pueblos have been paved over in the suburban spread at Albuquerque, Santa Fe, Farmington, and Las Cruces; that the building of the Navajo Reservoir on the San Juan River in the early 1960s resulted in the flooding of five hundred archaeological sites; and that other Indian burials have been obliterated by drilling pads built for oil and gas wells, while access roads and pipelines have caused further damage. Variants of the same problem arise everywhere on the American continent, and in the rest of the world. In Tunisia, the site of ancient Carthage may soon be covered by cement, and in Mexico road building has become a serious menace to Maya sites.*

As a result of both deliberate looting and the expansion of civilization, the material remains of the past are being churned up at an unprecedented rate. Sometimes the spoliation is rooted in greed; at other times its source is indifference. Either way, the consequences are the same—the wholesale devastation of the past. For the first time in our history we face the novel prospect of a future without a past. Given the present tempo of destruction, by the end of the century all unexplored major archaeological sites may be irrevocably disfigured or ravaged. We are witnessing the equivalent of the burning of the library at Alexandria by the Romans, the catastrophic bonfire in which much of the wisdom of antiquity was consumed in flames. One can see most of the ingredients of the conflagration in the relentless demolition of pre-Columbian sites, a problem to which we will now turn.

2. The Maya Mask

The pre-Columbian field is a prime example of what might be called a "growth" market in art. Forty years ago, the market scarcely existed, but today it is a flourishing specialty field attractive to thousands of collectors and tended by scores of

* The devastation of Maya sites by developers has been described in detail by Dr. Alberto Ruz Lhuillier, the excavator of Palenque and for twelve years chief of the Office of Pre-Hispanic Monuments in the Yucatán. Dr. Ruz was appalled by the sometimes wanton destruction of Maya pyramids for building materials. In the town of Akil, when he ordered a halt to such depredations, he was accused by the municipal president of "wanting to take the bread out of the mouths of our children." Dr. Ruz has written: "If this event had taken place in a less peaceful state than the Yucatán, where the price of a man's life is less dear, I would probably not have left the place alive." See Ruz, 1968.

dealers. Most of the art sold comes from three areas—Mexico, Central America, and the Andean republics of South America—and nearly all of it has been smuggled from the countries of origin. How the market works and what problems it poses are questions worth considering.

John Wise, a dignified man in his seventies who wears an old-fashioned watch chain across his vest, is the senior dealer in pre-Columbian art in North America, and he has witnessed the transformation in the market. He recalls that in the early 1930s pre-Columbian pieces were known as "specimens," which one could pick up for a few dollars in Latin America. For instance, a Colima dog—a clay figurine from western Mexico—then went for $2 in a Mexican market and cost about $25 in New York; by 1948 such a dog of good quality would bring from $250 to $400 in New York; now the price for a first-class example might be double or triple that figure. When Mr. Wise started out, only a few other dealers handled pre-Columbian art, preeminent among them the late Earl Stendahl in Los Angeles. Now there are about fifty dealers in the field, of whom a dozen sell pieces of outstanding quality. Some are "open" dealers who operate fancy galleries on Madison Avenue or who work (as does Mr. Wise) from a hotel suite in midtown Manhattan. But several of the most important are unknown even to the art public; they have no gallery, they never advertise and sell only to a select clientele.

Why has the market grown? The most obvious reason is that pre-Columbian art has become fashionable, along with the ethnographic art of Africa and Polynesia; it has an aesthetic kinship with contemporary art but with an added touch of appealing mystery. There is a practical reason, too: jet airliners, new roads, and light planes have opened up once inaccessible areas in Latin America, bringing new archaeological riches within reach of the market. Possibly more important is a third reason, the vast influx of new money into the art market and the enormous increase in the number of collectors.

The Times-Sotheby's auction price index offers one suggestive measure because it shows that the steepest rise in the public market has been, unexpectedly, in old master prints, which have multiplied in value thirty-seven times between 1951 and 1969. These prints are one of the few fields of fine arts within reach of the middle-income budget, and in commenting on the price increase, Geraldine Keen, chief compiler of the auction index, remarks: "The educated middle classes have taken up collecting on an unprecedented scale. This must largely be put down to the reverential aspect of the present-day attitude to art [which has] brought into existence a huge new clientele for minor prizes of the art market."

Pre-Columbian works are still among the major minor prizes available to middle-income buyers. For a few hundred dollars one can purchase a handsome Colima figurine or a polychrome Nazca pot, and one can even buy it at Bloomingdale's, which has a pre-Columbian department. A recent advertisement says: "Here is an extensive treasure-trove of over a thousand pieces that graphically records aspects of a long-lost civilization. . . . Here indeed is a haven for the connoisseur and a fascinating 'dig' for the arm-chair archaeologist." With an eye to middle-income collectors, one dealer—Hartwell Kennard of McAllen, Texas—sends out a fat mail-order catalogue of pre-Columbian pieces, many of them selling for under $50. Adds Mr. Kennard: "My location near the U.S.–Mexican border enables me to by-pass several middlemen and give you lower prices. Send your order now; I guarantee your satisfaction."*

There is thus a two-tier market in pre-Columbian works: the first a popular market in lower-priced pieces, and the second

---

* Kennard, who is also an automobile dealer, was arrested on looting charges by Mexican police in March, 1972. The case did not come to trial because the dealer jumped bail and returned to Texas.

a selective market for the rich collector willing to pay thousands for unique art of superior quality. Because most of the pieces derive from illicit excavations and necessarily have only a vague pedigree, buyers in both markets are bedeviled by the prevalence of clever fakes. A collector's suspicion that he has been cheated is the sour side of the market's sweet success, as the following story may illustrate.

First, a personal word. My inquiry into the illicit market began with a chance meeting, in April, 1970, with a dealer I shall call George Alpha. He operates from his home and sells only works of supreme quality. Like so many dealers, he is a man of polyglot charm and a likable iconoclasm about the ethics of his trade. He and I had been brought together for lunch by a friend. Alpha showed no reluctance to talk about his calling, and, thus encouraged, I asked if he was concerned about a UNESCO convention, then being proposed, which in theory would outlaw the smuggling of art. He looked at me as if pitying my innocence. "What does provenance mean?" he said. "It doesn't mean a thing. I have a warehouse in Europe [he mentioned the city] and I keep a lot of things there. If they ratify the UNESCO convention, then what? I know several indigent counts who would be delighted, for a price, to swear that any piece of mine was part of the family collection for centuries. I bring my things from Europe, and who is going to deny it? The treaty won't end the trade, it just means more trouble."

We talked about the problem of the destruction of archaeological sites. Alpha was not at all abashed. "Let me tell you," he said, "I take better care of my material than the archaeologists—in fact, the archaeologists are the worst looters. You should see how my men work, everything is done with love, and if you don't believe, I'll take you along so that you can see for yourself. What I'm doing is *saving* the art, saving it from the jungles and the ignorance of archaeologists."

15

A few months later, I saw Alpha again, and this time he showed me through his apartment, taking me into an inner room whose every crevice seemed to contain a pre-Columbian carved yoke, a funerary idol, or an exquisitely painted pot. As we talked, the name of a prominent museum official came up. Alpha said he wanted to show me something and he pulled from his file a document with an august letterhead and invited me to read it. It was a bill of sale for a pre-Columbian piece, ending with the interesting notation that one of the conditions of the sale was that neither the dealer's name nor the price would be divulged. "Look at the date," said Alpha. "It was the same week that our friend made a speech saying that his museum would never buy smuggled art."

During the same encounter, Alpha made a remark that strongly impressed me. I had asked whether he wouldn't prefer an open, completely legal market in antiquities so that he could operate as reputably as a bank manager. He thought for a moment, looked at me intently, and replied: "You must not forget one thing. I am a pirate. I enjoy piracy. I like the moment at the airport when they look at my passport [he carries several] and glance at my bag, for I take the very best pieces with me, on the airplane. You know, I don't like X [there he named a better-known dealer in the field] but I respect him—he's like me, he won't trust a runner with a really first-class piece. He takes it out himself. Once we saw each other at the same airport, each with our hand on a bag, and we pretended we didn't know each other."

These conversations persuaded me that an inquiry into the illicit market might be useful, would surely be interesting, and could possibly tell something about human behavior. During the following year, I made three trips to Mexico, and in the course of them I heard many bizarre stories, one of the most bizarre about a remarkable Maya mask.

* * *

Early in 1966, the telephone rang in the residence of Dr. Josué Sáenz on Paseo de Las Palmas, an avenue lined with prosperous homes, on the outskirts of Mexico City. The caller said: "Hello. I will have good news for you in two weeks," and hung up. After a few weeks passed, the telephone rang and the same voice said: "Hello, this is Gonzáles, but I can't talk now —the police are all around." Finally, there was a third call, and Dr. Sáenz was urged to take the first flight the following morning to Villahermosa, the capital of the State of Tabasco in the tropical south of Mexico. Dr. Sáenz promptly booked passage.

This was not strange or imprudent behavior on the part of Josué Sáenz, the owner of what is universally acknowledged as the finest private collection of pre-Columbian art in the world. In the Metropolitan Museum's "Before Cortés" exhibition, in 1970, no fewer than twenty-three of the pieces were from the Sáenz Collection, including a Maya openwork relief, showing a regal couple in intense discourse, regarded as the finest of its kind, which appeared on the cover of the Museum's lavish catalogue. His collection has grown through a willingness to take unconventional risks.

Dr. Sáenz, who is now fifty-seven, is an imposing figure in the collecting world. He is a banker, sportsman, public servant, and university lecturer. He has pedigree (his father was the eminent Mexican educator Moisés Sáenz), money, and social position (he was president of the national Olympics Committee during the Mexican Olympics). After attending Swarthmore and the London School of Economics, Dr. Sáenz studied monetary theory at Cambridge University and wrote his thesis under Maynard Keynes. In the 1950s, he also became a serious collector.

A North American friend who knew Sáenz in his early days as a collector has recalled his method: "Josué went about it the way he does everything, with intelligence and energy. He let it be known that he would pay the highest price on the market for anything he wanted, and as a result he got first refusal on everything of importance for sale in Mexico." In the process, he developed a discerning eye.

On his way to Villahermosa, after the strange summons by an unknown caller, Dr. Sáenz had no idea what to expect but he did become a bit apprehensive when he was met at the airport by two rough-looking strangers. He was told to leave his bags in the terminal and he was elbowed to a single-engine Cessna which was revving up nearby. Aloft, the plane seemed to head toward Chiapas but Dr. Sáenz could not be sure of the direction because the pilot, after takeoff, pointedly put a cloth mask over the compass. A rainstorm came up, and the Cessna virtually skidded over the foliage of the thick jungle. Finally the plane bumped to a landing on a recently cleared airstrip.

The party was met by a group of smiling peasants, but no names were given. "We have something to show you," said one of the peasants. He handed Dr. Sáenz a mosaic mask about six inches high encrusted with jadeite and bone. The eyes, nose, and mouth of the face were lined with a red resin material, but what was most striking were the teeth—a row of filed human teeth and two animal fangs. Dr. Sáenz studied the mask with a magnifying lens and concluded that it was probably post-Classic Maya and probably authentic. If so, it was one of only a handful in existence.

Dr. Sáenz suggested that before making any commitment he take the mask back with him to Mexico City for an expert appraisal, but the spokesman for the peasants, still smiling, said, "No, Señor Sáenz, you have to make up your mind right now." Having taken a hard look at the piece and its vendors, Dr. Sáenz offered the equivalent of $2,000. The smiles turned into laughter, and the spokesman, reaching into a ragged jacket, pulled out a Parke-Bernet catalogue and pointed to some of the recent prices of pre-Columbian art. A suitably higher sum was agreed upon, but Dr. Sáenz prudently—he thought—wrote out a check postdated to the following Tuesday; this was a Saturday, and he thought this would give him time to get the mask examined and stop payment if it turned out to be spurious.

Back in Mexico City, Dr. Sáenz took the mask to José Luis Franco, a gnomelike art expert who works in his own apartment—a cluttered walk-up filled with laboratory equipment—and who is considered one of the leading authenticators of pre-Columbian art. Señor Franco scrutinized the mask and didn't like it; he advised Dr. Sáenz that it was probably, though not certainly, fake.

On Monday morning the stop-payment order was put through on the check but under Mexican banking practice postdating is not binding and Dr. Sáenz, to his annoyance, learned that the check had already been cashed. He turned the mask over to one of his regular dealers, telling him to offer it for sale without any guarantee as to its authenticity and to get whatever he could for it. Within a few weeks the dealer proudly informed Dr. Sáenz that a North American had bought the fanged mask, and for a sum that matched the original outlay.

The North American was a dealer who had frequently worked with George Alpha. The mask made its way to New York, where it was shown to Dr. Gordon Ekholm, curator of Mexican archaeology at the American Museum of Natural History. Though Dr. Ekholm deplores the illicit art trade, he has long felt a scholar's obligation to see what comes out of Latin America, so that at least some track can be kept of it. He therefore agreed to examine the mask. He was puzzled by it. When he put it under a microscope, he noticed something curious: minute indentations on the cheek, little pocks in the resin, which showed that a beard had once been affixed to the mask. Other masks of known authenticity had similar markings, and Dr. Ekholm felt that a forger would hardly be aware of such a detail. His verdict was favorable.

The opinion considerably enhanced the value of the mask; the next problem was to find a customer. This can be an anxious

19

decision. If a major piece is shown to a potential buyer who refuses it, other purchasers may become wary, suspecting that something is wrong with the work. It was decided to offer the mask to the Robert Woods Bliss Collection, at Dumbarton Oaks, and the next journey the piece made was to Washington in a case wadded with foam rubber.

For a dealer, a museum purchase is important not only in financial terms but also as a certificate of reputability, and in the pre-Columbian field the Bliss Collection is held in special esteem. It was one of the first great private collections of ancient American art, and it was assembled by a notable couple. The collection had its beginning in 1912 in Paris, where Robert Woods Bliss, a career diplomat, was assuming a new embassy post. One day he visited the shop of an *antiquaire* on Boulevard Raspail and, in doing so, caught what he later called "the collector's microbe." Before long, he purchased the piece that had taken his eye—a jade figure. It turned out to be Olmec, and that was a touch of collector's luck, since the Olmec civilization was not identified as such until the 1940s, and hence the rarity of the piece was not known when he bought it.

Bliss was married to an heiress with a patent-medicine fortune (Castoria), a woman of regal bearing named Mildred Barnes. In 1920, the couple acquired Dumbarton Oaks, a handsome Georgian estate spacious enough to quarter, in 1944, the international conference that led to the founding of the United Nations. Mrs. Bliss made the garden her preserve, turning it into a fragrant labyrinth, while Mr. Bliss became interested in Byzantine as well as pre-Columbian art. Both collections grew steadily, and Dumbarton Oaks became a salon; Mrs. Bliss, wearing gloves and a hat, served tea at five P.M. precisely, and an invitation was a mark of social acceptance. Along with the Truxton Beales and the Robert Low Bacons, the Blisses comprised one of the "three Bs" of Washington society.

In 1940, the Blisses deeded Dumbarton Oaks to Harvard

20

University, and an advanced center for Byzantine studies was later established at the estate. By that time space was a problem, and, with some misgivings, the couple decided to add a special wing to house the pre-Columbian collection. Bliss died in 1962, and his widow supervised the completion of the wing, an eight-domed carrousel designed by Philip Johnson. When it opened in 1964, the wing was adjudged a success, its teak and glass blending gracefully with the Georgian lines of the old estate.

Here, in 1966, the fanged mask found its home as Item 449 in the Bliss Collection. The provenance is given as "Late Post-Classic. Mexico." It was one of the last major purchases approved by Mrs. Bliss before her death, in 1969, at the age of eighty-nine. The mask is believed to represent the Maya god Itzamná, the Lord of the Heavens. Had it not been for Dr. Ekholm's sharp eye, the unique mask might still be one of many fascinating pieces whose significance is clouded by doubts.

There were no such doubts when, in 1968, the Metropolitan Museum of Art was debating whether it should buy the entire façade of a Maya temple, whose story illuminates a more serious dilemma facing museums.

3. *The Winged Temple*

When a small object like a mask or a vase is offered to a museum, a dozen arguments can be made to justify its purchase, however questionable the route by which the piece came into the market. Small pieces are known as "tomb furnishings," and there are hundreds of thousands of pre-Columbian burials in the New World. Who can say where it came from? Who can begrudge a lucky peasant the few thousand pesos he may get if he chances upon a tomb? And if, out of fastidiousness, one museum does not buy the object, there are a score of others that will. But other objections arise when a dealer offers for sale an inscribed tablet, a painted wall, or a chunk of a monument.

All three have been available on the pre-Columbian market as collecting interest in the field has grown. No dealer has done more to meet the demand than the man I shall call Henry Beta, the most unabashed and enterprising *condottiere* in this particular market. Beta entered the trade in the 1940s, when his business took him regularly to Mexico City. He has a flair for the bold gesture, and in 1968 he undertook what for a dealer was a *coup de main.*

In the little-explored jungles of southern Campeche Beta's men discovered an entire Maya site, filled with plazas and pyramids. The site, which is called Calakmul, is notable for the great stucco masks flanking the stairs of its temples. Photographs were taken of some of the masks and Beta showed a set to Josué Sáenz, suggesting that an entire façade could be transported to the collector's lower-floor gallery. Dr. Sáenz declined the offer on the grounds that removing the façade would involve physical destruction of the site. In New York, however, stronger interest was expressed and Beta decided to airlift a large part of the temple façade.

The operation cost more than $80,000. A Mérida businessman organized the work crew to clear an airstrip for a plane flown by a pilot from Florida. Large rubber mother-molds were affixed to the temple façade, which was then sawed free. The power saws, however, struck stone pegs at intervals and the resulting vibrations shattered some of the stucco, but there was enough for a large shipment. The packed fragments were flown to Mérida and from there shipped in mislabeled crates to New Orleans, passing from that city to New York, where some of the façade was brought to the Metropolitan Museum of Art. The asking price was more than $400,000.

Thomas P. F. Hoving, the director, was then occupied with plans for the museum's 1970 centennial celebration, which was to include the most ambitious exhibition of Middle American sculpture ever held outside Mexico. "Before Cortés" was to have a symbolic importance. It had long been a source of distress to those interested in the art of the Americas that the Metropolitan had ignored pre-Columbian art, even though its first president, John Taylor Johnston, had urged in 1883 that the museum honor a "special duty" to show native art. Not until 1969 did the Metropolitan mount any major pre-Columbian display, and on that occasion, the pieces, on loan from the Museum of Primitive Art, shared billing with the primitive art of Africa and Oceania.

"Before Cortés," then, was an expression of tardy penance. The chief organizer of the exhibition was someone who had long pleaded for just such a show, the late Dudley T. Easby, Jr., who had been the secretary of the museum from 1954 until his appointment as first head of the Department of Primitive Art in 1969. A lawyer with a courtly manner, Mr. Easby was an expert on pre-Columbian metalwork and had standing as an authority in the field. Moreover his wife, Elizabeth Kennedy Easby, was a professional archaeologist and a former acting curator of primitive art at the Brooklyn Museum.

For three years, the Easbys traveled through Europe, Latin America, and the United States, pleading with often reluctant owners to lend pieces to "Before Cortés." In Vienna, their tact brought them successfully through an encounter with Professor Etta Becker-Donner, a formidable woman who is head of the Museum für Völkerkunde, which has as its prize pre-Columbian exhibit a brilliant feathered headdress sent by Cortés to Emperor Charles V. At the initial meeting, Professor Etta Becker-Donner opened the conversation by saying, "Not the headdress." "Madame," replied Mr. Easby in his most soothing manner,

23

"only a fool would ask for it, and only a madman would lend it." After that, negotiations for other pieces progressed successfully.

Now, in December, 1968, the Metropolitan had to decide what to do about the temple façade, parts of which were lying so temptingly in its laboratories. Before a decision was made, the Easbys happened to be in Mexico, where word of the winged temple was circulating among collectors. A dinner was held for the Easbys, and among those present were Dr. Josué Sáenz and Dr. Ignacio Bernal, Mexico's most prominent archaeologist and director of the National Museum of Anthropology. Dr. Sáenz at one point turned to Mr. Easby, who suffered from emphysema, and said, "There are funny stories going around. People are saying you came to Mexico by ship not for your health but to take temples away. They are also saying that the black bag you carry is not for medicine but to carry money to buy temples." Mr. Easby made no reply but absorbed the message.

In New York, meanwhile, the fragments of the temple were seen by Joseph Veach Noble, then the museum's vice-director for administration. Mr. Noble did not care for what he saw; in his view, to buy the temple would be like buying a chunk of the Parthenon. He expressed his objections in a forthright and vehement way to Mr. Hoving, and a decision was made to notify Dr. Ignacio Bernal, in Mexico, that a Maya temple had somehow found its way to New York.

Dr. Bernal, a tall man with an almost theatrical presence—he has great brows and a strong nose, which themselves suggest monumental sculpture—was soon in the Metropolitan to examine the booty. He identified the temple façade as Mexican property that had been illegally exported, and asked Mr. Hoving who was selling it. To Bernal's irritation, Mr. Hoving replied that it was against museum policy to reveal the names of dealers. Then the Mexican scholar noticed that the Metropolitan director was motioning curiously with his chin in the direction of the breast pocket of his jacket. A slip of paper was sticking out, and on it was the dealer's identity. Thus the code was honored; Dr. Bernal was not *told* the name.

A day or so later, Mr. Noble called Henry Beta and asked him to come to the museum. The unsuspecting Beta arrived with the genial air of a dealer about to close an enormous sale. Gruffly, Mr. Noble came to the point, telling Beta that the museum was not only not buying the temple but was urging its return to Mexico. The dealer's expression seemed to collapse like an exhaling balloon as Mr. Noble rose to excuse himself and returned to present Dr. Bernal. In that encounter, Beta had recovered his aplomb sufficiently to suggest that at least someone ought to reimburse him for the $80,000 or so it had cost him to take the temple out of the jungle. It took a moment for the startled Mexican to absorb this statement. Then he replied: "You mean to say that after you've stolen one of our temples, you want us to pay your expenses?" Beta was advised to write off the loss, and to bear in mind that he could easily run into legal troubles in Mexico.

The temple was repacked in some sixty crates and left New York aboard a special flight of the Mexican national airlines. Noble was at the airport when the cartons were loaded, and he was present in Mexico City a year later when the temple façade had its first public showing in the Maya Room of the National Museum of Anthropology.* Subsequently Mr. Noble left the Metropolitan to become director of the Museum of the City of New York. Among the photographs on his desk is one that

---

* There has been persistent confusion about the true provenance of the façade. At first, the site was believed to be Kohunlich in Quintana Roo; this is the place named on the label at the National Museum. Dr. Bernal asserts that Beta at different times gave him three different provenances, a third being in Chiapas. But the best evidence points to Calakmul, a vast, much plundered site in Campeche.

25

shows him standing beside the only Mayan temple façade that crossed the Gulf of Mexico twice.

In this case, the Metropolitan Museum resisted temptation, but American museums have not always been so scrupulous. Within the last fifteen years, a specialized market has been developed for the sale of large sculpture, carved lintels, and, particularly, stelae. Maya stelae are limestone tablets, inscribed with hieroglyphs, that are found at the bases of temples and pyramids. Most are in unguarded sites in Mexico and Guatemala, and to carry them away the looters—known as *esteleros* —cut them into pieces. They are reassembled by restorers and sold for prices that range from $50,000 to more than $200,000, depending on condition and the beauty of the carvings. No other form of looting has caused so much scandal.*

If one were to search for landmarks, an early one would be the publication in 1965 of a brief article in the *Journal* of the University of San Carlos in Guatemala City. Entitled "Two Maya Stelae Stolen from Guatemala: Their Presence in New York," the article was by Professor Jorge Luján Muñoz, an art historian at the university. Dr. Luján called attention to two fine stelae, one exhibited at the Brooklyn Museum, and the other at the Museum of Primitive Art. He reproduced photographs of the same pieces at their original site, Piedras Negras— photographs published in 1901 at Harvard by the Austrian scholar Teobart Maler. Both museums were now necessarily aware that they had purchased stelae illegally removed from a Maya ceremonial center. They were probably also aware that in engaging in such a transaction they were tacitly encouraging other museums and collectors to follow their example.

After prolonged negotiations—involving, in the case of the Primitive Art Museum, its founder and chief patron, Governor

* Two tables listing looted sites in Guatemala and Mexico are included in Appendix A.

26

Nelson A. Rockefeller—the museums agreed that the smuggled art would be returned to Guatemala. The Brooklyn Museum's decision was announced in a *New York Times* report in June, 1972, which said: "The restitution was made following the Museum's discovery that the pieces had been stolen." Whenever the discovery was made in Brooklyn, at the Primitive Art Museum the tablet was listed in a 1964 catalogue as "Stela, Guatemala. Piedras Negras, Maya ca. 600 A.D."

There were other episodes. In January, 1967, a large crate shipped from Central America and labeled "machinery" burst open as it was being taken to a warehouse in Houston, Texas. U.S. Customs agents found that the crate and five others contained a Maya stela broken into thirty-two pieces and weighing 2,918 pounds; when it was whole, the stela had stood at the site of Naranjo in Guatemala, close to the border of British Honduras. Customs officials learned that the stela had been hauled on muleback to British Honduras, where it was shipped to Houston. The fraudulent mislabeling helped make it a simple matter for Guatemala to recover the stela, but the federal action prompted some interesting comment in the Houston press.

In an article headlined "Buying, Selling Stolen Art Apparently Not Much of a Crime," the Houston *Post* carried an interview with Ben DuBose, proprietor of a pre-Columbian art gallery filled with art he admitted was stolen. The paper reported:

> This, he explained, is the simplest and most innocent kind of lawbreaking. "Those people need bread," he said. "They've got plenty of sex and too many people to feed. They really need food, shelter and money and their governments are not bringing it to them. . . . They've got more of this stuff than they can handle," DuBose said. "I've seen Mexican towns with big museums and starving people. . . . Every nation in the world is guilty of taking treasures from other countries. . . . Why should we start

27

giving them back? Why should the United States be different?"

Lowell Collins, identified as a Houston teacher and expert in pre-Columbian art, was also interviewed. "What the hell?" he was quoted as saying. "As long as U.S. laws are not broken, it's all right. After all, these things are not appreciated in those countries. They're brought here and given a home. Now cultured people can see them."

By and large, this has been the attitude of dealers, though it has not often been so bluntly expressed. A more sophisticated exposition has been given by André Emmerich, a leading New York dealer, who sells both pre-Columbian and contemporary art. Speaking at a College Art Association symposium in 1971 on the international illicit traffic in art, Mr. Emmerich declared:

> Like everyone else I would like to be on the side of virtue, motherhood, and so forth. I am not quite sure on which side virtue lies. . . . Do the descendants of the Turks who drove out the Greeks from Asia Minor have a better right to the art made by the ancestors of the Greeks? Do the destroyers of the Maya civilization [have more right] to its remnants than we do? I propose that it's a basic moral question. I beg the obvious fact that the art of mankind—the art of ancient mankind—is part of mankind's cultural heritage, and does not belong exclusively to that particular geographic spot where ancient cultures flourished. I think that this country more than any other has a special claim to the arts of all mankind. . . . American institutions have bought the objects they have acquired, and have not only paid with money, but we have paid the debt with scholarly contributions. . . . I would say that probably the majority of work on pre-Columbian art has

28

been done by American scholars. So I think we have paid our way.

It must be added that most scholars in the pre-Columbian field do not agree.

4. The Vanishing Glyphs

Early in 1971 an important archaeological exhibition opened in the Park Avenue mansion occupied by the Center for Inter-American Relations. It was called "The Art of Maya Hieroglyphic Writing" and was sponsored jointly by the Center and the Peabody Museum of Archaeology and Ethnology at Harvard. The exhibition had a double purpose—to publicize an ambitious new attempt to decipher Maya writing and to call attention to the destruction of precisely the material that contained the clues needed for such decoding.

The Center display had its genesis in a holiday trip to Mexico made in 1964 by a Washington lawyer, Edgar H. Brenner, who is normally concerned with civil and criminal cases at the firm of Arnold & Porter, where he is a partner. Mr. Brenner toured Chichén Itzá and Uxmal on a visit to Yucatán and was fascinated by the hieroglyphic inscriptions he saw at these Maya sites. On his return, he decided to try his hand at deciphering the script and found that the basic materials were not available —that there was no published corpus of all known hieroglyphs.

Mr. Brenner was a director of the Stella and Charles Guttman Foundation, established by a whiskey importer and chiefly devoted to medical research. The lawyer, who combines with a customary gravity a dry, deadpan wit, somehow persuaded the foundation trustees to sponsor a meeting of leading scholars to see what could be done about Maya hieroglyphics. The meeting was held in November, 1967, and it was agreed that a major contribution would be the publication, for the first time, of the texts on the 1,322 inscribed stones known to exist, most of them *in situ*, in Mexico and Central America.

The next step was to find a project director, who would have to be a Maya expert, a proficient photographer, a draftsman, a writer, a jungle explorer—and preferably a bachelor, since he would have to spend long months in the bush. Brenner heard about a Scotsman in his forties named Ian Graham who met every requirement, and early in 1968 Graham was appointed director of the Maya Hieroglyphic Inscription Study, a fifteen-year venture which will cost about $500,000. The Guttman Foundation provided seed money, and the Peabody Museum at Harvard added its support, naming Mr. Graham a research fellow in Middle American Archaeology and giving him the run of what is probably the best single Maya research library.

Like Brenner, Graham became interested in the Maya during a chance visit to Mexico, in his case in 1959. The Scotsman met some friends who spoke knowledgeably about the Maya and he visited the National Museum to learn more. The following year he was back in Mexico, and drove south in a 1927 Rolls-Royce, winding up in Guatemala, in whose remoter villages his automobile would bring out the entire populace, agape. Having some means (he is a son of Lord Alastair Graham and a Winchester graduate), he decided to become a free-lance Maya explorer.

He learned the ways of El Petén, the department in Guatemala with the largest number of sites, and he came to frequent a bar called the Green Twist, in Flores, the departmental seat, because that bar was a favorite haunt of the *chicleros*, the men who roamed the jungle collecting the sap used to make chewing gum and sometimes came upon ruins unknown to plodding archaeologists. He also befriended geologists working for oil companies, for they, too, sometimes chanced upon temples in the rain forest.

The first fruit of Mr. Graham's free-lance forays was a monograph published in 1967 by the Middle American Research Institute of Tulane University. It gave accounts of six little-known sites, illustrated with drawings and photographs by Graham, and interspersed with advice on how to make latex molds and where to look out for jungle insects. Thus, when he became director of the Hieroglyphic Study, the Scotsman was acquiring formal responsibility for what he had begun on his own.

Mr. Graham soon became aware that the very material he was recording was being looted at a dismaying rate. In the past decade, no fewer than forty stelae in Guatemala had been either stolen or badly mutilated. Of a hundred or so sites in El Petén, only one, Tikal, was guarded, and even there *esteleros* were at work. What especially troubled the explorer was that the carved stones were being eagerly bought by museums and collectors, most of them in the United States. It was partly to call attention to the problem that the Maya hieroglyphic exhibition was organized by the Peabody Museum and the Center for Inter-American Relations. Mr. Graham prepared the catalogue for the show, at which an entire room was devoted to photographs of defaced Maya monuments, with captions like "The Sack of El Peru," "A Stela Mutilated for the Second Time," and "The Destruction of History in the Name of Art."

The opening, on January 27, 1971, was a festive occasion. An audience in formal dress heard Mr. Graham give a pleasant account of various specialized matters, among them the best way to cook porridge in a jungle camp. A few weeks later, the Scotsman flew back to Guatemala to resume his work. He learned that looters had attacked the unrecorded site of La Naya, three miles north of Lake Macanaché, in El Petén; he decided to go there immediately, while there was something left.

Early in March, accompanied by three Guatemalans, Mr. Graham set out for La Naya. His guide was Pedro Arturo Sierra, a forest guard at Tikal National Park, who had recently visited the site, interrupted its plunder, and helped police identify several of the robbers. The party arrived at dusk and a camp was cleared, hammocks were hung, and the fire started for supper. Arturo was standing near the explorer when the clap of gunfire was heard. The Guatemalan was shot twice, first in the back and then in the chest, fatally. The survivors, badly shaken, stayed the night at La Naya, and when police arrived later the camp of the ambushers was found along with evidence that they had been chiseling away at a stela when Graham's party arrived. Graham, himself a lean six-footer, would have been an easy target; it was apparent that the forest guard had been singled out and had been killed in reprisal for his earlier identification of the La Naya looters.

In the fall of 1971, back in the United States, Graham learned that a La Naya stela was being offered on the art market; he also found, through a museum source, that a Santa Fe Springs, California, dealer was seeking a buyer for another tablet—Machaquilá stela 2, which Mr. Graham had discovered and recorded in 1962. Thoroughly angry, he told a colleague who, in turn, got in touch with the Department of Justice. On January 18, 1972, in what was the first such federal action, three agents of the FBI impounded the Machaquilá stela, which was in the home of Clive Hollinshead, the Santa Fe Springs dealer.

A federal grand jury heard the evidence and on August 28, 1972, an indictment was handed up charging Hollinshead and two other persons with conspiring to transport stolen goods in interstate and foreign commerce. The indictment charged that the stela was smuggled to Miami by an unindicted co-conspirator, who was met there by Johnnie Brown Fell of Mobile, Alabama, formerly in the fishing business. Fell delivered the stela to Hollinshead at a Holiday Inn at Raleigh, North Carolina. The stela, a large limestone slab, eighty-two inches high and forty-nine inches wide, has the figure of a priest on its face and hieroglyphs on its face and side. The asking price was $300,000.*

On February 28, 1973, the case went to trial in a Los Angeles federal district court. After hearing extensive testimony (one of the witnesses was Ian Graham), a jury deliberated for two days and found Hollinshead and Fell guilty of all charges against them. Subsequently, a Federal judge fined Hollinshead $5000, suspended sentence and put him on five years' probation; his co-conspirator, Fell, also received a suspended sentence and was placed on probation for three years. Both men are appealing. Whatever the legal precedent set by the case, the intervention of the FBI is a token of a new attitude toward the illicit trade, at least insofar as monumental pieces are concerned. But the range of other pre-Columbian material is vast, and scholars differ strongly as to how carefully they should examine suspect objects. The essence of the argument is embodied in the story of the new Maya codex.

5. *The Fourth Codex*

Of all the high Indian civilizations in the New World, only the Maya evolved what seems to be a fully developed system of writing. They were not only literate but gifted mathematicians

* A second Machaquilá stela was impounded by the FBI in West Helena, Arkansas, in January, 1972. The tablet was found in the home of Harry K. Brown, the owner of a fish processing plant in British Honduras. Machaquilá stela 5—which also had been discovered by Ian Graham—had been broken into about 25 pieces. In May, 1973, a Federal grand jury indicted Brown on charges of conspiring to transport a stolen artifact. Also indicted as a co-conspirator was George Alamilla, of Belize, British Honduras. The indictment alleges that the stela was shipped by Alamilla to Key West, Florida, where Brown took possession of it. The tablet was offered for sale to the Denver Art Museum. See Trimble, 1972, and Mitchell, 1973.

as well, independently inventing the concept of zero, and they are credited with calculating the length of the year with a precision unequaled in the West until the nineteenth century. But little of this was known before lost Maya sites were explored in the 1840s by a New York lawyer, John Lloyd Stephens, and an English artist, Frederick Catherwood. Stephens, an amateur archaeologist and a writer of some fluency, was especially impressed by the strange Maya script, of which he remarked: "I cannot help believing that the tablets of hieroglyphics will yet be read."

This hope seemed within easy fulfillment in 1863 when a long-lost key to the glyphs was found in a library in Madrid. The manuscript was by Diego de Landa, bishop of Yucatán, who in the 1560s had located Indians still able to read hieroglyphs. After getting a key to the symbols for numbers and dates, he thought it would be relatively simple to correlate the Latin alphabet with the Maya hieroglyphs. But many of the hieroglyphs were symbols for words; thus, when the bishop asked for the sign for the letter B he got the word in Mayan for "road" or "journey," which has the same sound. Hence many hieroglyphs were left unexplained, and Landa's key turned out to be less than a Rosetta Stone; even after a century of intensive international scholarship, the hieroglyphs can be only partly read.

Thanks in good measure to the bishop, dates and numbers can be deciphered along with isolated words, and something of the structure of the script is known. In 1960, an important breakthrough was made by the Harvard scholar Tatiana Proskouriakoff, who noticed that the dates on any one group of stelae at Piedras Negras did not cover a span longer than the average human life. Pursuing this insight, Miss Proskouriakoff was able to identify the symbols for specific rulers; she reasoned that two glyphs—known . as the "upended frog" and "toothache glyph"—were like bookends around historical information. The stelae, in short, may yet yield clues for the causes of the so far inexplicable collapse of Classic Maya civilization around the ninth century A.D. (Of the eight stelae she studied, it should be added, three were later uprooted and sold to foreign museums.)

For Maya scholars, a basic problem has been the lack of long texts. The Maya did compile books, which combined text and pictures on folded sheets of bark, known as codices, but most were burnt as pagan relics by Spanish friars. (Bishop Landa himself was responsible for an auto-de-fé in 1562 in which twenty-seven Maya picture books were destroyed.) Only three codices were known to have survived the Conquest, and these ended up in libraries in Dresden, Paris, and Madrid. Not a single Maya manuscript can be seen in a museum in this hemisphere.

One can thus understand the interest among Mayanists when, on April 20, 1971, it was announced that a wholly unknown fourth codex had come to light. The announcement was made by Professor Michael D. Coe of Yale, at the opening in New York of an exhibition entitled "Ancient Maya Calligraphy," sponsored by the Grolier Club of New York. By coincidence, this was only two months after the opening of the similar show at the Center for Inter-American Relations.

The fourth codex was an eleven-page fragment of a calendrical book written on bark cloth and apparently dating to the late post-Classic Maya period, from about 900 to 1520 A.D. Though its contents were specialized—it dealt with the cycles of the planet Venus—its mere preservation was, as Dr. Coe said, "nothing less than a miracle." But was it genuine? Who owned it? And where was it found?

Only on the first point did Dr. Coe feel free to talk. He said he would stake his reputation on its authenticity, which was proved in his view by its condition and by the inscriptions on it, so unlike anything previously seen. A piece of the bark was later carbon-dated to about 1250 A.D., plus or minus some 150 years, which put the organic material well within the post-Classic period. (Organic substances can be dated with rough accuracy since the radioactivity of carbon runs down at a fixed rate, a discovery made in 1947 that earned Willard F. Libby of the University of Chicago a Nobel prize.) As for the rest, the Yale scholar said the codex was a "real hot potato" lent to the Grolier Club by an anonymous owner, and nothing more could be said about it.

The Grolier Club is an association of booklovers founded in 1884 and bearing the name of the French bibliophile Jean Grolier (1479–1565). Its members meet regularly in handsome period rooms in the club's town house at 47 East 60th Street, and it maintains a fine library on the history of printing. It also from time to time sponsors exhibitions, one of which was the Maya show, a display of eighty-five objects of outstanding quality, most of them loaned by dealers and private collectors. No finer selection of Maya painted pottery has yet been put on public view; every piece was superb—and few had any pedigree. Here one could see what was available to a collector of means indifferent to provenance. And yet an eminent Yale scholar had organized the show. Why?

Though Michael Coe is in his forties and is the past chairman of Yale's Department of Anthropology, he can still be mistaken for a graduate student. He has a bouncy manner and a round, mobile face; he responds to anything new with a cadenza of exclamations. His car, a Volkswagen bus, has OLMEC inscribed on its license plates. His commitment to his field is not only total, but familial. In the mid-1940s he and his older brother William spent a college holiday in Yucatán, and the visit led to others; their interest in the Maya and pre-Columbian archaeology turned into an obsession. "I see this in students today,"

William R. Coe has said. "They become hooked—it's like falling in love and marrying, for better or worse."

William, who attended the University of Pennsylvania, earned his doctorate in archaeology and became director of the major dig his university carried out in Tikal. Michael followed similar interests at Harvard, joining the Yale faculty in 1960 after extensive field work. His wife, Sophie, is also involved with the Maya. The daughter of the Russian-born geneticist Theodosius Dobzhansky, she has translated the important Maya linguist studies of the Soviet scholar Yuri Knorosov. The Coes may fairly be called the first family in the Maya field, though the brothers are not always in agreement on many issues.

In Michael Coe one senses an impatience with the ponderous pace of research, and—more strongly—an irritation with the holier-than-thou attitude of many of his colleagues. For all the talk about looting, he will remark, archaeologists are among the worst offenders, since as many as half of all excavated sites are never published. "Think about that for a minute," he says. "Boxes of forgotten sherds lying in basements. The fellow who has dug them up has left long ago, his notes are scattered and labels vanish. The site could just as well have been destroyed, and yet every department of archaeology, every museum, is familiar with the problem."

Dr. Coe regards himself as a steward and not a policeman. He is interested in all objects, no matter how they have emerged from the earth, and points out that if qualified scholars did not examine these pieces they would vanish, unrecorded, into a hundred scattered collections. To him, the codex, and the Maya pottery at the Grolier Club show, are cases in point. He had been aware of the codex's existence for several years, and he also had known that Maya pottery, better than anything yet seen, was coming into the market. He saw a chance, by arranging the Grolier Club show, to bring these rich holdings into public view together. He is preparing a comprehensive catalogue so that other scholars will also be able to examine this otherwise vagrant material.* Coe has a quick answer to those who contend that any disturbance of context is a form of vandalism. "It depends on the object. It depends on the question you are asking," he retorts. "If someone brought me the Rosetta Stone, should I refuse to look at it because it was out of context and dug up by a pot hunter? Of course I'd look at it, because if it was genuine it would add immeasurably to our knowledge." Thus without a touch of defensiveness, he arranged for the exhibition and publication of the Grolier Club show.

Among the first people to put her name in the visitor's book at the Grolier Club was Mrs. Clemency Coggins, a Harvard art historian who has become the most forthright spokeswoman for the opposing view. More than anyone else, Mrs. Coggins has been responsible for forcing upon museums and collectors a debate on the ethics of acquisition, and she is looked upon either as heroine or harridan, depending on where one stands. She is a doctoral candidate in fine arts, and as it happens her specialty is Maya pottery. Her involvement in the dispute over the illicit trade began with her research. She was trying to work out a chronology and typology of Maya polychrome vases, and she found that much of the ware she studied had no provenance. Mrs. Coggins acquired an avocation as a free-lance detective.

A tall, dark-haired woman, Mrs. Coggins is married to a doctor specializing in nephrology at Massachusetts General Hospital. Periodically, she commutes from her home in Auburndale to the Fogg or Peabody Museum, in Cambridge, and returns home to cook for her family and retreat into her study. There she has the most extensive file in America on the theft and destruction of pre-Columbian art. She began it in the mid-

---

* Entitled *The Maya Scribe and His World*, the catalogue was published by the Grolier Club in autumn, 1973. It contains 278 black-and-white illustrations and 28 color plates.

1960s when she started tracking down the origins of pieces displayed in American museums. This led to a 1969 article in *The Art Journal* on the plundering of pre-Columbian sites, which ended with a long list, in fine print, of suspect pieces, many on exhibit in the United States. Her study thereafter became a clearinghouse for information about the illicit market. Field archaeologists sent her reports of fresh depredations: E. Willys Andrews of Tulane described a Maya site in Mexico as a "weird lunar landscape" after pot hunters had cleaned it out; Nicholas Hellmuth, a St. Louis archaeologist, listed stelae stolen while his work was underway at Yaxhá, in Guatemala; a Minnesota scholar told of a fine stela he had discovered near Tikal and deliberately kept secret, only to find it again, five years later, decapitated. Mrs. Coggins used the material for increasingly frequent articles and speeches.

On rare occasions she tours Madison Avenue to see what is new on the art market, talking to dealers with cold politeness. She gives an impression of old-fashioned integrity. Her mother is the novelist Anya Seton and her grandfather was Ernest Thompson Seton, the great nature writer and artist. In person, she has a humor, even a whimsy, not known to her detractors. In any event, Mrs. Coggins has become the conscience of her calling.

In May, 1971, she delivered a paper on the illicit trade to the annual meeting of the Society of American Archaeology in Norman, Oklahoma. She spoke about the Grolier Club exhibition, remarking on the extraordinary quality of the Maya material, and then asked what scholars could do about the economic realities of the art market. She went on:

First, perhaps, we should try to examine what the relationship is between the world of the specialist and that of the art dealer. Particularly salient, it seems to me, is the fact that the present nature and the success of the antiquities business has imposed a great strain on that relationship, one which has in the past been largely benign and cordial.

There is a sense of betrayal, and of confusion, on the part of many archaeologists and art historians whose dealings with dealers have always been correct, and carried on in an atmosphere of antiquarian scholarship, and of aesthetic pleasure in the objects involved. Their opinions, freely given, have been offered in the hope of enhancing the objects in an historical sense, and of ferreting out forgeries. In return for such information art dealers have traditionally kept such specialists informed on what objects were where; and they have given them photographs. But somehow this time-honored relationship has gone bad.

The size, the destructiveness, and the money now involved in what used to be a relatively innocuous trade have turned the scholar, who would only authenticate a piece, into an accomplice. His opinion, however cautiously given, may determine the market value of a piece. For many who have mediated between dealers and collectors and museums, the new turn this relationship has taken is a source of agonizing and perhaps insoluble conflict, often compelling a choice between an ethical abstraction and long-term friendships.

In those few words, Mrs. Coggins caught the essence of a complex situation, and at least pointed the way to a civilized approach to a partial solution.

First, a digression. A few months after the opening of the Grolier Club show, I had an encounter with the dealer I am calling George Alpha. We talked about many things, and inevitably the new Maya codex came up. I asked if he thought it was genuine and, with some emphasis, he answered yes. How could he be so sure? "Because I know its father and mother, and they are both honest." What did he mean by that? "That codex," he said, "was found in a wooden box—I happen to know about it though it is not mine—and the box was tightly closed, so tight that the bark paper was not spoiled by the humidity. The codex was discovered in a cave in Chiapas, and was part of a funerary group. I expect that it will be sold for six figures and disappear from sight for a number of years. Then it will reappear again, with a collector's name attached to it." Alpha paused for a moment, as if debating whether to say more. "You know," he added, "it was found with some other first-class objects, including the mosaic mask in Dumbarton Oaks."

If Alpha was telling the truth—and I believe he was—an archaeological find of major significance was made at the site to which Dr. Sáenz was summoned in Chiapas. Whatever was in the cache has been dispersed, and the item of most importance —the only Maya codex found in modern times—has simply vanished, its owner unknown, its whereabouts uncertain. Such is the high price we pay for the high price of art. What can be done about it?

6. *A Question of Law*

The dilemma that faces a scholar in deciding whether to examine or authenticate a piece of suspect art cannot be resolved by legislation. Nevertheless public policy can have some effect on the market forces that underlie that dilemma. This can be brought about in two ways, the first being through legislation that outlaws the sale and trade of illegally excavated cultural property. Such laws are already in force, with little noticeable effect.

Nearly every country rich in antiquities has legislation that seeks to restrict the export of rare works of art.* In Mexico,

* A table summarizing the provisions of various national antiquities laws is included in Appendix B.

for example, there is virtually no legal market in pre-Columbian antiquities. But because Mexico has thousands of archaeological sites, because much of the country is poor, and because prices for pre-Columbian art are high, the law is about as effective as the Prohibition Amendment was in America. The United States, for its part, has responded to appeals for action by imposing import controls on some forms of looted art. In 1971, a treaty with Mexico was ratified that provides for the return of stolen archaeological and cultural material of "outstanding importance." A year later the Senate gave preliminary approval to the UNESCO convention which in theory proscribes the trade in contraband art, and Congress passed a law making it an offense to bring into the United States monumental pre-Columbian sculpture exported contrary to another country's laws. Yet as even those responsible for formulating these measures will despairingly admit, the combined effect will only be to lessen, not eliminate, the plunder of ancient sites.*

There is a second approach which has not yet been tried. This would be to qualify the invisible subsidy which American tax laws now give to the international art market. The nature of that subsidy can be simply explained. Since the 1950s, the United States has allowed gifts of art to museums to be taken as deductions in the donor's tax return up to a level equivalent to 30 per cent of his gross income in any one year. Thus, the wealthy collector can have the choice of paying taxes or making tax-deductible gifts to a museum, with his gifts valued at current market prices. No other country has made so generous a fiscal gesture to the arts, and unquestionably this tax formula has been a success in terms of the huge flow of art to museums.

Just as unquestionably, American tax laws have been a powerful factor in the postwar art boom. In his comprehensive sur-

---

* The complete texts of the UNESCO convention and of the treaty between Mexico and the United States are included in Appendixes E and F, as is a summary of a law imposing import controls on monumental pre-Columbian art.

vey, *The Economics of Taste,* Gerald Reitlinger says the change in the tax laws "is reflected in some of the more abnormal prices that are bid at European auction," adding, "It is the main source of the champagne and television-screen entertainment of the sales room." One can question, however, whether those who give looted art to museums should also benefit, as they now do, from this exceptional provision—whether, in effect, the American taxpayer should subsidize the devastation of archaeological sites.

No one has thought harder about the matter than William D. Rogers, the president of the American Society of International Law, a former deputy coordinator of the Alliance for Progress, and, like Edgar Brenner, a partner in the Washington firm of Arnold & Porter. A few years ago, because of his interest in Latin America, Mr. Rogers became concerned with the illicit traffic in smuggled art, and at his instigation a special panel was formed to study what could be done. The panel, sponsored by the Society of International Law, made proposals which were later embodied in the 1972 legislation protecting monumental pre-Columbian art. But Mr. Rogers came to feel that a more fundamental step was needed. Specifically, he suggested that no antiquity given to a museum should qualify for a tax benefit if the donated object is without convincing pedigree. This limitation would not apply to art already owned by a collector at the time the suggested law might go into effect, but it would be up to the owner to prove that he possessed any object prior to that date.

Such a reform would end the anomaly whereby American laws reward those who purchase pillaged art. It would take, as well, a good deal of the speculative money out of an inflated market.

CHAPTER TWO

SAILING FROM BYZANTIUM

The obsession with expansion—bigger collections, bigger audiences, more "services," bigger staffs, bigger budgets—constantly undermines the activity of intelligence in America. Institutions that permit themselves to be dominated by the spirit of annual statistical growth (see the Met's Annual Reports) are doomed to lose sight of their original reason for existence.

HAROLD ROSENBERG, "On the Metropolitan Museum," 1970

1. The Migration of Art

The rise of the art museum in America is an event that could not have been predicted and cannot be easily explained. Although the United States, according to a favorite European myth, is imbued with materialism and motivated almost entirely by the soulless business ethic, it now spends more on art museums than does the rest of the world combined, and most of the money comes from businessmen. A good estimate is that from a third to one-half of all of mankind's museums are in a country that has rarely been accused of an excessive devotion to art.

Before the Civil War, there were only a few museums in the United States, the oldest being the Wadsworth Atheneum in Hartford, which opened in a Tudor Gothic building in 1844. (There is some dispute over priority, but Hartford seems to have the strongest case.) By 1910 there were about six hundred museums. A census in 1939 recorded twenty-five hundred, and thirty years later that total had more than doubled. In one spurt, between 1965 and 1970, new museums were opening at the rate of nearly one a day. The expansion continues; there were major openings in 1972 in Texas at Corpus Christi and Fort Worth, and in Washington, a $15-million building will soon enclose the Joseph H. Hirshhorn Collection of contemporary art, which is valued as high as $50 million.

Fifty years ago, one European who sensed what was occurring was the French art dealer René Gimpel. During a visit to the United States in 1923 he was particularly impressed by the Toledo Museum of Art, which had been munificently endowed by a glass manufacturer, Edward Drummond Libbey. Gimpel was the brother-in-law of Sir Joseph Duveen, the great dealer, but unlike him he was wary of superlatives. Yet in this provincial city he was struck by the selfless dedication to art of Mr. and Mrs. George Stevens, the director and assistant director of the Toledo Museum. The visitor noted in his diary: "Mr. and Mrs. Stevens, who are only moderately well off, are devoting their lives to the museum. He gave up a fine situation for the post, which has obliged them to live, if not drably, at least quite unpretentiously. This devotion to the cause of art is found throughout the United States, and gives an idea of the fervor that convulsed the Middle Ages, when its churches were erected."

A prescient remark, but something that Gimpel could not have guessed was that this fervor, this altogether creditable obsession with art, would in time have as a regrettable side effect the negation of the museum's nominal purpose—the preservation of the past. He could not have foreseen that museums, acting out of the loftiest of motives, would be indirectly subsidizing the devastation of antiquity. How and why this came about is the subject of our present inquiry.

In the history of American museums, a landmark year was 1870, when two great institutions were incorporated—the Metropolitan Museum of Art and the Boston Museum of Fine Arts. These were the first of the encyclopedic galleries, each determined to display the best of the world's art of all periods and regions. The timing was formative. The Civil War was over, there was a freshened air of nationalism, a new competitiveness with the older cultures of Europe. Fittingly, the first directors of both the new museums were Civil War officers—Major General Charles G. Loring in Boston and General Luigi Palma di Cesnola in New York. The trustees were men of great wealth. There was big money, and there was an aggressive spirit of acquisition. A poem by Walt Whitman, "Song of the Exposition," written in 1871, eloquently catches the spirit:

> Come Muse migrate from Greece and Ionia,
> Cross out please those immensely, overpaid accounts,
> That matter of Troy and Achilles' wrath, and
>   Aeneas', Odysseus' wanderings,
> Placard "Removed" and "To Let" on the rocks of
>   your snowy Parnassus,
> Repeat at Jerusalem, place the notice high on
>   Jaffa's gate and on Mount Moriah,
> The same on the walls of your German, French and
>   Spanish castles, and Italian collections,

For know a better, fresher, busier sphere, a wide
untried domain awaits, demands you.

So the great migration began. In the next half century, empty
galleries filled with Old Masters, Greek statuary, medieval
tapestries, Chinese vases, Egyptian mummies. And in the process it became apparent that the museum, essentially an eight-
eenth-century European invention, was going to take a different
form in the New World. American museums, to begin with, were
decentralized and invariably private, while the British Museum and the Louvre, like other great European collections,
were under state authority. This meant that American museums
could operate with free-wheeling enterprise, unhampered by
bureaucratic controls; it also meant—the obverse side of the
coin—that they could operate with less public accountability.

Equally important was the difference in approach. European
museums tended to ignore the mass audience in favor of the
minority of connoisseurs. In America, the net was cast wider.
Art, great art, was often seen as a form of moral therapy. At a
founding meeting of the Metropolitan Museum, a principal
speaker was the poet William Cullen Bryant. "My friends," he
said, "it is important that we should encounter the temptations
of vice in this great and too rapidly growing capital by attractive entertainments of an innocent and improving character."

From this impulse evolved the notion of the multipurpose
museum; the gallery was not, as in Europe, simply a collection,
it was also a campus. With energy and imagination, American
curators invented junior wings, prepared lecture and concert series, and devised visually dramatic displays. Frequently, the
measure of success was attendance figures—the democratic
justification of an institution with an aristocratic pedigree. To
swell attendance, publicity was needed, and one method of obtaining it was by putting on elaborate special exhibitions. There
was another method: a continuing inflow of spectacular acquisitions. Accordingly, art museums sought out wealthy trustees

who might be persuaded to loosen their purses for such acquisitions. When a journalist recently asked the architect Philip Johnson, a Museum of Modern Art trustee, what he looked for in a fellow trustee, the answer was "Money." "Is that all?" the reporter pursued. "That's three things," came the reply. "Money, money, money."

Yet even as the explosive growth of museums was beginning, some saw dangers in an outlook which they feared could evolve into high-minded rapacity. An early warning was sounded by Henry James. In 1905 the novelist made a long visit to New York, his native city, for the first time since 1883, and one of the many things that struck him was the transformation of the Metropolitan Museum of Art. It no longer occupied an eccentric mansion on West Fourteenth Street but had moved grandly uptown to Fifth Avenue and Central Park. "It is a palace of art, truly, that sits on the edge of the Park," James wrote in *The American Scene*. He was qualifiedly impressed by the emphasis given education in the enlarged museum, but otherwise had doubts. He saw in the huge new edifice "an object lesson" of a large presence in the New York future. He would not attempt to foretell it but felt it sufficient to define its announcing shadow, "that Acquisition—acquisition if need be on the highest terms —may, during the years to come, bask here as in a climate it has never before enjoyed."

To the novelist, there was money in the air, "ever so much money—that was, grossly expressed, the sense of the whole intimation." The money was to be "for *all* the most exquisite things . . . except creation, which was to be off the scene altogether," he noted, adding, "The Museum, in short, was going to be great." One reads this with a certain awe: James was able, with a few words, like an aerial flare, to illuminate a troubled landscape.

That the museum world was troubled was already clear in the 1940s. One problem was that the art museum had too many functions, with a resulting confusion of purpose. The point was mordantly expressed in 1945 by Francis Henry Taylor, then director of the Metropolitan. "If the term 'museum' strikes terror in the heart of the average layman," he remarked in a book called *Babel's Tower*, "it is nothing compared with the sense of panic which its sound produces in the poor innocents who spend their life rationalizing its very existence." Dr. Taylor continued:

> Going back into the far reaches of time, the word "museum" has succeeded in meaning nothing vital to anyone in particular, yet at the same time it has strangely meant all things to all men. Through a metamorphosis lasting many centuries, it has emerged from the simple designation of a temple of the Muse to be the encompassing catch-basin for all those disparate elements of hereditary culture which are not yet woven into the general fabric of education of modern society.
>
> And since education has been defined as "the art of casting artificial pearls before real swine," it is only natural that museum workers have concerned themselves with the elaborate furnishing of the trough at the expense of the digestive capacity of the feeders.

So disenthralled was Mr. Taylor that in 1954, without warning, he resigned as the Metropolitan's director and returned to a post he had held earlier as head of the small but still manageably intelligible Worcester Art Museum, in Massachusetts. Before his decision, he said with irritation to a colleague: "Dammit, we've got them into the museum, but what do they look at? One thing after another—if they come to a fire hose, they look at that, too."

In the ensuing years, other museum workers attempted to define the aims of their institution, with results that frequently remind one of the fable of the blind men and the elephant. An example is the "Museum Manifesto" published in 1970 by

Joseph Veach Noble, who was then the Metropolitan's vice-director for administration and is now director of the Museum of the City of New York. Mr. Noble had questioned his brethren about the museum's proper role, and the only common denominator he found was a spirited lack of unanimity. Undiscouraged, Mr. Noble nevertheless listed the five major tasks of a museum, the first being acquisition.

Acquisition, he maintained, was "our lifeblood, our *raison d'être*." Any museum that shirked this duty might be a useful exhibition gallery "but it is not a museum." Acquisition took priority over the other purposes, which he defined as conservation, study, interpretation, and finally exhibition. But one thing Mr. Noble did not settle, and possibly could not, and that was the increasingly familiar curatorial dilemma: What does a museum do when there is a conflict between acquisition and conservation—when one value can be realized only at the expense of the other? It is this conundrum we will now examine.

2. The Mutable Collection

The dilemma arises in two places—at the entrance to a museum collection and at the exit. In the first case, there is the problem of suspect art, which may have been smuggled into this country contrary to another nation's laws. In the second, there is the question of whether, and how, a museum should dispose of anything it already owns. The two matters are linked, because money earned through sales—or "de-accessioning," in museum parlance—is often used for acquisition.

To Europeans, the ease with which American museums dispose of art has long been a source of wonder and concern. A prevalent view has been expressed by Germain Bazin, the former chief curator of the Louvre. In his book *The Museum Age*, published in 1967, the French scholar asserts: "Endeavoring to create more space, several American museums went to the extreme of selling less popular works—an adventurous practice, because a revolution in taste might very well restore to fashion works formerly considered *démodé*. It is quite conceivable that the Barbizon painters, many of whose works the Metropolitan Museum sold as 'surplus' a few years ago, might return to vogue one day." (As has happened, for example, to Art Nouveau—deemed an ugly curiosity a few years ago and now squarely back in fashion.)

There are other risks as well. In a series of auctions in the 1920s, the Metropolitan realized $100,000 by selling "surplus" Cypriot antiquities from the Cesnola Collection; later, it was discovered that two heads from an important statuary group representing Geryon, the triple-bodied monster of Greek myth, had been erroneously "de-accessioned." (Ultimately, the museum bought the heads back.) Nevertheless the practice is widespread, and since World War II there have been major museum sales in Boston, Minneapolis, Providence, Chicago, and by the Frick Collection and Guggenheim Museum in New York. About twenty years ago the Art Institute of Chicago sold a group of Impressionist paintings in order to acquire a Tintoretto. The aim was to "upgrade" the collection, but the Tintoretto was later reappraised as a workshop product with little market value, while Impressionist prices soared.

The biggest controversy over de-accessioning concerned the Metropolitan and raised so many issues of importance that the underlying question—the priority given acquisition—was obscured in the smoke.

This scandal, like so many others, began with an official denial. On February 27, 1972, John Canaday, the chief art critic of the *New York Times*, asserted with alarm and indignation that the Metropolitan was secretly offering for sale a large number of modern masters, including works by Manet, Picasso, Gauguin, and Cézanne. A week later, with equal indignation, Thomas P. F. Hoving, the director of the Metropolitan, replied that the charge was "99 per cent inaccurate." Mr. Hoving found it truly confounding that anyone of Mr. Canaday's stature should imply that the museum was engaged in "equivocal, clandestine, and even possibly unethical" practices. It was true, the director said, that in twenty years the Metropolitan had disposed of some 15,000 works by a variety of methods, but, he explained, the risks in such "de-accessioning" were "not more significant" than the risk of missing a great work of art for lack of funds. Moreover, he promised, if any pictures were sold, the museum would announce that fact.

Six months later it developed that Mr. Canaday's original assertions were closer to being 99 per cent accurate, though, in the general hubbub, some of the paintings he mentioned were removed from the de-accession list. In September, Mr. Canaday learned in London that the Metropolitan, five months before, had secretly sold two important works, Van Gogh's *The Olive Pickers* and Rousseau's *Tropics*, for a total of $1.45 million to Marlborough Galleries, the most aggressive international purveyor of art. No announcement had been made. In embarrassing installments, the rest of the story was pried from the museum. It appeared that the Metropolitan had secretly traded or sold at least fifty paintings from the collection of modern masters bequeathed it by Adelaide Milton de Groot, a member of a wealthy old New York family. While alive, Miss de Groot had been courted by many museums, but around 1950 she was persuaded to leave the Metropolitan the bulk of her collection— which, the Metropolitan's representatives apparently told her, was too important to be dispersed. She died in 1967 at the age of ninety-one, and her wish, expressed in her will even if not in terms that were legally binding, was that the Metropolitan give to other museums in New York or Connecticut any works it did not want. Five years later, the collection had been dispersed, and among the de Groot pictures that had been returned to private hands were works by Modigliani, Bonnard, Beckmann, Léger, Dufy, Degas, Renoir, Redon, Toulouse-Lautrec, Picasso, and Gris.

There was an uproar. The secret sales were denounced by art historians, the College Art Association, the Art Dealers Association, and the friends and kin of Miss de Groot. There was a host of objections. Did the Museum get a fair price in its private sales, or was Mr. Hoving (in the phrase of Mr. Canaday) "a small boy setting up his first lemonade stand"? Was the spirit of the bequest violated by ignoring a donor's wishes? Were the de-accessioned works indeed weak and inferior examples of the artists involved? Had the departmental curators approved the sales? By what right did Mr. Hoving tell a reporter, "It's none of your business," when the reporter inquired as to the whereabouts of still another missing painting, the *Odalisque* by Ingres?

Yet the overriding question was why the Metropolitan was dumping its art. The tersest explanation was given by the chief curator, Theodore Rousseau: "What really sparked all this was the acquisition of a really great work of art—the Velázquez—and we had to make some sacrifices." In his candid way, Mr. Rousseau was referring to the purchase, in 1970, of *Juan de Pareja* for $5,544,000, the highest price paid for any work of art at a public sale. To finance that purchase, the museum dipped heavily into its endowment funds, and to restore the principal it was forced to sell what it could at the best possible price. Was the Velázquez worth it? An almost identical portrait has been on exhibit for a half-century at a smaller New York museum, that of the Hispanic Society of America. The portraits are so similar that some nineteenth-century scholars thought they were equally good, but the present view is that the Hispanic museum work is a product of Velázquez's studio, in the production of which the master may or may not have had a hand.

53

What is unquestionable is that Velázquez has a star quality, and that the purchase of the painting at a record price stimulated publicity. This is symptomatic of an outlook deeply troubling to some scholars, among them John Coolidge, a retired director of the Fogg Museum at Harvard. At an early stage in the de-accession dispute, Mr. Coolidge was quoted as saying that leading museums of the Northeast were no longer engaged in true collecting but instead, with the full support of their trustees, were shopping for masterpieces. "The museum which stops collecting in favor of shopping stops thinking about the issues which matter most," he said, "and, what is worse, can no longer effectively help those who do think about such things."

There is still another problem that has been generally overlooked. In the United States, works of art given to a museum provide a tax benefit to the donor or his estate, partly on the assumption that the public, too, will benefit from seeing the art. However, when a museum returns such a legacy to the private market it is negating the spirit of that tax benefit. Furthermore, a commercial gallery may turn over a handsome profit on art intended solely for public enjoyment.

All of this is part of the price paid for the priority given acquisition. A more serious cost is the physical destruction of historical evidence, the problem to which we now turn.

At the museum exit, there is the de-accession dilemma, and at the entrance the question of buying suspect goods. The question arises every week in major American museums. It happens like this. A dealer comes into a curator's office and spreads on the desk marvelous treasures, or photographs of marvelous treasures, that can have been unearthed only in clandestine excavations and that clearly were smuggled from the country of origin. There is a pleasant patter of conversation, an exchange of gossip, as the curator looks—without seeming too eager—at the prizes before him. Are they genuine? On this point, the curator must rely on his educated scrutiny while he listens to the tale told by the dealer. (There is always a tale, and it usually sounds more or less convincing; Norbert Schimmel, a New York collector of great discernment, says it is his maxim "to buy the piece but never the story.") If he wants the object, the curator will next plead for time. He must consult others, the price seems high, the budget is tight this year—these are ritual moves in the courtly saraband, while both parties make their hard private calculations.

The pressure to buy can be palpable. An American curator is known by the acquisitions he recommends. (Mr. Hoving's rise at the Metropolitan dates from the museum's purchase, at his urgent plea, of the Bury St. Edmunds Cross in 1963 for a still undisclosed price from a collector in Switzerland.) The curator in many cases submits his choices to a special committee of museum trustees, whose members esteem enterprise. Price is often not a consideration, at least in the usual sense; rather, it may be a means of giving a special halo of merit to the piece under consideration. If a dealer does not ask for a high price for a unique work, the museum may feel that the vendor does not believe in his own works—a feeling that is all the stronger when the origins of the piece are obscure.

Still, there may be a problem of scruple, or a fear that a foreign government may cause an unpleasant fuss. The dealer is equal to such doubts. He will suggest that if the museum does not buy, the treasure could vanish into the vitrines of a private collector, or that a rival museum is interested in it. What is the curator's first obligation? Surely it is to see that the public, his public, has access to a supremely interesting piece. Even if the piece has been smuggled, the dealer may point out, no American law has been broken, and why should a museum be responsible for another country's failure to enforce its own often absurdly inflexible laws? So persuasive are these arguments that established American museums, acting in good faith, have wound up subsidizing the wholesale devastation of antiquity. Nowhere can results be more clearly seen than in Turkey.

3. *The Washington Treasure*

Turkey has so many archaeological sites that no one has yet been able to count them. An educated estimate is that there are some 40,000, ranging from scattered burials to the magnificent remains of sumptuous cities. As the land bridge between Asia and Europe, Anatolia has witnessed a unique procession of peoples and civilizations. In this varied landscape one finds Neolithic settlement and Bronze Age cities, and, in a continuous chronology, the mingled artifacts of the Hittites, the Assyrians, the Phyrgians, the Lydians, the Ionian Greeks, the Persians, the Armenians, the Hellenistic Greeks, the Romans, the Byzantines, the Arabs, the Seljuks, the Frankish Crusaders, and the Ottoman Turks. The great majority of sites are in unpoliced rural areas, many of them only recently opened up by the building of roads.

Rich in its past, Turkey is otherwise poor. In 1970, the gross national product per head in Turkey was calculated at $350, compared with $660 in Portugal, $3,020 in West Germany, and $4,850 in the United States. For a Turkish peasant, the sale of antiquities can mean the difference between poverty and a marginally better life, and there is always the hope of a lucky strike. In theory, the export market is illegal, but the law that protects antiquities is a rickety 1906 statute providing only nominal penalties. (A stronger measure has been stalled in the national parliament for a decade, reportedly because of opposition by landowners fearful of losing a source of added income.) Turks who are professionally involved in archaeology receive wages low even by Turkish standards: the starting wage of a guard is 413 lira, or about $30 a month; the director of a museum begins at

1,250 lira, or some $89 a month; and the average rate for an unskilled digger is 30 lira a day, or about $2.25.

At the same time, foreign tourism has increased tremendously in Turkey, as in other once remote areas rich in antiquities. In 1964, there were 168,054 tourist arrivals, and six years later the total was 664,702; in a year or so from now it is estimated that there will be a million.

For all of these reasons, more ancient treasure has left Anatolia in the past generation than at any time since the fall and sack of Constantinople during the Fourth Crusade, in 1204. A scholar who has seen the change is Cornelius Clarkson Vermeule III, curator of classical art of the Boston Museum of Fine Arts. He recently remarked: "Fifteen years ago I could go into any muddy village in the Near East and step backward in time; today, in the tiniest Turkish town, you walk into the local merchant's and see tacked to the wall a list of Auction Prices Current issued by Sotheby's–Parke Bernet. The era of the stupid peasant is over, assuming it really existed."

Like narcotics, Turkey's other illegal crop, antiquities reach the market by established routes. Thousands of Americans are stationed on military bases or in diplomatic missions, and it is easy to gain access to the inviolable APO-FPO mails. Art can be smuggled by ship or truck, or can even be sent through the regular mail in camouflaged packages. (One American collector found an exquisite gold pendant within a lump of Turkish delight.) There is an active internal market, too. "Virtually every foreigner's house in Turkey was a miniature museum," David I. Owen, a Pennsylvania archaeologist, reported at a 1971 symposium on looting. "And all the objects managed to leave with them at the end of their residence. Even American agencies like CARE and AID contributed in their small way. Their staff members had the added advantage of going to outlying areas far removed from the usual tourism and they literally had the pick of the material, which would then be sent out of the country."

Dr. Owen believes that continued pillage, combined with urban growth and the mechanization of farming, will result by the end of the century in the obliteration of all remaining unexcavated sites near present urban areas. "If this seems somewhat alarmist in tone, I can allude to the tragic destruction of underwater sites throughout the Mediterranean in somewhat less than fifteen years. This destruction is nearly total as far as ancient shipwrecks are concerned." His estimate of the gravity of the situation is shared by Professor Machteld J. Mellink of Bryn Mawr, the acknowledged *doyenne* of American archaeologists digging in Turkey. She has said, "This is the murder of man's history, and it's a tragedy."

Tragedy it may be, but it is also a business. For years, one of the major dealers in Istanbul was a man of undisputed charm whom I shall call Gregory Omega. He used to operate a shop not far from the Grand Bazaar, and had a shrewd eye not only for the piece but for the customer; he could tell in an instant how much a buyer might be willing to pay, and whether it was worth taking him home to see the best wares. In 1962, the dealer found a dream realized when a unique cache came to light.

As Omega tells it, the episode literally began with a dream. A peasant woman who lived in an obscure town called Kumluca (pronounced "Kuhm-lu-ja"; the Turkish *c* is phonetically a *j*) one night dreamed that a treasure was buried beneath a tree. The following day, accompanied by her incredulous family, she found the very tree, and everyone began to dig. They came upon a chain, which as it was unearthed led directly to a trove of Byzantine silver—liturgical dishes, engraved crosses, candlesticks, dining implements, repoussé book covers, and a censer (to which the chain may have been attached).*

Kumluca is about twenty miles from Antalya, on the Aegean coast of Turkey, and news of the discovery reached Gregory

* The precise site of the find has been pinpointed—it is a mound four miles from the shoreline known as Büyük Asar.

Omega, who was then on a holiday trip with his striking, dark-haired wife. The dealer arrived in Kumluca in time to buy a substantial part of the treasure, which comprised at least a hundred pieces. When word of the find came out, the rest of the cache was obtained by the Antalya Museum and later sent on to Istanbul. When Omego studied his share of the find (he is a specialist in Byzantine art), he found inscriptions naming a bishop, Eutychianus, and a monastery named Holy Sion. There were five stamps on each implement, which, like a hallmark, showed that the silver was made between 565 and 575 A.D., one of the best periods of Byzantine art. The monastery was north of Myra, the port from which St. Paul sailed to martyrdom in Rome, and sixty miles from Kumluca. (Holy Sion is also associated with St. Nicholas the Sionite, who died in 564 A.D., and who, through the alchemy of time, ultimately took on a new identity as Santa Claus.)

Omega's next move was to get in touch with an old customer in Washington, D.C., Dr. John Seymour Thacher, then the director of Dumbarton Oaks, home of the Robert Woods Bliss Collection of Byzantine and Pre-Columbian Art. For years, Dr. Thacher had been prominent in the museum and social worlds; he had ascended the accepted rungs, from Yale to the Fogg Museum and then to the Bliss Collection, a logical lateral movement since in 1940 Dumbarton Oaks had been deeded to Harvard by Mr. and Mrs. Bliss. Dr. Thacher had worked hard over the years to see that its Byzantine art was the finest of its kind in the United States.

Early in 1963, Dr. Thacher received a letter from Omega describing the treasure, and he shortly booked passage to Switzerland, where he met the dealer. On being shown the treasure, he recognized that this Byzantine hoard, the finest of its kind ever found, would assure the preeminence of the Bliss Collection. The price was high—$1 million—but somehow Dr.

Thacher was able to meet it, and in due course the Kumluca trove traveled from Switzerland to the United States.

There were two other developments. Omega was aware that the sale of the treasure would become known in Turkey; he therefore closed his shop and moved, first to Athens, and later to Switzerland. Meanwhile, the Turkish share of the cache was being studied by Dr. Nizeh Fıratlı, a curator of the Istanbul Archaeological Museum, who was preparing the material for publication. Dr. Fıratlı had no idea where the missing portion of the treasure might be; he knew that Omega had acquired most of it and had left Turkey, but otherwise he was in the dark. In the summer of 1964, at an international meeting of Byzantine specialists in Athens, Dr. Fıratlı read a paper on the Kumluca silver, mentioning that much of the treasure was missing, in the hope that others present would give him a clue about the missing half. He learned nothing.

During this period, Dr. Thacher and the curator at Dumbarton Oaks were in a state of nervous indecision about the magnificent collection, which by now was in the museum laboratory. The eighty-fifth birthday of Mrs. Robert Woods Bliss would fall in September, 1964; and at about the same time there would also be an international museum conference in the capital. Impatience prevailed over prudence, and the Kumluca treasure made its public appearance that autumn. A subsequent catalogue entry gives this information about its provenance: "The following objects are from a large treasure of ecclesiastical silver found near Antalya in southern Turkey and now divided between the Archaeological Museum in Istanbul and Dumbarton Oaks."

Once the secret was out, the Turkish authorities demanded the return of the smuggled silver. The State Department explained that the United States government had no control over Dumbarton Oaks. Unable to recover the hoard, the Turks retaliated by refusing official permits to scholars affiliated with Dumbarton Oaks who wished to do field research in Anatolia. Though Dr. Thacher retired as director in 1969, the ban persists. One reason for the Turks' unforgiving attitude is that three other treasures, which may all be from Anatolia, have since turned up in American museums. Each treasure posed a special dilemma to the museums involved, and in each case the outcome provides a case study on the most emotional controversy that has ever unsettled the American museum community.

4. The Boston Treasure

Whatever the ethics of the Dumbarton Oaks decision to hold on to the Kumluca silver, Dr. Thacher at least knew that the treasure was authentic and was able to learn something of the circumstances of its discovery. But what does a museum do when it is offered a dazzling find of obscure pedigree? This problem faced the Boston Museum of Fine Arts in 1968, when it had to decide whether to buy a cache of 137 pieces of gold jewelry— the apparent remains of a royal burial—which included bracelets, rings, a handsome diadem, a necklace, pectorals, and, most striking of all, a Fifth Dynasty Egyptian gold cylinder seal in superb condition.

As it chanced, the vendor was again Gregory Omega, who had acquired the trove after his departure from Turkey. Omega either cannot or will not say where the treasure was discovered, though it seems likely that it came from southern Turkey. It was a difficult sale for Omega, partly because the Egyptian cylinder, though of outstanding interest, seemed culturally out of place in the hoard. He offered the treasure to museums and collectors in Europe, without success, and to the Metropolitan in New York, where it was also rejected. Mr. Hoving later dismissed the find as a "dealer's bag"—meaning that it consisted of unrelated objects grouped together to fatten the price.

But in Boston, the treasure appealed to Dr. Vermeule, the curator of classical art, a scholar of charm and erudition. Dr. Vermeule inclines to poker-faced sarcasm and the contrary argument, spoken with High Table self-assurance. He is capable of extracting a dog biscuit from his pocket and, without losing the thread of his discourse, disposing of it to a friendly animal. His wife, the former Emily Dickinson Townsend, is also a classical archaeologist and is a Fellow for Research at the museum and holder of the Samuel Zemurray, Jr., and Doris Zemurray-Stone-Radcliffe Chair, the only full professorship at Harvard reserved for women. She is equally fluent, and her papers attract overflow crowds at professional meetings. Together the couple have roamed the Mediterranean, where dealers speak of them as of mythic personages. In his spare time, Dr. Vermeule has been writing a memoir tentatively entitled *The Exporters* about the antiquities trade.

When he examined Omega's treasure, he decided it was not a "dealer's bag." The decision was made to buy the gold for a six-figure price, which was donated by a museum trustee, Landon T. Clay. When the treasure was examined by the museum laboratory, tiny flecks of clay were found on the Egyptian cylinder seal, indicating that it had been buried with the rest of the gold. With the full concurrence of the late William Stevenson Smith, the museum's respected Egyptologist, the Vermeules concluded that the trove belonged stylistically to the Early Bronze Age, roughly in the years 2500–2200 B.C., and that it was a find of major importance.

A special circumstance favored the purchase: the Boston Museum was planning the celebration in 1970 of its centenary. The normal eagerness to attract attention was quickened by the fact that the Metropolitan Museum would also observe its hundredth birthday in 1970. So anxious was the Boston Museum for a coup that its director, Perry T. Rathbone, gambled, in 1969, on the purchase in Italy for a reported $600,000 of a portrait attributed to Raphael, which Italian authorities claimed was taken illegally from Italy and brought into the United States without being declared to customs—circumstances that later led to the return of the smuggled portrait to Italy. (The story is told in the next chapter.)

The Raphael and the golden treasure were among the main attractions at the museum's initial anniversary exhibition, "Art Treasures for Tomorrow," which opened on February 4, 1970. The "birthday treasures," which numbered 130 and which the museum valued at $10 million, included other objects of great interest—a Cycladic idol (one of the largest yet found), a rare bronze crown from Korea, a Persian hunting carpet of mellow beauty, and two arresting steel sculptures by David Smith. But it was the gold that caught press attention. Where did it come from? The museum was evasive, saying simply that it originated in "one of eleven or twelve countries located in the eastern Mediterranean." This prompted an international outcry. The London *Sunday Times* said the treasure was "almost certainly smuggled out of Turkey," and Turkish authorities angrily made the same claim. Other scholars complained that the trove was a hodgepodge, of little archaeological value, since its provenance was unknown and its authenticity open to serious question.

The Vermeules made their reply with elegant coolness in an article about the treasure which appeared in the *Illustrated London News*. They wrote:

> A couple of journalists in London have tried to create "a scandal" over the acquisition of this group, which had been offered on the international art market in Switzerland, Germany and England before reaching New York. It would have been far more scandalous for it to continue its peregrinations, with a prominent American museum bidding for the cylinder alone because the rest was "non-Egyptian" and private collectors wanting bracelets and hair-rings for their wives.

The loss of archaeological context, with which this group came equipped, was guaranteed by the greed of whoever dug it up and peddled it abroad; and this loss is nothing to that which would have ensued had the collection been dispersed into scattered pieces. The donor deserves credit for recognizing this impending danger and acting promptly to save what still could be saved for historical study by serious scholars.

One can only hope that the site, with its new regional style, will be discovered and responsibly excavated in the near future instead of continuing as a playground for brigands, and that ministers of education in the eastern Mediterranean will increase their support of their antiquities services and their education of their people in the importance of not breaking into ancient monuments.

This able defense, however, did not do full justice to Gregory Omega, who insists that he never considered breaking up the collection. Dr. Cornelius Vermeule has elsewhere conceded as much; in an interview, he remarked to the *Christian Science Monitor*: "The seller wasn't going to split up the collection. He realized its value as a whole." Nevertheless, the Boston Museum acted in good faith in reaching a difficult decision and openly defending it. By coincidence, the Metropolitan Museum was at that moment coping with the same dilemma, and resolving it in a different way.

5. *The New York Treasure*

Competition between museums for major acquisitions has its roots in the national rivalries of the nineteenth century. Going even further into history, one discovers that in classic times great art was a form of booty, and its capture a means of gain-ing prestige; thus Sulla looted Athens, Verres plundered Sicily, and Titus returned to Rome with the treasures of the Second Temple. In the modern age, the history of pillage begins with Napoleon, who filled the Louvre with the uprooted art of Italy. What Napoleon began was continued in other ways but to the same end in the decades that followed; each national museum had its agents combing the Mediterranean for portable art. The spirit of the epoch was expressed by the French commander of an expedition that removed an obelisk from Egypt: "Antiquity is a garden that belongs by natural right to those who cultivate and harvest its fruit."

This harvesting had its positive results. Much was preserved that might have been lost or destroyed: the Rosetta Stone, the winged lions of Nineveh, the Venus de Milo, and perhaps (it is arguable) the Elgin Marbles. A less welcome result has been the enduring resentment of plundered countries, which has often given rise to laws prohibiting the export of all ancient art. One expression of nationalism has, in effect, stimulated another, while the past has continued to be destroyed.

The United States was a late entry in the competition for prizes and, since there was no national museum in the European sense, the rivalry took a different form. Here the encyclopedic galleries began competing with each other as well as with the European national museums. Intermuseum as well as international contests have been pursued vigorously, so much so that museums have acquired the outlook of independent principalities, each with the jealous sensitivity of a royal court.

A measure of this deep-rooted enmity is the use of the mischievous leak to embarrass a rival institution. It was by this technique that the first hint appeared that the Metropolitan had in its cellar a treasure of suspect origin. The initial report was in the Boston *Sunday Globe,* in an article by art writer Robert Taylor which defended the Museum of Fine Arts for buying and displaying its golden cache. Mr. Taylor contrasted this action with the secretiveness of the Metropolitan, which, he suggested, had purchased a rich Lydian hoard taken from tombs in the Hermus River Valley of Turkey. The treasure, he wrote, "would be just the thing to celebrate an anniversary . . . if a sister museum hadn't hogged the headlines with a smaller gold collection."

The story reached Turkey, and formal inquiries were made to the Metropolitan. The *New York Times* assigned a reporter to question the museum authorities; since Mr. Hoving was away, the Metropolitan spokesman was Theodore Rousseau, the chief curator. He denied that the museum had exported anything illegally from Turkey but added candidly that what he heard "seemed to be hearsay fabricated around something that might have a kernel of truth to it." This was in August, 1970, but not until February, 1973, was a further press inquiry made about the treasure.

Fern Marja Eckman, of the New York *Post*, had heard of the trove's existence, and when she inquired at the Metropolitan's press office on a Friday she was told that no qualified curators were available to comment but that an interview could be arranged the following Monday. Over the weekend, the story was leaked to the *Times*, whose account made it seem the Metropolitan was announcing the treasure's existence—the headline was "Met Proud of a Rare Greek Pitcher."

The pitcher was part of a collection of 219 pieces acquired in three· lots between 1966· and 1968 from J. J. Klejman, a Madison Avenue dealer. Originally, the intention was to unveil the treasure during the centenary, but when the Boston controversy developed, the Metropolitan had second thoughts. It did exhibit a pitcher and four companion pieces at its final anniversary show, "Masterpieces of Fifty Centuries." But there had been no formal announcement of the purchase (the price was around a half million dollars), and any reference to the new objects was omitted from the published catalogue of the exhibition. When "Masterpieces" closed, the five silver pieces vanished into the vaults, until their disclosure was forced by the *Post*'s inquiry. Eventually, Mrs. Eckman did talk with Dietrich von Bothmer, the curator of Greek and Roman art. She asked him where the treasures came from. "You should ask Mr. J. J. Klejman that," was the reply. Didn't the museum ask Mr. Klejman? "I think you should ask him." Did this mean that the Metropolitan paid half a million dollars without asking where the cache originated? "Well, it's a long time ago. All I know is he acquired them on the Continent. That's what he told us at the time." (Klejman, according to the *Times* story, "purchased the bulk of it on two occasions in different cities of continental Europe very early in 1966. He called the vendors 'traders,' ignorant men . . . who themselves did not know the places of origin and could not distinguish the good pieces from the masses of 'junk' they also offered.")

A scholar who spotted the five pieces at the "Masterpieces" show was Dr. Kenan T. Erim, a classical archaeologist at New York University and an experienced excavator in Turkey. To him, the style was Lydian or western Anatolian, and in his view the group must have been part of a trove illegally excavated from a tomb in Lydia. For his part, Dr. von Bothmer insisted that, wherever the treasure came from, he was at least responsible for keeping the group together.

In any event, by withdrawing the pieces from sight, the Metropolitan acted in accord with an old museum practice. Objects will sometimes vanish for a decade until it is felt safe to display them. An earlier instance was the decision of a Berlin museum to delay for ten years the public debut of the great limestone bust of Queen Nefertiti, which had been exported from Egypt in 1912–13 through misrepresentation. There was a furious protest anyway, and as a result Egypt refused excavation permits to all German archaeologists, a prohibition that was only recently lifted.

67

Conscientious curators have long had misgivings about such sharp practices, but along with this attitude there has been a disposition to dismiss objections as nice-Nellyism. James J. Rorimer, who was director of the Metropolitan from 1955 to 1966, used to admonish the overscrupulous that "no major work of art ever crosses a national frontier without at least two laws being broken." This accords with what can be called the Cesnola tradition.

Luigi Palma di Cesnola, the Metropolitan's first director, arrived in New York in 1858, a penniless Italian immigrant of noble descent. During the Civil War he became a colonel in command of New York's Fourth Cavalry Regiment. Recklessly brave, he was taken captive by the Confederates, and subsequently released in a prisoner exchange. (After the war he said he had been orally promoted to the rank of general by Lincoln the day before the President's assassination, and he called himself General Cesnola thereafter.)

In reward for his war services, Cesnola was appointed United States consul in Cyprus, which was then part of the Ottoman Empire. He was on the island from 1865 to 1876, and became an amateur archaeologist, exhuming a total of 35,573 objects in excavations that were for the most part conducted without Turkish permission. He then put his finds up to international auction, and though the Louvre and The Hermitage were interested, the winning bid came from the newly founded Metropolitan Museum. "All right!" the consul cabled, "three hearty cheers for our dear New York museum." Alerted to the sale, Turkish authorities issued an order forbidding export of the art, but Cesnola, forewarned, shipped his treasures off the island.*

---

* The plunder of Cyprus has continued, and tomb robbing has mounted alarmingly during the political turmoil on the island in the past decade. An entire Mycenaean city, at a site located north of Sinda, has been destroyed by robbers. Thousands of tombs have been rifled in areas around Polis, Ayia, Irini, Ambelikou, Paphos, Louroujina, Krini, and Margi. Peter Hopkirk of the London *Times* reported in 1971 that the pillage in Cyprus is probably worse than in any other Middle Eastern country. When Hop-

Back in New York with his collection, the General next proposed that he be named director of the new museum, and the appointment was made in 1879. An impressive figure with a bristling moustache, Cesnola presided with vigor over the Metropolitan's early growth, and took the brave step of opening the museum on Sunday. He was at his desk until the day before he died in 1904. J. P. Morgan, the president of the Metropolitan, speaking for the trustees, extolled him as an "independent figure" devoted to duty if somewhat impetuous in speech and action.

The Cesnola legacy is a fine collection of Cypriot antiquities and a tendency to ignore the export laws of art-rich countries. The Lydian purchase was squarely in that tradition, and fortuitously, it was made just before publication of the first biography of Cesnola, *The Glitter and the Gold,* a lode of information. The author, a journalist named Elizabeth McFadden, confirmed that Cesnola himself had invented still another treasure which he called the "Treasure of Curium"—a rich collection of Cypriot jewelry that he erroneously said came from a single cache. Miss McFadden said she was certain that some pieces from that Cesnola treasure were still hidden away "in the depths of the massive museum." Metropolitan curators insist that she was mistaken, and that there may be some confusion with the Lydian treasure, but Miss McFadden maintains this was not the case. In any event, it was a fuss that the General himself would have relished.

---

kirk asked about the source of a hundred pieces from Cyprus at a London auction, he was told by a Sotheby's spokesman: "Provided we are persuaded that the person selling an antiquity is its rightful owner, we do not normally Old Master paintings or Chippendale furniture." See Hopkirk, August, 1971.

6. *More Treasures*

Whether one approaches the acquisition problem from the viewpoint of Turkish officials, or from that of working archaeologists, whose concern is quite different, one finds an increasing alarm over what seems to them the casual rapacity of American art museums. Ethics aside, there is a practical matter which makes the field archaeologist the ally of the Turk: every digger is dependent on a permit.

In 1970, there were thirty-four foreign-financed excavations in Anatolia, of which seven were sponsored by Americans, the sponsors ranging from Harvard to Miss Iris C. Love, of Long Island University, who has been operating at Knidos. When the Boston scandal developed, all seven were threatened with the loss of permits. As an Ankara official put it to the *New York Times*: "Either America does something tough to stop this racket or a lot of your classical archaeologists are going to have to develop an interest in early Navajo culture."

The appearance of a mysterious treasure in America is a feature story outside of Turkey; inside Turkey, it is a political story with emotional overtones. Like other Near Eastern countries, Turkey is resentful about what it regards as past Western exploitation of its patrimony. When treasures are smuggled, Turkish officials are made to look impotent and foolish, and their feelings are not soothed when American museums loftily— as it seems to them—insist that the fault is Turkey's for not adequately protecting national property.

A special circumstance added to Turkish irritation over the Boston affair—the publication of the Vermeules' article about the treasure and pictures of it in the *Illustrated London News*. As it happens, that British magazine is identified in Turkey with the scandal known as the Dorak Affair, which has been a source of lasting ill will toward foreign archaeologists in Turkey. It is a puzzle with the bizarre overtones of Hitchcock and Eric Ambler, and though the details are known to archaeologists, most laymen have never heard of it.

It began, innocently enough, in November, 1959, with the appearance of an article in the *Illustrated London News*, "The Royal Treasure of Dorak." The author was James Mellaart, then assistant director of the British Institute of Archaeology in Ankara. The article, which was accompanied by detailed sketches of handsome figurines, fluted cups, fine daggers, and a marble scepter, described a treasure of great beauty and importance that had been found in a clandestine excavation in Turkey. But the only view of the treasure was that given in the pages of the magazine—all trace of it has otherwise been lost, and there are those who doubt its very existence.

Dr. Mellaart, a scholar of international standing and a man of direct manner, is of Dutch birth and Scottish blood. While still a young man, he discovered two major Neolithic sites in central Anatolia, Hacılar and Çatal Hüyük; at the first site, he came upon art of museum quality that was 7,000 years old, and in the second, an urban settlement that was even older. Çatal Hüyük yielded what seems to be man's first pottery, textiles, mirrors, and painted buildings. Then, in mid-career, Mellaart was somehow drawn into the compromising Dorak Affair.

By Mellaart's account—quoted in *The Dorak Affair*, by two British journalists, Kenneth Pearson and Patricia Connor—it began with a chance meeting in 1958 while he was on the train to Izmir. "We were getting near the coast and it was getting dark. My compartment started to fill up, so I moved further down the train to an empty one. Soon after that a girl came and sat down opposite me. She was attractive . . . in a tarty sort of way. But the thing that made me stare was what she was wearing on her wrist. She had a solid gold bracelet. It looked prehistoric.

71

"I said I was an archaeologist and asked her if I could have a look at it. It was the kind of thing that has only been found at Troy. She said she'd got lots like it at home, and asked if I would like to see them. Well, you know, it sounded important. I said I would."

The girl, who said her name was Anna Papastrati, spoke English with an American accent. She took Mellaart to a house in Izmir, where the scholar stayed several days examining finds that he was told had been dug up illegally in the town of Dorak, near Troy, during the early 1920s. Studying the trove, Mellaart concluded that it had come from a royal burial of the Yortan culture, which had once flourished in that region.

For Mellaart, the Dorak cache had a special fascination. It had been one of his theories that seafarers from ancient Anatolia had reached Egypt, and in the Dorak treasure he saw strips of sheet gold with hieroglyphs and a royal cartouche, which enabled him to date the find to about 2500 B.C. He was allowed to make all the sketches he wished, and he returned with them to Ankara. His colleagues recall his excitement over the treasure, whose existence he reported to Turkish authorities and to Professor Seton Lloyd, director of the British Institute. He omitted any reference to Anna.

Mellaart was anxious to publish the sketches, and in October, 1958, he received a short, typewritten letter from Anna authorizing him to do so. With Lloyd's concurrence, he submitted the report to the *Illustrated London News*. Nothing was said in Turkey about the Dorak find until 1962; then the popular newspaper *Milliyet* published a series which accused Mellaart himself of smuggling out the Dorak finds. There was a police investigation. No trace of Anna could be found, and by that time the house in Izmir could not be traced. The British scholar was then barred from field work in Turkey and his digs remain unfinished. He is now a lecturer in Anatolian archaeology at the University of London.

One published theory is that Dr. Mellaart invented the story simply to get publicity. But he had already made his name, and the Dorak Affair has come close to ruining Mellaart's career. More ingenious is a second theory—that the treasure did exist, that it was held by parties unknown, and that its very novelty made it difficult to sell. A scholar's opinion was needed to authenticate the trove, and the girl on the train was the lure used to catch Mellaart. If this is true, the Dorak Treasure exists and may yet come to light again.

To Turkish officials, the Dorak Affair is an exasperating example of foreign culpability in the plunder of Anatolia. To archaeologists, it is an instance of the damage done to historical evidence by illicit excavation. Even if the treasure exists, there is no assurance of its integrity; the gold sheet imprinted with hieroglyphs could have been inserted in the cache to enhance its interest. The scholar who publishes an undocumented find always risks giving credibility to worthless evidence.

The archaeologist, then, finds himself doubly imperiled by the illicit antiquities trade: he can be penalized by the loss of his excavation permit and compromised by unwittingly publishing falsehoods. Precisely these concerns have been at the root of a revolt against the acquisitive tradition of major American art museums. The revolt began at the University Museum of the University of Pennsylvania, and the case for reform found its focus in yet another treasure smuggled from Turkey.

In 1966, the University Museum acquired from a Philadelphia dealer a small hoard of Trojan and Sumerian jewelry. Publication of details of the purchase was assigned to an associate curator, George F. Bass, a balding Southerner who is a specialist in underwater archaeology and whose interest has centered on ancient trade routes. In Dr. Bass's eyes, the treasure was important because it seemed to provide the first definite evidence of trade contact between Troy and the Sumerian city

73

of Ur. The hoard—twenty-four pieces—included five pendants in a style that Sir Charles Leonard Woolley had found in the Royal Cemetery at Ur, and a pin and several earrings resembling jewelry Heinrich Schliemann had come upon at Troy in 1873.* According to the dealer, the treasure came from the area near Troy.

But were the pieces really found together? As Dr. Bass pursued his examination, his mood changed to irritation; he had to accept on faith a dealer's assurance, and if his faith was misplaced he was wasting his time and misleading other scholars. When he completed his report on the Philadelphia treasure for the *American Journal of Archaeology*, he added to it a paragraph deploring the illegal market in antiquities. It read, in part:

> If we, as archaeologists, are truly interested in artifacts as evidence for ancient history, rather than as possessions to be selfishly prized because of their rarity, it is time to take a firm stand. The clandestine excavator and antiquities smuggler are criminals to be abhorred; museums and private collectors who encourage their illegal work, however, are held in high esteem by society.

When the *Journal* received his article, Dr. Bass was asked to eliminate the last paragraph, and he did. He was at the time on sabbatical leave in England, and with some misgivings he gave the terminal paragraph to the British journal *Antiquity*, where it was published in June, 1970. He had an uneasy feeling that his institution would disapprove his bluntness.

In this he was mistaken. Independent of Dr. Bass, another Pennsylvania archaeologist had reached the same conclusion.

---

* Schliemann, the famous rediscoverer of Troy, smuggled from Turkey the great hoard he erroneously called "the Treasure of Priam." The gold jewelry was part of a collection of one thousand items that Schliemann later presented to a Berlin museum. Most of the Schliemann collection was lost during the fall of Berlin in 1945, but reports persist that the gold of Troy still survives in a clandestine collection. See Nicholas Adam, 1972.

This was Dr. Robert H. Dyson, Jr., who is the curator of the Near Eastern Section of the University Museum, and who first became concerned by the looting problem while he was directing the university's excavations in Iran. Early in 1970, he approached Dr. Froelich Rainey, the director of the University Museum, who was about to attend a UNESCO meeting in Paris called to draft a convention to prevent the illicit movement of cultural properties. Wouldn't it be appropriate, Dyson suggested, for the University Museum to show its good faith by taking a unilateral step in the same direction?

The director concurred, and on April 1 the University Museum announced that on the unanimous recommendation of its curators it would no longer purchase any antiquities unless accompanied by a convincing pedigree. With what was to be known as the Pennsylvania Declaration, the question of museum-acquisition ethics became for the first time, a matter for open debate. And that debate revealed a conflict between archaeologists and art museums.

After the Pennsylvania Declaration, other museums followed the same course. At Harvard, Dr. Stephen Williams, the director of the Peabody Museum, was among those who took the lead in persuading the Harvard Corporation to adopt, in 1971, a policy barring acquisition of suspect art by any of the Harvard museums—the Peabody, the Fogg, Dumbarton Oaks among them. At the Field Museum of Natural History in Chicago, a similar restriction was approved in 1972.*

* The full texts of all museum statements are included in Appendixes C and D, along with relevant resolutions and reports adopted by the Archaeological Institute of America and the American Association of Museums. The record should note that the Art Museum Directors' Association did endorse the UNESCO convention in a resolution adopted at its meeting in New York in January, 1973. A similar resolution had been rejected the year before. There was only one vote against the statement that was finally adopted—that cast by Merrill C. Rueppel, the director of the Dallas Art Museum. Mr. Rueppel was later appointed director of the Boston Museum of Fine Arts. Questioned about his stand, Mr. Rueppel told the Boston *Globe*, "I did not feel and don't feel the UNESCO resolution is adequate.

By contrast, not a single one of the largest art museums took the same step. Senior curators discussed the Pennsylvania Declaration with an air of annoyance or condescension. The Vermeules expressed the consensus in a note in *Antiquity* commenting on the Pennsylvania Declaration. The University Museum, they pointed out, "is primarily an excavating institution" and thus has a steady inflow of new objects, whereas the Boston Museum relies principally on gifts and purchases to expand its collection. Moreover, the Vermeules said, there was a striking contrast between the harshly restrictive export laws of countries like Turkey and the total freedom that prevails in the United States. "Any Arab," they wrote, "can possess the most basic examples of American heritage, as did the late King Farouk of Egypt on repeated occasions, from George Washington's sword given at one of the British surrenders to the gold seals of the Confederate states, without a murmur of nationalistic antiquity control. Free enterprise works both ways."

One does not have to be very clever to detect a certain overstatement in arguments like this. America, however rich, is poor in art, and by favoring free trade in the arts it has gained far more than it has lost. In the short space of a century, the United States has filled an empty continent with people, and empty galleries with art. It has achieved both results by means of liberal immigration policies. What the Vermeules did not discuss was the large, more important matter—the primacy of acquisition in the hierarchy of museum values. It is to this point that we will finally turn.

... Any country can state what its culture properties are as the UNESCO resolution urges, but for heaven's sake, I could state that my son's paintings were a national treasure. Mexico and Guatemala need effective export controls, just as we do in the United States. Due to the lack of export controls here we're losing our North American Indian heritage daily. . . . The problems involved here are social and political. They are not the fault of the art market." Mr. Rueppel is a specialist in the pre-Columbian field, and he plans to expand the pre-Columbian holdings of the Boston Museum. See Robert Taylor, 1973.

7. *A Question of Values*

"The Money Is the Message." The unflattering headline appeared in March, 1971, over a front-page review in the London *Times Literary Supplement* of centennial histories of the Metropolitan Museum and the Boston Museum of Fine Arts. The anonymous author, who was obviously well informed, made some telling points about the deficiencies of great American art museums. He spoke of the unceasing pressure to mount new exhibitions and make new purchases, invariably with the aim of increasing museum attendance. He referred to the "severe trial" imposed on young curators by the need to cultivate rich patrons who might be potential benefactors—an obligation that distracted them from their primary responsibility. A department head at the Metropolitan was quoted as saying: "Nowadays they serve us boot-blacking sandwiches in the canteen to get us properly used to the taste."

The review noted, further, that few American museums have published catalogues of their holdings comparable with those issued by British and European museums, and that such catalogues as have been published have been written by Europeans imported for the purpose—for example, the catalogue of the Metropolitan's French paintings, written by the European art historian Charles Sterling, and the catalogue of sculpture at the Frick written jointly by Sir John Pope-Hennessy, the director and secretary of the Victoria and Albert Museum, and Terence Hodgkinson, the keeper of the Department of Architecture and Sculpture at the same museum. The writer went on to ask:

> Is it too old-fashioned and too puritanical to suggest that too much money is at the root of the Metropolitan's problems? Too much money and too many people. Not bigger but *better* museums are what is wanted; not more visitors

77

but more perceptive visitors. It may be platitudinous to say this, but platitudes are, after all, truths.

Anyone who takes the trouble to speak with younger museum curators about the *TLS* review will find that it touched a nerve. The same misgivings that led Francis Henry Taylor to resign as Metropolitan director in 1954 cause many younger museum workers to wonder whether their jobs are, in the end, really worthwhile. Statistics are not necessarily a measure of excellence, whether the figure is the price tag on a work of art or the number of people who have come through museum turnstiles. The truth, as these dissidents see it, is that their institutions have come to reflect all too accurately a national obsession with quantity, and a national weakness for the star system.

In this sense, the debate over museum acquisition policies really comprehends a larger dispute over the values of American life. The museum is a mirror as well as a public gallery, and it may be unrealistic to expect that even such a special institution can evince an outlook at odds with that of the society around it. Yet even if this be so, there is evidence enough to suggest that American art museums could benefit from a period of pause, from a hiatus for reflection.

In concrete terms, this could be achieved by a moratorium on acquisitions.

The moratorium idea occurred to a number of people in 1973. One of them was Allen Wardwell, curator of primitive art at the Art Institute of Chicago. In its evolution, his outlook has been very much like that of other museum workers; when he assumed his post in 1960, he bought freely, even when he knew that what he was buying was "hot," and on being reproached for buying a Mexican fresco, he replied that if the Institute didn't make the acquisition someone else would, and, moreover the museum was preserving the fresco. Later, there was a furor over museum acquisition of large-scale monuments, and, like other curators, Dr. Wardwell decided it was justifiable to purchase only smaller, portable objects.

But this was no solution. The demand for the smaller figurines and ornaments was so great that it stimulated the large-scale destruction of burial sites. Wardwell came to feel that a more basic answer was required—that it was time for all American museums to declare a two- or three-year moratorium on the acquisition of antiquities. This would provide time for them to think through their own priorities, and it would also encourage antiquity-rich countries to rethink their laws with the aim of creating a legal market in exportable art. In a paper on the problem, presented in 1973 at a symposium at Columbia University, Dr. Wardwell reached this conclusion: "Fine as many of these antiquities may be as works of art, they are unfortunately tainted by suggestions of dishonesty, corruption, and greed. It is the responsibility of our museums to cooperate with the nations of the world so that these objects may truly fulfill their primary purpose: to express the greatest qualities of man."

One has the sense that the notion of a moratorium is an idea whose time is coming. New works would continue to flow to museums through gifts and bequests, and the money saved on purchases could be used to fulfill currently neglected museum functions. Moreover, new and imaginative loans and swaps could be arranged between museums; an example of this is the spectacular success of the Tutankhamen loan exhibitions in Paris and London in 1967 and 1972. Acquisition, it can be reasonably argued, has reigned long enough. Conservation, study, interpretation, and exhibition—the other purposes named by Mr. Noble in his "Museum Manifesto"—could well be given a larger role in the American art museum. Otherwise the muses of art and history will continue obscenely to consume each other.

CHAPTER THREE

SEE ITALY QUICKLY

Beauty is a frail good.
Ovid, Ars Amatoria, II

1. The Slums of Art

For every dollar spent on the acquisition of art, less than a penny is spent for its preservation. This is a discrepancy as appalling to scholars as it is generally unknown to the public. Art acquisition is a growth industry, so much so that the *Wall Street Journal* reports that the potential market for fine arts in the United States alone could eventually climb to $5 billion a year. By contrast, the preservation field has roughly the glamour of tsarist bonds, with as much immediate prospect of greater cash inflow. The result is that the very moment when the demand for art of every kind is soaring, a pittance is spent on maintenance and no proper inventory of the world's important pieces and collections really exists. To a businessman, this would seem worse than irrational; it would seem insane.

Without undue exaggeration, one can say that the world of art consists of three elements: a casino, a palace, and a slum. The casino is the international market, with its perfumed chic and its golden counters, where buyers wager on tomorrow's taste. Here no price seems outrageous. "In its upper reaches, the art market has been afflicted with a kind of collective hysteria, a St. Vitus's dance of zeros across the checkbook," Robert Hughes, the art critic of *Time*, has written. Thus, the National Gallery in Washington, has been able to raise upwards of $5 million to buy a Leonardo da Vinci portrait from Lichtenstein; Norton Simon, the business executive and collector, has written a check in excess of $3 million for a Raphael Madonna; and J. Paul Getty has offered $4 million for a Titian. Even antiques command astronomic prices; in 1971, an Iranian oilman paid $415,800 for a Louis XVI table, the most expensive bit of furniture in auction history.*

Some of the prizes go to the palace—the great museums of the world, the richest of them in the United States. Here lovely things are sumptuously displayed and lavishly published. But next to the Palace is the slum—the decaying patrimony from which much of the art is taken, a place of squalor and ignorance where things of beauty and importance are routinely stolen or negligently permitted to crumble away. The focus for the inquiry that follows will be on the slums of art, of which the most flagrant example is in Italy.

Italy, in Byron's phrase, has a fatal gift of beauty. Nowhere else is so much of such supreme interest in art, extending over

* A word about estimates. How can one say that the annual turnover in the international art market is at least one billion dollars? Most sales are private, but auctions are entirely public. In 1972, Sotheby's–Parke Bernet and Christie's together accounted for at least $160 million in sales (the figure must be rounded, because the total of $60 million at Christie's includes an undisclosed number of buy-ins for objects that did not reach reserve prices—the rule of thumb being that this is 10 per cent of sales). By the most conservative estimate, all auction houses together sold at least $200 million worth of art in 1972. The accepted trade view is that auctions represent only 5 to 10 per cent of total art dealings in the world. Using the lower figure, total turnover must have been $1 billion dollars in 1972. One per cent of $1 billion is a hundred million, and nothing like that amount is spent worldwide on conservation of art. It thus can be sensibly said that less than a penny is spent on preservation for every dollar spent on acquisition.

so many epochs, visible to us. One calculation is that the cultural resources of Italy are worth something like $50 billion —the value of objects in 30,000 churches, 20,000 castles, 60,000 religious buildings, and 200 state museums, not to speak of uncounted archaeological sites. Still, the monetary measure is degrading. What is Michelangelo's *Pietà* worth? Its market price might be set at $15 million, but its value to humanity is incalculable. Yet deficient security permitted the statue to be attacked in 1972 by a demented vandal who, claiming he was Jesus Christ, smashed it with a hammer, shattering the Virgin's face and one of her arms.

There was an international outcry; the Vatican has since improved its protective measures, and the statue has been more or less restored. Little else in regard to the neglected art treasures of Italy has changed. In that same year, every conceivable plague visited the Italian past. In September, the Colosseum was closed when thirty large blocks toppled from its upper vaults as a result of heavy rains, traffic vibrations, and air pollution. At the same time, the Roman Forum, flooded by storms, was closed for safety reasons. An ominous crack opened in the fourth floor of the Leaning Tower of Pisa. "The tower is very, very ill," said the Pisa superintendent of monuments, who went on to explain that basic remedial work could not begin before 1975. Meanwhile, the Italian press reported that the sonic booms from jets were flaking the Giotto frescoes in Assisi, while humidity was fading frescoes by Mantegna in Padua. Milan Cathedral is crumbling; the Ghiberti *Doors of Paradise*— damaged by the 1966 floods in Florence—are deteriorating; and the total work of art that is Venice is sinking away.

Thefts increased. In 1971, there were 290 thefts, and the next year the total, which includes only verified thefts, was 342. Officials estimate that in the past thirty years works of art valued at $400 million have been stolen in Italy. A symptomatic episode was the theft, in December, 1972, of one of the few paintings universally attributed to Giorgione. His *Madonna Enthroned* had always hung in the Cathedral of Castelfranco Veneto, about thirty miles from Venice. The church has no alarm system, although on at least three occasions the Italian Fine Arts Administration's superintendent for the region had urged the installation of one; even after an attempted break-in at the Cathedral, nothing was done. The church was easily entered by thieves, who removed the Giorgione from the wall and simply carried it through the main door to a waiting van. (The painting was later recovered, and it is said an alarm system has been installed.)

So slight are Italian security precautions that art thieves work with a certain nonchalance. While taking a Titian and thirteen other works from a church near Cortina d'Ampezzo in 1971, the brigands paused to drink Communion wine. (Later, the Titian was recovered.) No less carefree are the *tombaroli* —as tomb robbers are called—who for a century have been stripping Etruscan sites. A skilled *tombarolo* knows the surface indications of a tomb and pilfers the treasure inside after using an ingenious probing device known as an *asta* (lance) or *chiave* (key). The tombs are nearly always unprotected; when police are around a ritual game is played, for the hunters and the hunted both know that there is only a small fine for being caught.

"We have no special judges or courts for those who steal from tombs or traffic in antiquities," one officer has explained. "And our courts are as crowded as anywhere else in the world. You can imagine: a judge who deals mostly with cases of assault, perhaps, or fraud doesn't think stealing a vase is so very bad."

An Italian who has watched the pillage with special sorrow is Carlo Maurilio Lerici, an engineer and industrialist, who retired in 1955 as head of a Milan geophysical exploration firm, and, after a chance visit to the Etruscan collection of the Villa Giulia in Rome, decided to apply his technical skill to archaeology. He invented electronic "spades" for the location of Etruscan tombs—a potentiometer for finding cavities in the earth, and a periscopic drill that could scan and photograph unopened tombs. Within a decade, Dr. Lerici and a trained staff were able to identify a thousand Etruscan graves in the necropolis of Cerveteri and fifty previously unknown painted chambers in that of Tarquinia. Far too often, thieves had preceded the scientists. In a 1958 speech to the Rotary Club of Rome, Dr. Lerici reported that of 550 chamber tombs he discovered in Cerveteri, nearly four hundred had been previously stripped by

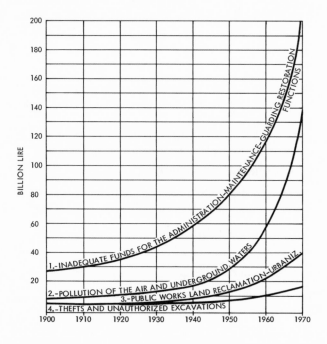

Carlo Maurilio Lerici's graph shows the sources of the progressive decay of Italy's artistic and archaeological resources. Based on many reports published from 1956 to 1966 by Italian and foreign newspapers and magazines. The graph represents one of the few attempts at systematic analysis of the destruction of the past. (Courtesy Carlo Maurilio Lerici.)

84

tombaroli, who, he said, clumsily destroyed a good half of what they found, sometimes demolishing painted walls with picks. He bitterly remarked that in one site plagued by brigands his team could not even get a permit for a survey from local authorities—who, his audience did not need to be told, were in the pay of the looters.

Dr. Lerici nevertheless pursued his work. He attempted an analysis of all the forces that together were destroying the Italian past and published the results in a rigorous monograph in 1969. He identified four major destructive factors—inadequate funds for maintenance and protection of sites; water and air-pollution damage; public works and urbanization; and illicit excavations. Of the four, he contended, the first is by far the most devastating. He wrote: "It is inconceivable that the country with the most important archaeological heritage in the world should have an administration and resources inferior to those of a single museum in the United States (the Metropolitan of New York)."

In 1972, an austerity year, the Metropolitan employed a staff of 761. In the same year, the Italian Fine Arts Administration employed 92 art historians, 95 archaeologists, 107 architects, and 58 technicians. The financial comparison is still more revealing. A Metropolitan professional will earn in a week what his Italian counterpart gets in a month; a qualified state archaeologist in Italy will receive the equivalent of $265 a month, meaning that most men doing this work must take a second job to support a family. Those in the service refer ironically to their remuneration as *"stipendi stupendi."*

Even if more money were available, the difficulties would surely persist, for there is worldwide lack of trained conservationists. Until recently, one of the leading training centers was the Central Institute of Restoration in Rome. The institute was housed in a crumbling Franciscan convent which had fallen into such disrepair that an extra state appropriation beyond the

85

institute's usual $43,000 was required to restore the building. The Italian Parliament failed to vote the additional money, and the institute was forced to close. That was in the fall of 1972, when the Colosseum was collapsing, the Leaning Tower had cracked, and the Roman Forum was barred to tourists for the first time since the end of World War II.

It *is* a slum. Italy's failure to protect her own cultural heritage evokes a patronizing contempt among those who buy what the Italians show no willingness to guard. At one point, a California financier, Thomas Merrick, impudently offered to buy the Colosseum for $1 million, saying that he would patch it up, charge admission, and split the profits with the Italians. Merrick's million-dollar offer was rejected as a bad joke, but, shortly before it was made, a great antique vase, of probable Italian provenance, was en route to the United States because a similar sum had changed hands.

The transaction underlined with embarrassing clarity how much is available internationally for acquisition, how little for conservation. It also threw light on the behavior of those in the palace when they go slumming.

2. *The Million-Dollar Pot*

At a museum conference in New York in June, 1970, Thomas P. F. Hoving, the director of the Metropolitan, said that the smuggling of looted art was not simply growing but leaping. It created, he said, "the most serious issue facing the museum profession." He went on to assert that the Metropolitan, for its part, had decided it would respect the export laws of pillaged countries, and that whenever there was any doubt about provenance it would consult with appropriate authorities. But Mr.

Hoving's later failure to take account of such doubt contributed to the worst turmoil in his museum's history.

The episode opened publicly on a wholly festive note. "A New (6th Century B.C.) Greek Vase for New York," said the headline on an exclusive account in *The New York Times Magazine* for Sunday, November 12, 1972, which proudly reported that the Metropolitan had acquired what its classical curator would later call "the finest Greek vase there is." The director was quoted in the article as saying that "histories of art will have to be rewritten" as a result of the purchase of an entirely unknown calyx krater executed by two great Athenian artists, the potter Euxitheos and the painter Euphronios.

Later, writing in the Metropolitan *Bulletin,* Mr. Hoving said that the vase was "majestic without pomp, poignant without a shred of false emotion, perfect without relying on mere precision." It was, he declared, one of the two or three finest single works ever obtained by the museum, and he added: "Appropriately enough, this unsurpassed work was acquired with funds obtained through the sale of ancient coins of its realm and time, which had not been on exhibition for years."

The price of the krater was reported to be $1 million, but the museum was vague about its origin. The official story was that the vase had been in a private European collection since about the time of World War I, and that the name of its owner could not be divulged, because he was the source of future acquisitions. This account was repeated by Mr. Hoving, appearing with Dietrich von Bothmer, the curator of Greek and Roman art, on the NBC "Today" show.*

A few months passed, and on February 19, 1973, the *New York Times* published an entirely different account of the origin of the Euphronios vase. Nicholas Gage (who normally covers the Mafia for his paper) cabled from Rome that the pot had been sold to the Metropolitan by an expatriate American

---

* The complete transcript of the program appears in Appendix G.

with a record of legal difficulties who lived in Rome, and that European scholars and dealers believed that it had been dug up in 1971 from an Etruscan tomb by bootleg excavators—an accusation put forward three days later by the Italian police. As the story unfolded, in increasingly bizarre installments, many Americans came to understand for the first time why Mr. Hoving had said that buying suspect art was "the most serious issue facing the museum profession."

The chief supporting figure in the drama was Dr. von Bothmer. He has glacial eyes, a massive square jaw, and blond hair, and only the absence of a monocle spoils his resemblance to the archetypal movie Prussian. But appearances mislead: the fact is that Dr. von Bothmer takes on a positively Mediterranean animation when visitors show an informed interest in his life-long passion, Greek art. Words cascade, his eyes flash, his gestures become emphatic. One believes him when he says that in an instant he can transport himself back to the fifth century B.C. He was a boy of twelve when he visited a Berlin museum and saw Greek art, including a Euphronios vase, and he decided then and there to become an archaeologist. As one of the last German Rhodes scholars at Oxford in the interwar years, he studied under Sir John Beazley, the reigning authority on Greek pottery. Dr. von Bothmer came to America in 1939, earned his doctorate at the University of California at Berkeley, and later enlisted in the United States Army, where he won a Bronze Star for saving a wounded comrade in the New Guinea campaign. He became an American citizen, and after his demobilization, in 1946, he applied for a job at the Metropolitan and was named an assistant in the classical department. (An older brother, Bernard, is an Egyptologist, and is now a curator at the Brooklyn Museum.)

At the Metropolitan, Dr. von Bothmer quickly became known for his uncanny visual recall. A glance at a pot would suffice

for the departmental curator (as he became in 1959) to determine its authenticity, its date, and its kinship to all other known
vases. His sharp eye also enabled him to quickly decipher the
alphabetic codes written by modern dealers on Greek ware to
show the original purchase price. In these codes the ten letters
in a key phrase stand for numbers. At Spink's, in London, the
revealing phrase was "Come and Buy," while Münzen & Medaillen, in Basel, used "Goldschmit." Ancient potters also used
to code their vases, and, to his amusement, Dr. von Bothmer
would sometimes find himself reading classical and modern
price inscriptions on the base of the same pot.

Dealers learned to respect Dr. von Bothmer's acumen and to
cater to his passion for the best. In February, 1972, Dr. von
Bothmer received a letter from a dealer who was an old friend,
Robert E. Hecht, Jr., of Rome, asking if the Metropolitan
would be interested in buying a krater of a quality comparable
to the Louvre's G103 and suggesting that the price would be in
the range of that asked for a first-class Impressionist painting.
The curator did not have to consult a reference book; he at once
recognized the catalogue number of the Louvre's Euphronios
vase showing Hercules wrestling with Antaeus. He replied immediately, "The answer is yes. Tell me more." Mr. Hecht had
sent an identical letter to John D. Cooney, curator of ancient art
at the Cleveland Museum of Art, and had also approached
Copenhagen's New Carlsberg Glyptotek. The dealer knew that
the Metropolitan was about to sell its ancient coins, and would
therefore have purchase money; he knew that the Cleveland
Museum, with its Hanna bequest of $30 million, had ample ac-
quisition funds; and he knew that the Danish museum was unusual in Europe in its private resources, thanks to its having been
founded by a brewer with a passion for archaeology. (Every
bottle of Carlsberg beer that anyone drinks contributes to the
Glyptotek's funds.)

Cleveland asked for photographs, and then decided that the

asking price was unreasonably high while the Danish museum reached the same conclusion, so the Metropolitan had a clear edge. In early June, Mr. Hecht checked into the Stanhope, the plushly genteel hotel facing the Metropolitan that has become the art dealers' canteen. On Sunday, June 4, the dealer took photographs of the krater to Dr. von Bothmer's country home on Centre Island, Long Island. On Monday, in high excitement, the curator showed the pictures to Mr. Hoving and, a day later, to Douglas Dillon, former United States Secretary of the Treasury and the president of the museum's Board of Trustees. It was decided that Mr. Hoving and Dr. von Bothmer should fly to Switzerland on June 26 to examine the vase.

In Zurich, the curator saw the vase for the first time in the garden of a private home, and it was for him an overwhelming experience. He was, according to the *Times Magazine* article, "speechless, bowled over." He saw a vivid depiction of the death of Sarpedon, a Homeric hero, with the gods Thanatos and Hypnos holding the bleeding body. It was, he said, like a new work by a great composer: "You're prepared for heavenly music, but you don't know how heavenly until you've heard it." Meanwhile, Mr. Hoving began negotiations with Mr. Hecht. By the director's later account, he asked first what the price was, and then he asked if it was a "hot pot." He was assured that the vase belonged to an "old collection" and that its owner— an Armenian living in Beirut—did not want his identity known because he planned to move to Australia and there might be tax problems.

At this point, one must pause. The "old collection" and the owner in difficult straits are among the hoariest dodges in the illicit trade. When the Dutch forger Han van Meegeren was selling his fake Vermeers, he said the paintings belonged to "an old Dutch family" living in Fascist Italy, whose name he invented. Dr. Cornelius Vermeule of the Boston Museum of Fine Arts says that he has invented a fictitious Polish family

—impecunious aristocrats with bad luck—whose misfortunes can explain the otherwise doubtful pedigree of all the suspect art in the world. "Despite their bad luck," says Dr. Vermeule, "the family somehow was able to get its art to the vaults of a Zurich bank."

It would have been simple prudence to inquire further into Hecht's story, especially since it was asserted that the vase's purported owner had other objects of such importance that his name could not be revealed. As Mr. Hecht may have known, by this time the Metropolitan had a $1.5-million guarantee from Sotheby's on the sale of its coins, so that money was figuratively in the bank.* The bargain was sealed, and on August 31 the vase was flown from Zurich to New York on a TWA 747, in the company of Mr. Hecht. The crate filled a seat; as Dr. von Bothmer proudly remarked later, "Euphronios went first class." Mr. Dillon, who was at the museum when the pot arrived and was cleared by customs, was especially pleased when the customs inspector said, in effect, "I don't know anything about Greek art, but you've really got something beautiful here."

The Metropolitan had every reason to believe that it had brought off a coup, and for Dr. von Bothmer the announcement was the high point of his curatorial career. He had long deplored popular indifference to his specialty, and he saw in the Euphronios purchase a way of giving deserved glamour to Attic painted vases. His mood was exultant when, on December

* Three sales were scheduled. In the first, at Zurich, in November, 1972, a total of $2.12 million was realized. A record price of $55,000 was paid for an ancient gold piece. A second sale, also held in Zurich, took place in April, 1973, and fetched $700,000. The highest price—$44,600—was paid for a silver tetradrachim. Swiss banks were among the most active bidders, according to a spokesman for Sotheby's. A third sale, due to be held in autumn, 1973, was cancelled as a result of protests. The Numismatic Society was given time to raise $150,000 to buy the 6,000 coins that were to have been auctioned—the appraised value of the coins was $185,000. Thanks to a flood of contributions, the Society was hopeful of raising the full amount.

27, he headed for Philadelphia to attend the annual meeting of the Archaeological Institute of America, the chief forum for archaeologists in the United States. By chance, he had just been nominated to be a trustee of the AIA, and he was also giving a talk on the great acquisition. He was prepared for congratulations, but in Philadelphia he encountered what was to him inexplicable hostility. Why?

"Archaeology is not a science, it's a vendetta," the British scholar Sir Mortimer Wheeler has written. Envy may have played a part in Dr. von Bothmer's humiliation, and the scars left by his sometimes peremptory manner may also have been involved. But there were also more substantial reasons. To begin with, few believed that the krater had come from an "old European collection." The study of Greek pottery has a long tradition, dating to the time of Lucien Bonaparte, a brother of the Emperor's, who, in the 1820s, first found magnificent vases in Etruscan tombs. (His discoveries inspired an Italian pun: when one asks how many Italians are likely to steal antiquities, the answer often is, *"Una buona parte,"* a good many.) So much has been published about Attic vases that few of the Metropolitan curator's peers were prepared to believe that so magnificent a work could have been utterly unknown for half a century.

The presumption was, rather, that the vase had been looted recently from an Etruscan tomb. Laymen are generally unaware that the greatest Greek pottery has been found in Italy, but everyone in the field knows it. (The point was ably made by Dr. von Bothmer himself, in a 1957 catalogue to the William Randolph Hearst collection of such works displayed at his museum: "Almost all the vases shown in this exhibition were found in Italy, where they had been exported in antiquity. So preponderant in fact is Italy among the known provenances of Greek vases, that early excavators took them to be of local Italian, or Etruscan, manufacture.")

Archaeologists concluded, then, that *tombaroli* had come upon a magnificent cache, in which there most probably were other objects of great value. This conviction was reinforced when it was learned that the Boston Museum had obtained another important Greek vase, for around $25,000, and that a hitherto unknown Euphronios cup, far smaller than the krater, had been placed on the international market. In his talk at the AIA meeting, Dr. von Bothmer showed a slide of the cup, which was immediately spotted as a new prize by specialists present. (The whereabouts of the cup is still a mystery; Dr. von Bothmer says it may be in Norway, and Mr. Hoving confirms that a photograph of it was shown to the Metropolitan.)

When Dr. von Bothmer made private explanations about the Armenian owner who was emigrating from Beirut to Australia, the story was greeted with derision. "Why not an Eskimo moving to Florida?" inquired a New England curator, while a Harvard archaeologist, when a reporter sought his view of the Metropolitan story, replied, with a smile, "My boy, there is an old Russian proverb that the earth is kept warm by people who believe."

Equally troubling to archaeologists was the price. The reported cost of the vase represented an immense increase in existing levels, since the highest known asking price for a Greek vase was $125,000, the price sought by Münzen & Medaillen in 1968 for a piece decorated by the Greek artist known as the Berlin Painter, which was exhibited at the Emmerich Gallery in New York. There were no buyers, and the vase subsequently went, probably for around $100,000, to a German museum.*

* Auction prices for Greek painted ware have been far lower. According to one survey, the top price paid in the period from 1741 to 1962 was only £2,150, the amount bid in Basel in 1954 for a black-figure pinax, or platter. See Reitlinger, 1963, p. 372. In *The New Yorker*, where much of this chapter was published, the author erroneously said the Berlin Painter vase was now on loan to the Basel Antikenmuseum. A red-figured mixing bowl, or *deinos*, decorated by the Berlin Painter is indeed on loan to that museum, but it is a different vase. In fact, the vase in question was sold to the

The implications of a tenfold increase in prices were set forth in the Fall, 1972, newsletter of the Association for Field Archaeology.

> The inflation brought to the antiquities market by such a price . . . cannot fail to encourage speculators whose objective in acquiring ancient art may have nothing to do with resale but lie instead in the tax benefits to be gained by donating objects to museums. . . . And the thieves; not merely the thieves who may assault picturesque castles with dusty old collections, but the brigands whose work has scarred archaeological sites around the world? What visions of quick riches are not conveyed to them in this one transaction?*

Lastly, there were doubts about the wisdom of the sale of much of the Metropolitan's coin collection. One of the critical archaeologists at the AIA meeting was Margaret Thompson, a former president of the organization and chief curator of the American Numismatic Society. Some 11,000 coins and medals owned by the Metropolitan had been on deposit at the society's quarters in New York until the museum suddenly decided to sell the great majority of them. Miss Thompson pointed out, in a letter to the society's members dated December 12, 1972, that

---

Badisches Landesmuseum in Karlsruhe, where it has the inventory number 68/101. The author regrets the error.

* This prediction proved all too accurate. In March, 1973, the *New York Times* reported that the vase had stirred fresh visions of vast riches in Cerveteri, the center of tomb robbing in the Etruscan area. The paper's correspondent wrote: "Even small shacks around this ancient town bear television aerials, and shepherds talk knowingly about Euphronios since they saw a picture of his vase on the screen. . . . Something like an archaeological gold rush is on in Cerveteri and nearby places." See Hofmann, March, 1973. For his part, the humor columnist Art Buchwald recalled that he once met Paolo, the chief of all Cerveteri *tombaroli*. Mr. Buchwald added: "I'm sorry the Met didn't contact me first. I could have sent them to Paolo and they could have avoided middlemen. I wouldn't be surprised if Paolo would have sold the famous vase to the Met for $198, plus four bottles of a decent red Chianti." See Buchwald, 1973.

most of the coins had little commercial value but had great importance as a study collection. She wrote:

> As we begin to withdraw material from our trays, the full extent of the loss to scholarship becomes apparent. Whereas formerly we had one of the most comprehensive cabinets in the world in certain areas, such as Roman Alexandria and Southern Asia, we now discovered that certain Moghul rulers were disappearing entirely and other series were being drastically reduced.
>
> Although we had known that the coins involved were here on loan and therefore subject to "de-accessioning," we had never been in a position to use our scanty coin-purchase funds, ranging from $10,000 to $15,000 a year for all departments, for the acquisition of duplicates against what seemed the remote contingency of future recall.

Miss Thompson, a spirited and dedicated woman, pointed out that the Metropolitan collection had never been published, and that its dispersal to private collectors and dealers would therefore mean that no record would remain of what had been lost.

All of these reservations, perhaps combined with personal factors, contributed to a decision to oppose Dr. von Bothmer's candidacy as a trustee. On Saturday, December 30, the organization's council met in closed session and in the vote the Metropolitan curator was defeated by a floor nominee, James McCredie, of the American School of Classical Studies in Athens. It was a personal humiliation for Dr. von Bothmer, and a hint of trouble to come.

Mr. Hoving, of course, had long been aware of rising concern about American museum acquisition policies. Among other things, he had attended, in April, 1970, a meeting of experts to study the ethics of museum acquisition. The meeting, held in Paris, was sponsored by the International Council of Museums, and one of the papers presented was entitled "Indirect Museum Acquisition through Middlemen." The author, Xavier de Salas, the director of the Prado in Madrid, had this to say:

> One of the greatest temptations to which a museum director or curator may succumb is that of buying objects from middlemen. The exhibits made available in this way may be of interest to the museum, are easy to obtain if one has the means and are sometimes offered on the very best of terms. Thus circumstances unite to create a strong desire to buy them and a temptation to do so. . . . Whether they were honestly or dishonestly acquired by the owner or intermediary who offers them for sale, it is difficult—and even in most cases impossible—to reconstruct their history or guarantee that their owner has the right to possess them.

In a closed session, Mr. Hoving himself presented a paper discussing the problems of acquisition. He also supported the draft conclusions, one of which was that museum workers ought to observe "the highest ethical standards not only in the very important process of acquisition but also in the other fields of their professional activity."

In due course, as Mr. Hoving had promised, the Metropolitan instituted a new policy in regard to the purchase of unpedigreed objects. Although the change received little publicity at the time, it was announced by Dr. von Bothmer in a speech given in November, 1971, at a conference in Florence called to counter the illicit traffic. The curator said:

> Whenever such an object without bibliography or pedigree is proposed for acquisition, a letter is sent to the responsible governmental offices in the countries that might consider the object part of their cultural or artistic patrimony. In this letter the object under consideration is described briefly, the condition and the dimensions are

given, and a photograph is enclosed. Only if no claim is made within 45 days after receipt of the letter does the museum feel free to go through with the acquisition.

The new policy indeed marked a change in hitherto uninhibited museum traditions—traditions in which both Mr. Hoving and Dr. von Bothmer had been trained. Much of what was done, even as recently as the 1960s, looks worse in the light of these changing standards than it did to the more scrupulous curators at a slightly earlier time. Implicit in the new policy is an awareness that museums must now operate within stricter legal limits, and that foreign countries must be given a chance to reclaim suspect pieces.

But the new policy, for all its merits, has two loopholes. If an object has been illegally excavated, the country of origin will have no record of its existence, and therefore will be unable to make an effective claim; this is particularly the case where Greek art is involved, since such ware is to be found in a score of Mediterranean countries. A second loophole is that the museum is its own judge as to whether a piece has an adequate pedigree, and its judgment hinges on its willingness to believe a dealer's story.

The vital question in the Euphronios affair is whether the Metropolitan exercised sufficient care in inquiring into the story about the calyx krater's origins and previous ownership. It is pertinent to say that Mr. Hecht—known to friends in Rome for his urbanity, his quick temper, and his passion for tennis— had a good reputation in the art world for connoisseurship and for returning money promptly and without question in the event a doubt arose about the authenticity of any piece he had sold. But also pertinent is the fact, known to everyone in the field, that Hecht had had his problems with Italian and Turkish authorities. According to official Italian records, he had lived in Rome for most of the time since 1955 on a moderate private income (his grandfather founded department stores in Baltimore and Washington). In 1961, he was accused of being a receiver of looted antiquities, but the charge was dismissed in June, 1967. In May, 1963, he was asked by the Ministry of the Interior to leave Italy, but in the absence of a formal expulsion order he was able to return later. From 1967 to 1971, he was on the "frontier list," which is to say that his baggage was routinely checked as he left the country—something that rarely happens in Italy. He had been a frequent visitor to Turkey, where his antiquarian activities had been watched with increasing suspicion, and he was banned from that country in April, 1967. A few years earlier, the Turkish authorities had found in his possession a hoard of ancient coins. Although he had quickly explained that he had been about to present the coins to a Turkish museum, when he subsequently attempted to get into Turkey he was denied entry. (For all his troubles, he has been able to say, "I have never spent one minute in a cell.")

Mr. Hecht told Mr. Hoving that the man for whom he was acting as an intermediary was Dikran A. Sarrafian, an Armenian coin dealer living in Lebanon, and that Sarrafian's father had bought the vase in London in 1920. The director was purportedly shown documents to this effect, but at no point was there a serious effort to meet Mr. Sarrafian and find out how he had obtained so extraordinary a work of art. Possibly one reason was that at the time Mr. Hoving was particularly anxious to bring off a coup. The vase purchase occurred as the Metropolitan was in the midst of a controversial de-accessioning process, for which Mr. Hoving was being attacked by John Canaday, the chief art critic of the *New York Times*. In defending his museum's sale of "surplus" works, Mr. Hoving pointed out that without adequate funds the Metropolitan might risk losing forever a masterpiece when it appeared on the market. The vase, clearly, was such a masterpiece; during his appearance on the "Today" show, Mr. Hoving said, in part, "[T]his is one of those moments in museum collecting that in my opinion is the perfect example and the perfect justification for trading out the stuff we no longer want to show and to put in their place things that indeed will be one of the top pieces in the entire museum, which has three million works of art in it."

It happens that the publisher of the *Times*, Arthur O. Sulzberger, is a Metropolitan trustee and a member of the museum's acquisition committee. With some enthusiasm, Mr. Hoving told the publisher about the vase, and proposed that the *Times* carry an exclusive report on the acquisition. The Sunday department duly assigned a reporter to the story, without informing Mr. Canaday—who, on his own, had already learned of the purchase, and was preparing a story about it. A spare man with a sturdy sense of independence, Mr. Canaday was furious when he learned of the Sunday *Magazine* project—all the more so because he felt that facts from his story, which was by now set in type, had been borrowed for the *Magazine* article. He told friends he was adding up his savings to see if he could afford to resign. As a mollifying gesture, his editors suggested that his article, in truncated form, could be run the same day as the *Magazine* piece. He was not mollified. He sent a memorandum to his editors, saying among other things: "It is bad enough to be castrated, without showing my wounds in public."

Later, when the *Times* began publishing a less reverent version of the vase's acquisition, it was suggested that the paper had a vendetta against Mr. Hoving. Mr. Canaday is not known as a hater of museums or as a petty and vindictive person. There was, in fact, a strongly felt disagreement on principles. Many who have dealt with the Metropolitan have been offended by what they regard as that institution's arrogance and its air of conspiratorial secrecy. Though the museum enjoys tax exemption and occupies a public park, though it is asking for a $3-million city appropriation for its expansion program, and though its building is largely maintained by the city (it received $2,414,499 of municipal funds in the fiscal year ending June, 1972), it tends to regard itself as an autonomous duchy, accountable to no one but its trustees.

The question of whether, as the Italian police believe, the Euphronios was found in a looted Etruscan tomb is a criminal matter, which will presumably be settled in court. No court finding is needed to determine that the museum failed to inquire fully into the clear title of a suspect piece. Enough discrepancies have appeared in varying accounts of the vase's history to make suspect the Metropolitan's title to it and to increase distrust in utterances of all privately endowed art museums. When Mr. Sarrafian was finally tracked down, he said he was not emigrating to Australia. There was no evidence of any other great objects in his fourth-floor walk-up apartment in Beirut. He reportedly said that his father had acquired the Euphronios vase "by an exchange with an amateur," and that he had never seen it intact. The krater had been lying in pieces in a hatbox, he told Mr. Gage, the *Times* reporter, adding, with charming insouciance, "I wasted most of my life with whores and archaeologists." The line is worthy of Aristophanes.*

* In a further interesting statement, Mr. Sarrafian denied that he had received anything like $1 million for the vase, though the Metropolitan had released letters allegedly written by him saying that that figure was his price. The phrase "New South Wales," it might also be noted, is used as an idiom in Lebanon when one doesn't wish to name a country or when one means no country at all. When an old customer once told Mr. Sarrafian she was going to Israel, the dealer said, "Don't say Israel—just say 'New South Wales,' and everyone will know what you mean." This gives a piquant flavor to a sentence in a letter purportedly written by Mr. Sarrafian and produced by the Metropolitan Museum as documentation. Allegedly dated July 10, 1971, and addressed to Mr. Hecht, the letter states: "In view of the worsening situation in the M.E., I have decided to settle in Australia, probably in N.S.W."

100

The Grand Acquisitors. *Thomas P. F. Hoving, left, director, and Douglas Dillon, president of the Metropolitan, disclose that the museum has acquired the most expensive painting in auction history—Velásquez's "Juan de Pareja." The portrait was knocked down for $5,544,000 at Christie's in London, in November, 1970, and six months later the museum announced that it was the secret bidder.*

A Curator's Prize. *Dietrich von Bothmer, curator of Greek and Roman art at the Metropolitan, poses with the calyx krater painted by Euphronios, said to cost about $1 million and said to be from an old private collection.*

The Boston Raphael: I. *An unknown portrait attributed to Raphael is examined by Perry T. Rathbone, right, former director of the Boston Museum of Fine Arts, and George C. Seybolt, then president of the Museum. The purchase was announced in December, 1969, on the eve of the Museum's centenary; just over a year later, U.S. Customs impounded the tiny portrait, which was later returned to Italy as smuggled art.*

The Boston Raphael: II. *Italian art sleuth Rodolfo Siviero, a guardian of his country's cultural patrimony, reclaims the purported Raphael, which now hangs in his office in Rome, pending a court determination of its ownership.*

The Explorer. *Ian Graham, a lean Scotsman who directs the Maya Hieroglyphic Inscription Study, photographs stela 38 at Naranjo. Graham is in a race with looters, in an effort to record all of the 1,322 stelae known to exist.*

The Stelae Hospital. *One of the saddest sights in the Western Hemisphere is the jumble of smashed Maya stelae kept in the inner courtyard of the National Museum of Archaeology and Ethnology, in Guatemala City. All were shattered by looters seeking wares for the international art market.*

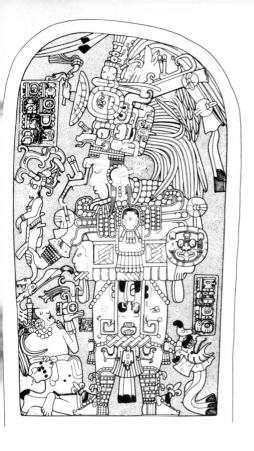

Stolen Stelae. *Ian Graham drew both Machaquilá stela 2* (LEFT) *and stela 5 in 1963, publishing his sketches in 1967. A few years later stela 2 was seized by the FBI in California, and stela 5 in Arkansas. Both had been smuggled to the United States after being stolen from a remote and unguarded site in El Petén, Guatemala.*

The Fourth Codex. *Only three Maya picture books are known to have survived the Conquest, and all are in European libraries. In April, 1971, the discovery of a hitherto unknown fourth codex was announced. These four bark pages from it illustrate the phases of Venus, with the lines of dots showing the duration of each phase.*

The Steward. *Michael D. Coe of Yale announced the existence of the codex, which was shown publicly for the first time at a special exhibition at the Grolier Club in New York. The Yale scholar does not regard himself as a policeman, but rather as a steward of the past.*

The Fanged Mask. *An anonymous telephone call in 1966 summoned the eminent Mexican collector Josué Saénz* (BELOW) *to the jungles of Chiapas, where peasants showed him this tiny (less than six inches high) Maya mask of polychrome beauty. Later advised that it might be a fake, Dr. Saénz sold the mask to a North American dealer; it was resold, after another expert proved its authenticity, to Dumbarton Oaks, in Washington.*

Decapitated Stelae. *When Jimb‹* *stela 1 was first found, near Tik‹* *archaeologists kept its discovery* *secret in order to thwart looter* *However, looters soon hacked ‹* *its inscribed top with a saw an* *chisel.*

In the Name of Art. *Among the most* *pillaged Maya sites is Naranjo, in* *Guatemala near the frontier of British* *Honduras. This is stela 21, shattered* *prior to its mule-back journey to British* *Honduras, where it was discovered by* *police.*

Rescue Campaign. *Alarmed by the theft of stelae, concerned Guatemalans in 1970 organized "Operación Rescate," to protect or remove imperiled Maya monuments. Here Naranjo stela 38 is being hoisted onto a truck.*

Smuggled Goods. *This crate was addressed to a warehouse in New York, and supposedly contained marble. A suspicious Guatemalan customs inspector found within it Dos Pilas stela 17. The person or persons to whom the shipment was destined could not be determined.*

The Nay-Sayer. *"It would be like buying a chunk of the Parthenon." This was the view of Joseph Veach Noble, then the chief administrator of the Metropolitan, when the purchase of the Campeche temple façade was being debated. He is shown here inspecting the stucco wall as it made its debut at the National Museum of Anthropology, in Mexico City.*

The Winged Temple. *Now a prized exhibit in the Maya Room of Mexico's National Museum of Anthropology, this temple façade was originally shipped to New York in 1968, and was offered for sale, for around $400,000, to the Metropolitan Museum. The Metropolitan decided against the purchase, and the dealer—who had organized its removal from a remote site in Campeche—was persuaded to make it a gift to the Mexican Museum.*

The Washington Treasure. *In 1962, peasants in the Turkish village of Kumluca came upon the most important hoard of Byzantine silver yet found. A part of the treasure was taken to an Istanbul museum, and most of the rest was sold to Dumbarton Oaks, in Washington. Among the Washington acquisitions were* (ABOVE LEFT) *the leaf of a book cover,* (ABOVE RIGHT) *a cruciform polycandelon, and* (BELOW) *two silver patens. The inscription on the paten at left reads: "This was provided in the time of our most holy and blessed bishop, Eutychianus," which helped scholars date the find to between 565 and 575* A.D.

The Boston Treasure. *A model displays the striking treasure of obscure provenance acquired in 1968 by the Boston Museum of Fine Arts. Turks claim the 137 pieces of gold were illicitly excavated in Turkey. The model holds in her upraised hand a Fifth Dynasty Egyptian seal, an object whose unexpected presence caused other possible buyers to hesitate.*

The New York Treasure. *Acquired during the 1960s from a Madison Avenue dealer, this superb group of 219 gold and silver pieces was sequestered in the Metropolitan Museum of Art. Shown are* (ABOVE LEFT) *a silver oinochoe, or wine jug, about nine inches tall, with a figure of a youth on the handle, late 6th century B.C., Greek;* (ABOVE RIGHT) *a silver phiale, a small bowl with lobes in the form of heads, each containing pellets (for use as a rattle), late 6th century B.C., East Greek;* (BELOW LEFT) *a gold brooch, with pin, adorned with a hippocamp, a winged marine horse, same period, East Greek;* (BELOW RIGHT) *a silver kyathos, or ladle, with two sphinxes overlooking the bowl, same period, Lydian style. Five of the pieces, including the wine jug and the phiale, made an unannounced debut at a Metropolitan centenary exhibition. Turkey contends the trove was looted from a Turkish site.*

Tombaroli at Work. *Three Italian tomb robbers plunge into a promising Etruscan site; the figure with a stocking cap is using an* asta *or* chiave, *the pointed implement employed in prospecting for tombs.*

Unprotected Art. *The deranged Hungarian-born Lazlo Toth sprang on Michelangelo's "Pietà" in May, 1972, and was photographed by a startled tourist in the Vatican.*

A Mock Attack. *To dramatize official negligence, a reporter for a Rome newspaper, Paese Sera, staged a mock assault on Michelangelo's "Moses" in St. Pietro in Vincolo, two days after Toth's assault.*

Decline and Fall. *The Colosseum is buttressed with scaffolding in September, 1972, to prevent its collapse as a result of traffic vibrations—huge blocks had been falling from the Flavian amphitheater.*

An Olmec Treasure. *A great find of Olmec jade was made at Arroyo Pesquero, in the Mexican state of Veracruz, in 1969–1970. Most of the best pieces wound up in New York, including these superb masks, for which a Madison Avenue dealer was asking $110,000 (top, left and right), and $90,000.*

Shopper's Portfolio: I. *In Costa Rica, where tomb robbing is a popular avocation, the author was offered an abundance of pre-Columbian art, including* (LEFT) *a fierce burial vase of the Chortogas culture, and three pots dug up in the Linea Vieja region.*

Shopper's Portfolio: II. *These pottery figurines, purportedly made by the Maya on the island of Jaina, were offered in Mérida. Experts who examined the photographs said the pieces were fakes, probably made in Campeche. The Colima dogs* (LEFT) *were offered by a North American dealer, who brought them in a station wagon to the author's house. The four West Mexican figures* (ABOVE LEFT) *were among many pieces for sale at low prices in the state of Guerrero, the bargains attributable to a momentary police crackdown. The figures were said to belong to the Xochipala culture.*

Shopper's Portfolio: III. *The author, in the course of his research, was offered innumerable pieces. This Roman glass* (ABOVE), *dating to about the 2d century* A.D., *was shown in Turkey, along with* (BELOW) *three pieces of Roman bronze, about 1st century* A.D. *The glass was intact, and came from a tomb; the bronze includes an oil lamp in the shape of a satyr's head, a figure of Eros, and a statuette of a bull.*

A COGNOCENTI contemplating y.º Beauties of y.º Antique.

In the Beginning. *A little-known caricature by Gillray, dated 1801, catches in amber popular attitudes when antiquities collecting became a craze among the wealthy.*

The Collectors: I. *Norton Simon, a California tycoon and collector of princely tastes, favors Impressionist and Post-Impressionist art and the artifacts of Asia. In 1972, for a reported $1 million, he acquired a bronze Shiva (BELOW), which had been stolen from a village temple in southern India. "Hell yes, it was smuggled," Mr. Simon conceded. "I spent between $15 million and $16 million over the last two years on Asian art, and most of it was smuggled."*

The Collectors: II. *Mr. and Mrs. Leon Pomerance of Great Neck, Long Island, collectors of conscience, with some prize pieces in their home. The couple helped finance a major Minoan excavation in Crete, and Mr. Pomerance—a New York businessman—has become an authority on the Mediterranean Bronze Age.*

The Collectors: III. *Lord Elgin, modern patron of collectors, won the Elgin Marbles for Britain and made his name notorious in Greece. Here a contemporary portrait shows the seventh Earl as he was about to assume his post as British Ambassador to the Ottoman Empire.*

3. The Boston Raphael

Even if Mr. Hoving had followed his own precept and had
sent a photograph of the Euphronios to Italian authorities, it
would have made small difference. An attribute of the slums of
art is that no inventory exists—not even of objects in museums,
to say nothing of pieces in the clandestine market. For years,
the Italian Fine Arts Administration has, in theory, been working on a national catalogue, but not one finished section has
appeared and completion of the project seems light years away.
Recurrently, Greek and Etruscan pottery is stolen from the
crowded cellars of the Villa Giulia, in Rome, and on several
occasions Dr. von Bothmer has been offered pieces he recognized as part of that collection. (He was able to bring about
their return.) Once, Dr. von Bothmer was visited by two Italians
who showed him a travel brochure of Sicily that included a
picture of the famous Ephebus of Selinunte, a three-foot-high
bronze statue of a youth owned by the town of Castelvetrano.
Did he want to buy the statue? When Dr. von Bothmer replied
that it was Sicilian property, the visitors said he must be crazy
to pass up such an opportunity. Three weeks later, the Ephebus
was stolen, but no official news of the theft was sent the museum
—Dr. von Bothmer learned of it only because he happened to
see a tiny item in the *New York Times*. (The statue was recovered in 1968, five and a half years after its theft.)

There is a void of information. Not only is there no inventory of what exists, but there is only the scantiest information
on what has been stolen. Interpol, the international police organization, maintains a tiny office specializing in art thefts at its
Paris headquarters, but at best it serves as a post office to
circulate fliers describing major missing pieces. The strange
truth is that the best intelligence service on the whereabouts of

101

art is operated by a leading international dealer, the Wilden-
stein Gallery, which has cultivated a network of confidential
informants for commercial purposes.

Against this void, one can better understand a scandal that
recently took place in Boston, over a Raphael.

As with the Euphronios, the affair began with a festive public
announcement. On December 15, 1969, the Boston Museum of
Fine Arts announced a sensational acquisition—an apparently
unknown portrait by the Renaissance master Raphael. It had
taken extended negotiations, and the price was reported to be
around $600,000, but the museum had somehow found a lost
masterpiece just in time for its forthcoming centenary exhibition. The painting's authenticity was attested to by an English
scholar, Dr. John Shearman, a reader in the history of art at
the Courtauld Institute, who said the portrait, which measured
only eight and a half inches by ten and a half, was "unquestionably" a Raphael and that the attractive young girl depicted
was very likely Eleonora Gonzaga, daughter of Isabella d'Este
and Francesco Gonzaga. It was probably painted, Dr. Shearman
said, on the occasion of her betrothal in 1505 to the future Duke
of Urbino.

And, as with the Euphronios, the affair ended with an international uproar. On January 7, 1971, United States Customs
officials entered the museum and impounded the tiny portrait,
pending a decision to return it to Italy, from which it had been
illegally smuggled. At the same time, the painting's authenticity
came under serious attack, and it was later conceded that the
portrait, even if by Raphael, had been heavily overpainted.
(The same suspicion of extensive restoration was also to cloud
the Metropolitan's claims to the excellence of the Euphronios
krater.)

There were other parallels. The then director of the Boston
Museum, Perry Townsend Rathbone, was an older, tweedier

version of Thomas P. F. Hoving. Even the jokes about the two directors were similar. The most familiar about Mr. Hoving (he had made it on himself) was that his middle initials stood for Publicity Forever. Of Mr. Rathbone, it was said that he shared more than his initials in common with P. T. Barnum. A Harvard graduate (Mr. Hoving is a Princetonian), Mr. Rathbone had made his name in the museum field as director of the City Art Museum in St. Louis, a post he assumed in 1940.

In St. Louis, Mr. Rathbone—an affable man of considerable charm—had indeed used circus techniques to increase attendance. He had hired a band of Comanches to perform tribal dances in order to publicize an exhibition entitled "Westward the Way." He had a Dutch windmill installed on the museum grounds to promote the Van Gogh centenary. For a show called "Italy at Work," he had dispatched a Sicilian donkey cart, filled with pretty girls, through downtown streets, and a circulating show on Viennese treasures had been promoted with knights on horseback.

When he came to Boston, in 1955, Mr. Rathbone used less flashy means to promote the museum, but his concern with attendance and publicity persisted. Mr. Rathbone's great coup was the Raphael. The painting, according to the museum, had come from an "old European private collection." In due course, a photograph of the Boston Raphael appeared in the international press. Among those who saw the picture was Rodolfo Siviero, who heads Italy's Commission for the Recovery of Works of Art. Signor Siviero, a Florentine bachelor in his sixties who lives with his sister in a house on the banks of the Arno, became involved with art during World War II when he kept records of works stolen both by the Germans and by Allied liberators, and he has served in successive postwar governments. A stolid man who looks a bit as one imagines Hercule Poirot might, Siviero has, over the years, cultivated an extensive acquaintance with everyone in the Italian art world.

103

What struck him, when he saw the illustration of the Raphael, was the frame. According to historical records, such a portrait had been done by Raphael but had lost its frame; therefore, the handsome gilt carving around the picture had to be modern. Signor Siviero consulted with members of the Florentine art community and found a dealer who said he had sold the frame to another dealer, named Ferruccio Ildebrando Bossi, then in his eighties, who lived in a villa near the village of Recco, about twelve miles east of Genoa. Mr. Bossi, it later developed, had a police record in Italy going back to 1924. He had been convicted for smuggling both currency and works of art, had served five years in jail for smuggling antiques, and had been outlawed as a dealer by both the Italian police and the Italian art dealers association. Hotel registers were searched, and it was learned that on July 12, 1969, Mr. Rathbone had checked into the Aquila Reale, in Genoa, along with John Goelet, a Boston trustee, and Hanns Swarzenski, the museum's curator of decorative arts. Under direct questioning, and on being confronted with his criminal record, Mr. Bossi finally admitted that he had sold the Raphael to Boston.

In Boston, meanwhile, Mr. Rathbone was sticking to his original story—that the Raphael had come from an "old European private collection" and had been legally imported into the United States. When he was asked about Mr. Siviero's initial charges, he said: "Pure supposition on the part of that fellow in Rome. How can he make such a claim when a painting was entirely unknown, uncatalogued, unlisted, unillustrated, and unpublished up till now?" Unfortunately for Mr. Rathbone, Signor Siviero had a strong case. And then, amid general astonishment, it was found that the Boston Museum had failed to declare the Raphael when it was brought into the United States.*

* By chance, as the Boston scandal developed, a special meeting of the American Association of Museums was held in Washington to discuss "the ethics of acquisition." Reporters inquired about the Boston episode. The late Armand G. Erpf, the chairman of the association's trustees, a trustee of the

This meant that, in addition to Italian law, which prohibits the export of unlicensed art, American laws had also been violated. The small painting, the Italians charged, had been tucked in a suitcase carried by Mr. Swarzenski. In October, 1971, Mr. Swarzenski, an erect and striking figure with an impressive mane of white hair, retired as curator, remaining at the museum as a senior research fellow. In December of that year Mr. Rathbone announced that having reached the age of sixty, he was retiring "in order to write and pursue independent research." Bossi in the meantime had died, and the Boston Museum found it had lost not only the painting but a substantial part of the price paid for it. (Bossi's estate is still in the courts.)

Early in 1971, the Raphael controversy was brought to the attention, in Washington, of Eugene Telemachus Rossides, then the Assistant Secretary of the Treasury responsible for the Customs Bureau. Mr. Rossides is of Greek ancestry and has strong feelings about the Elgin Marbles, but is otherwise not involved with the art world. (He was a football star at Columbia University and a racket-busting investigator for the New York County District Attorney's office before joining the Treasury.) He met with the trustees of the Boston Museum to discuss the smuggled painting, and he was surprised to discover that they were so obviously ashamed of what had happened that they were very willing to do anything that might make matters right. As a result, the return of the painting to Italy was smoothly negotiated, and, pending a final determination of its ownership,

Whitney Museum, and general partner of Loeb, Rhoades & Co., commented: "Of course the Boston should have declared it and put in the proper papers. But I'm sure that's just a technicality. I get tired of the real effrontery of the Italians. They're also wanting us to pay to restore their treasures damaged in the floods of Florence so they can attract American tourists to come to Florence to spend U.S. money." One gentleman, who put his hand over his identifying name tag, said that "the whole Boston affair was political. A group of Italian policemen in Boston were riled up." See Conroy, 1971.

the portrait now hangs in Signor Siviero's office in the Palazzo Venezia.

There was, however, a further embarrassment. The very authenticity of the Raphael for which the museum had risked so much came into serious question, beginning with a letter to *The Times* of London on March 3, 1970. The letter was signed by Sidney F. Sabin, a London art dealer, and said flatly that the picture was "entirely meretricious and demonstrably a fake." In language equally as warm, the portrait was defended by its original authenticator, John Shearman. And yet Shearman, after listing all the technical points in the painting's favor, did make this admission:

> Faking (which is something I meet too) has its own evolution. I would not deny that an exceedingly clever faker in 1970 could reproduce most of the physical properties that I have described. But every year backwards from this date makes the suspicion less plausible.

> So far all that has come to light in the way of facts, not traditions, about the history of this picture is that it was in the collection of the Fieschi (an ancient family based in Genoa and Rome) until about 1946, and that when it had been in their hands it was seen and approved by a number of distinguished Italian scholars.

Here, surely, one comes to the gravamen of the scandal— that a painting responsibly attributed to one of the supreme masters of Italian art could be swallowed up in darkness, only to reappear on the walls of the Boston Museum, its provenance a mystery to be solved by diligent police work. There is no unified, comprehensive inventory of art, though all experts agree that the very first step in any practical preservation campaign must be to compile such a register. The techniques for compiling the inventory exist. What is lacking is the money.

The key to such an inventory is the computer. In 1967, a

106

promising program aimed at using computer technology for recording art was initiated when fifteen New York museums and the National Gallery of Art, in Washington, formed an unincorporated consortium known as the Museum Computer Network. The idea was to create a unified, indexed data bank for cataloguing the collections not only of museums but also, ultimately, of major art in private hands. Of the many potential benefits, the first would be that a scholar, having access to such a unified index, could get a printout summary (say) of every known painting by Raphael, or the School of Raphael, or works attributed to Raphael. Each work would be briefly described and its whereabouts identified. Or, to take another example, an archaeologist studying Attic red-figure pottery depicting the death of Sarpedon could likewise get a printout locating and describing all known specimens.

A further benefit would be that a computer inventory would provide an opportunity for a rigorous appraisal of the world's art. Optimistic attributions could be reexamined and fakes weeded out in a systematic study of mankind's cultural legacy. Emphasis on scholarship could supplement the already sufficient emphasis on acquisition. Finally, an inventory would be an obviously useful security measure. If the Villa Giulia's cellar were rifled, a record of its contents could be consulted and descriptions of what had been taken could be instantly transmitted to museums and dealers—a vast improvement on the rudimentary informational network that now operates.

In 1968, a two-year experimental program was undertaken by the Museum Computer Network, and the feasibility of such inventories was confirmed. In 1970, funding for the project, provided from foundation grants, was not renewed, and the group has since proceeded in low gear, and only in the United States. In a complementary initiative, prominent members of the New York art community also founded, in 1968, an organization called the International Foundation for Art Research. A nonprofit body with a distinguished board of trustees, the foundation has as its major purpose the gathering of information on controversial works that are brought to it for examination. It could, in theory, evolve into a multinational clearinghouse for computer data, and for descriptions of lost, stolen, and plundered art.

The foundation's aims are as widely applauded as they are indifferently supported. With some small grants from foundations and public contributions, it maintains a small office in New York, which has a staff of one—its executive secretary, Mrs. Margery Torrey, who is a trained art historian. Mrs. Torrey says she has an annual budget of about $20,000, of which $7,000 goes for office rental. Much of her time is necessarily devoted to raising money to keep the organization going. The foundation, too, subsists in the slums of art.

4. The Fake Factory

Since no inventory of art exists, and since museums and collectors continually buy unpedigreed works, there is a chronic hazard of being taken by a forgery. The prevalence of fakes is the venereal disorder of the illicit art market—the punishment for excessive desire and bad judgment. When a piece is exposed as a fake, the usual museum practice is to hide it away, as if its mere presence would infect the worthier works around it—and in the process, years of scholarly labor may be wasted in arguments over the virtue of an object.

Italy, without question, has been the world's premiere fake factory. In the days of Hadrian, Roman artisans were already making cunning copies of Greek art for sale as originals to Imperial collectors. When antiquity came back into fashion in the Renaissance, the forger's art was reborn, its greatest prac-

108

titioner being Michelangelo. One of the master's earliest works was a marble god of Love, lying as if asleep. When Lorenzo di Pier Francesco de' Medici saw it, he slyly told the sculptor: "If you arrange to make it look as if it had been buried under earth, I will send it to Rome and it will pass as an antique, and you'll sell it much more easily." An early biography (1553) of Michelangelo, by Ascanio Condivi, continues the story:

> Hearing this, Michelangelo, from whom no technique of craft was hidden, immediately fixed it up so that it seemed made many years ago. Then it was sent to Rome. The Cardinal di San Giorgio bought it as an antique for two hundred ducats; although the man who took the money wrote to Florence that Michelangelo should receive thirty ducats, such being what he had received for the Cupid, deceiving both Lorenzo di Pier Francesco and Michelangelo.

Furious when he later learned that he had been underpaid— even though he himself was perpetrating a fraud—Michelangelo went to Rome to see the cardinal and recover the fake Cupid. ("Afterward, it wound up, I don't know how," says Condivi of the statue, "in the hands of Duke Valentino, and was given to the Marchesana of Mantua, who sent it to Mantua, where it still is." The Cupid is now lost.)*

With a single essential difference, the episode anticipated the experience of Alceo Dossena, the greatest modern Italian master of the fake antique. The essential difference is that Dossena, a simpleminded stone mason who died in 1937, was by all accounts not a party to deceit. Dossena had a passion for every kind of ancient art and could uncannily imitate the style of any period, producing works that were never literal copies but, instead, brilliant originals. He said of himself: "I was born in

---

* The author is grateful to Sidney Alexander, of Florence, Italy, for locating and translating this passage from Condivi.

our time, but with the soul, taste, and perception of other ages."
His work caught the attention of local dealers, and during the
1920s he was given small sums for pieces he thought were being
sold as modern imitations. Orders flowed in to his Rome work-
shop, and Dossena happily turned out Etruscan terra-cottas,
hewn Greek gods, and Gothic saints by the dozens, often adding
to each work an ancient patina of subtle perfection. Eventually
he learned the truth—that his customers were inventing fake
pedigrees for his work and selling them as originals at large
prices. The naïve artisan was appalled and angry at being
cheated and at having his art misrepresented. By then, Dossenas
were on exhibit in museums throughout the West; some of his
production is still displayed as ancient art.

When Dossena learned what had been happening, he swore
he would make no more antique sculpture, but, according to a
son, he did do one more—a terra-cotta Diana, in the Etruscan
manner—around 1937. The best evidence is that this figure appeared on the art market and may have been sold in 1953 to
the City Art Museum in St. Louis, then under the directorship
of Perry T. Rathbone. The museum had an affidavit of authenticity, asserting that the sculpture had been found in a heap of
fragments north of Rome in 1872. According to the affidavit,
the alleged original owner was Count Mancinelli-Scotti, whose
niece later inherited the statue, which passed through several
more hands before reaching Adolf Loewi, a Los Angeles dealer.
The City Museum was reported to have paid $56,000 for the
statue, which had its old Etruscan colors still apparently visible
on it. When it later developed that the museum had quite possibly acquired Dossena's last work, the statue was sent to Europe for further opinions, which were inconclusive—Italian
experts refused even to examine the statue. In 1968, the Diana
was quietly withdrawn from exhibition.

Museum curators talk about the work of eminent forgers with

an affectionate relish—that is, when it is someone else's fake that is exposed. The products of various workshops have come to be known by their stylistic kinship; for example, there were the Riccardi cousins of Orvieto, who collaborated with Alfredo Adolfo Fioravanti in creating the three Etruscan warriors exhibited at the Metropolitan from 1933 until 1961. The reigning master today is a superb workman living in an ancient town not far from Rome, whom I shall call Alfredo Kappa. His work is on display in many museums, and he made some Etruscan wall paintings on terra-cotta that cost a European collector $1.2 million.

Kappa is in his forties, a good-looking, ruddy-complexioned man. I spent an evening with him in May, 1972, at the home of friends in Rome, and when I asked how he had acquired his skill, he said he had learned nothing in school, but, in his twenties, while employed as a furnace worker in a tile factory, he was befriended by *tombaroli* and went on their tomb-hunting forays. He became acquainted with dealers, learned the rudiments of the market, and then tried his hand at making fakes, using firing techniques he learned at the factory. He quickly showed a gift for making a convincing Greek vase or an authentic-looking Etruscan terra-cotta. But he found there was a problem—a need to prove a provenance for his pieces.

A man of superior intelligence, Kappa devised a brilliant solution: to fabricate his own Etruscan site. In the 1960s, working with twelve other men, he began to dig a tomb; as luck would have it, he hit the remains of an authentic ancient chamber. He now had a place to which he could bring dealers, and he sowed it with his own wares, coating his pots with its distinctive earth. In a four-year period, he sold hundreds of objects to leading dealers from Rome, Geneva, and Basel. He followed the progress of his art with satisfaction as it went from dealer to museum; sometimes pictures of it appeared on the covers of archaeological books or magazines.

111

Kappa's technique improved. He bought and studied carefully a handsome book written by Joseph V. Noble, *The Techniques of Painted Attic Pottery*, published in 1965 and intended for scholars. At this time, too, he met a leading European collector whom I shall call Pedro Sigma—American-educated, Paris-bred, and now living in Geneva. Though Sigma's specialty is classic bronzes, he collects everything antique, and knows all the dealers in the field. Having suspected that he was being overcharged because he was wealthy, Sigma decided to bypass middlemen and go directly to the source—the *tombaroli* themselves. Sometimes this led to trouble; in 1963 he was accused by Italian police of attempting to smuggle out a truckload of antiquities; the Italian press reported that he was associated at the time with Robert E. Hecht, Jr., then in enforced exile from Italy.

In his explorations, the collector met Kappa, who told him that there was something incredible that could be seen *in situ*, in an underground Etruscan temple. Kappa, according to one account, led his victim to his contrived site and, with flashlights, showed him some extraordinary painted plaques which, the collector was told, could be transported to Geneva. There were tortuous negotiations, and Sigma eventually agreed to pay the equivalent of $1.2 million for the unique treasure. In due time, it was sent to his villa in Geneva.

Some years earlier, the collector had come to know Dietrich von Bothmer, one of the scholars the forger had been unable to fool. The Metropolitan curator first saw the terra-cotta forgeries in June, 1967, in Munich, Basel, and Geneva. He thought he also saw the same forger's hand in a piece owned by Sigma which was submitted the following year to a New York benefit for the American preparatory school the collector had attended. There was a correspondence about that suspect piece, and on a subsequent trip to Geneva, Dr. von Bothmer sadly informed the collector that the costly Etruscan terra-cottas he owned were probably fake, and all from the hand of the same forger.

The collector was indignant. He was sure his terra-cottas were original. An opportunity for a decisive test arose when a new technique, known as the thermoluminescence test, was developed by scientists at Oxford and Cambridge. In the test, a crushed sample of ancient pottery is heated and its age is proved by its glow. A sample was taken of Kappa's Etruscan terra-cottas, along with other suspect art. In July, 1972, the scientists reported that their tests showed the terra-cottas to be of recent manufacture. Their report was carried in an issue of *Archaeometry*, whose pages were carefully studied by Kappa. He has since told me he has figured out a method of defeating the thermoluminescence test.

In the case of the Etruscan terra-cottas, only money was lost. More serious is the mindless waste of time as curators spend years arguing about the authenticity of major works. The most celebrated instance was the debate over the Greek horse that the Metropolitan Museum acquired in 1923 from Georges Feuardent, a Paris dealer, for a still undisclosed sum. The dealer's story was that the provenance of the horse was "the famous shipwreck discovered near Mahdia, in Tunisia, in 1908." This, he said, was "very confidential information," not to be disclosed because if it were, "Paris journalists might cause trouble."

The horse is undoubtedly beautiful, and from 1923 to 1961 it was proudly displayed by the Metropolitan as one of its supreme prizes, along with the Etruscan warriors. The late Gisela Richter, then curator of Greek and Roman art, called the horse "without doubt the artistically most important single object in our classical collection." The horse was illustrated in nearly every volume on Greek art, and was given a full-page photograph in the *Encyclopaedia Britannica*. Nevertheless, there were doubts. A leading skeptic was Mr. Noble, then chief administrator of the Metropolitan and an authority on ancient art techniques. As he passed the horse one morning in 1956, he noticed for the first time a line running down the horse's spine and under its stomach—and it struck Mr. Noble that this might be a mold-mark, a telltale sign that the sculpture had been made by sand-casting. The trouble was that sand-casting was a technique not invented until the fourteenth century. Classical artisans used a lost-wax process, in which a mold was assembled around a wax model, then heated until the liquid wax emptied through a hole in the bottom. Bronze was then melted and poured into the mold, resulting in a seamless sculpture.

Mr. Noble conferred with Dietrich von Bothmer, who, during a subsequent business trip to Greece looked carefully at other horses, because the curator was suspicious about a small hole on top of the Metropolitan horse's head. The hole apparently was intended to be filled with a *meniscus,* or spike, of a kind once placed on equestrian statues to discourage birds from dirtying them. But why would a *meniscus* be employed on a fifteen-inch-high statuette? After his return from Greece, Dr. von Bothmer joined Noble in recommending that the horse be withdrawn from exhibition. A few years later, the horse was submitted to a special test using gamma rays, which can penetrate thick metal more effectively than X-rays. A gamma-ray shadowgraph disclosed that within the horse there was a sand core, and that an iron wire was used as a frame, confirming that it had been made by the sand piece-mold process, and not the lost-wax process. In 1967, at a Metropolitan Museum seminar on forgeries, Mr. Noble announced the new findings, saying of the bronze horse, "It's famous, but it's a fraud."

In an issue of the Metropolitan *Bulletin* devoted to the announcement, Mr. Hoving said that the "tension of apprehension" over the authenticity of any piece was a normal part of museum work. It takes study and expertise to prove that something is good, he said, but "at the same time you have to watch very carefully that you don't commit the sin of branding something a falsehood when it is, in fact, a genuine piece." What Mr. Hoving did not explain is that this risk is the normal price every museum pays for knowingly buying unpedigreed objects.

But the controversy over the horse was far from over. Carl Blümel, a German scholar, published a lengthy monograph contending that iron cores *had* been used in classical times and that the horse could have been made in sections. An equally rigorous monograph by Lewis S. Brown of the American Museum of Natural History then attacked the horse on entirely new grounds —its too-perfect gait. Until the first publication in 1887 of serial photographs of animals in motion, so Brown contended, all ancient representations of moving animals were anatomically wrong, save for the Metropolitan's horse. On stylistic grounds, too, the once-beautiful horse seemed suddenly suspicious. As Calvin Tomkins put it, in his centennial history of the Metropolitan, the horse looked "horribly wrong," and its eyes, instead of being round, as in other Greek examples, "were seen to be almond-shaped like those of Bambi the Deer—a sentimentalizing tendency that had appealed unconsciously to our own twentieth century taste."

Whether or not the horse looked like Walt Disney's Bambi, there were those who still believed it was ancient, and in 1971 it was decided to submit the horse to yet another test—this time a thermoluminescence test. (The same test had already confirmed that the Etruscan warriors were only about sixty years old.) Core ingredients, including grains of quartz and zircon, were taken from the horse and heated for the test—with special allowances made for the artificial radiation produced by the earlier gamma-ray shadowgraph. Scientists duly informed the museum that the core material demonstrated that the horse was between 2,000 and 4,000 years old. Laboratory analysis also showed that the horse *was* seamless, and that the suspicious

115

lines that Mr. Noble had observed were only wax ridges easily swabbed away. The seams were apparently the result of reproduction casts made of the horse. On Christmas Eve, 1972, the Metropolitan solemnly reversed itself and announced that the horse was an "irrefutably genuine work of antiquity."

The announcement could hardly have come at a worse time for Mr. Noble. He had left the Metropolitan in 1970 to become director of the Museum of the City of New York. In December, 1972, he went to Boston to be interviewed by the trustees of the Museum of Fine Arts as a candidate to succeed Mr. Rathbone. The Metropolitan released the story vindicating the horse just as Mr. Noble came under consideration in Boston. (Mr. Noble did not receive the appointment; the new director is Merrill Rueppel, formerly of the Dallas Art Museum.)

But the arguments are not yet over. Mr. Noble concedes that the horse might just possibly be a late Hellenistic or Roman period eclectic piece, but is not fifth century B.C. Greek. "Even if it is Hellenistic it is still a copy," he said, "and, as such, a forgery. All forgeries are like vampires. They should have a knife driven through their heart." Forgeries can be wicked in another way—they can needlessly blemish a scholar's reputation, waste years of time, and gratuitously bring museums into disrepute.

Still, however much time has been wasted in scholarly arguments over the authenticity of museum pieces, the fake factory acts, in a negative way, to defend the past. Money that might be spent on buying genuine, if stolen, art is diverted into the forgery market. And when a museum or collector has been defrauded, there is no one to blame, because without the original covetousness the purchase would not have been made. This circumstance led one museum worker, James L. Swauger of the Carnegie Museum in Pittsburgh, to write an article entitled "In Praise of Forgers." The author declared:

116

It was with grim amusement the other day that I heard a comment of David Owsley, curator of decorative arts at the Carnegie Institute's Museum of Art. He remarked that the number of experienced forgers has grown so large that buyers are becoming wary of purchasing antiquities; this to the extent that such buyers may soon demand certification of excavation by a reputable working field archaeologist and processing of the transaction through legal channels.

Ha! The sun rises. More power to the forgers. May their tribe increase! They, at least, harm no one and nothing but the buyers. And the con man has always had a respectability that the thief can only envy!

5. *Question of Money*

It would be apt if the money that goes into buying fakes could be matched by funds committed to the conservation of the genuine articles. In Italy, however, one can surmise that far more is spent in the fake factory than on preservation, and this is another instance of the root problem that crops up at every point in our inquiry—the disordered priorities of the art world. What can be done about it?

To begin with, what happens to art should surely be viewed as an international responsibility. What Italy does with its patrimony is not of concern solely to Italians, and in effect this fact has been recognized by Italians themselves in their appeals for international aid after the flooding of Florence and in the effort to salvage Venice. The same impulse prompted Egypt to invite world support for its campaign to preserve the Temple of Abu Simbel and other Nubian antiquities imperiled by the rising waters of the Aswan High Dam. Recently the United Nations

Educational, Scientific and Cultural Organization launched another such drive to raise money to save the site of ancient Carthage before it is consumed in the urban development of greater Tunis.

When it comes to commerce, the art world unquestionably has an international outlook. This has been evident in the special pleasure that dealers and auction houses have lately taken in the entry of Japan into the market. "They're buying these things the way the Dutch bought tulip bulbs in the seventeenth century and American bankers bought Impressionist works from 1890 to the 1920s," says the director of the New York branch of Christie's auction house. The estimate is that Japanese buyers purchased between $50 million and $75 million worth of art during 1972, and that sales will be even bigger in 1973. At one Parke-Bernet auction, in October, 1972, the Japanese, it is said, accounted for $1,015,000 out of a $5-million sale. "No hammers go down nowadays either at Christie's or Sotheby's," a Japanese buyer told a reporter, "without at least one of us raising his pudgy hand." Hiroko Saeki, a Japanese dealer who buys art extensively in New York, told the *Times* recently that her clients acquire paintings not only for aesthetic reasons but also for social status. "Let's say Mr. Yamamoto buys a Renoir nude," she said. "So Mr. Fuji has to get one too. The Japanese buy names rather than quality."

Whatever their motives, no one should begrudge the Japanese their new place in the international sales room—least of all Americans. But one can be distressed by the contrast between the internationalism of the market and the frugal concern with sovereignty that appears as soon as preservation is at issue. An obvious instance in point was the outcome of a UNESCO meeting held in Paris in April, 1972. The purpose of the conference was wholly laudable—to create a World Heritage Fund, modeled on the World Wildlife Fund, which could provide a steady source of revenue to countries caring for imperiled cultural properties. The UNESCO Secretariat had proposed that the Fund be supported by compulsory contributions, fixed by periodic votes, not to exceed one per cent of any member nation's UNESCO dues. This would not have involved a huge amount; if all 129 UNESCO members had agreed, the total tax would have been at most about $406,000 a year. At the Paris meeting, however, the Secretariat proposal was decisively rejected; voting against it were the United States, the Soviet Union, and other wealthy member-states. As a result, the World Heritage Fund will be financed on a voluntary basis, and a realistic budget is unlikely.

Another way of providing a steady flow of money into an international fund has been suggested by Robert Hughes of *Time.* His idea is ingenious. In an article written in 1971, he proposed the imposition of a conservation tax of five per cent on every work of art sold at auction that fetched more than $100,000. Not only could this painlessly yield money to a suitably organized international fund, but, as Mr. Hughes wrote, "most of all, it could mitigate the crushing sense of waste and meaninglessly flamboyant consumption that anyone who cares about art and its priorities is apt to feel" when reading about record auction prices.

An even bolder idea has been discussed by Hugues de Varine-Bohan, the brilliant director of the International Council of Museums, which is an affiliate of UNESCO. Though he is still in his thirties, he has held his job for nearly a decade, in the course of which he has visited more than seventy countries and attended many international conferences on the world cultural heritage and its preservation. He has seen at firsthand the contrast between the rich museums and those subsisting on pennies, and when he was asked to comment, in 1972, on the financial distress of some American museums, he replied: "Your museums have deficits. You don't find deficit museums in Europe. You find starving museums." A trained archaeologist himself,

119

he did not have to make the further obvious point—that in Asia, Africa, and Latin America, the financial plight of museums is often far more precarious.

During a Paris visit, I met M. de Varine-Bohan and we talked about the problem. The idea of an international tourist tax arose, and he elaborated upon it. "Suppose that everyone over twenty-five who is going on a pleasure trip paid a dollar tourist tax at the airport," he said. "Suppose that the money was split between an international fund and those countries the tourist was visiting—why, for the first time, there could be sufficient money available to protect and restore precisely that which the tourist is traveling to see. In the process, the tourist would become aware of an otherwise invisible problem—the gradual degradation of our cultural patrimony. But"—and here his face clouded—"the idea is simply not politically feasible. Not now."*

The reason that the idea is not feasible is because the past is an interest without a constituency; it has no effective lobby. As a Guatemalan with a concern for the devastation of Maya sites remarked, "The truth is that stelae don't vote." Yet if the human past has a doubtful future, it is not because most people wish to see its remains destroyed or mutilated. Most people are not even aware that there is a problem. They don't understand, for

---

* The idea of a permanent trust fund to support the arts could also be tried on a national or local level. For some years, the City of San Francisco has collected a Cultural Affairs Amenities Tax, levied on transient hotel rooms, to provide assured funds to local cultural activities. A New York investment banker, Donald M. Blinken, has proposed that a Federal Arts Excise Tax should be imposed on the sale of television sets, with the proceeds used solely for a national Arts Trust Fund. (See "A Trust Fund for the Arts?," East Hampton, Long Island, *Star*, March 22, 1973.) As a result of Mr. Blinken's personal lobbying, a bill that would create a Cultural Resources Endowment in New York State was introduced in the Albany legislature by State Senator William T. Conklin, the deputy majority leader. It seems unconscionable that a multimillion-dollar highway trust fund should be supported by gasoline taxes, while museums and the performing arts are denied an assured source of annual funding.

example, that the past is menaced by the very civilization that has evolved from it.

The point has been made with visual brilliance in the film *Fellini's Roma*. In one episode, a camera crew accompanies workmen who are digging a tunnel for a new subway under the Eternal City. They unexpectedly come upon an ancient Roman villa, a ruin filled with marvelous wall paintings. But as the cameras record the discovery, the murals melt ineluctably away, their colors dissolved by the inflow of modern air. This fantasy has taken literal form at Lascaux, the site of the greatest of all prehistoric painted caves. The cave, discovered by schoolboys in 1940 and opened to the public in 1948, was attracting 122,000 visitors by 1962, and thus was the fourth most popular tourist attraction in France. The cave was equipped with fancy hatches and its air was purified by elaborate machines, yet by 1963 it was apparent that something was drastically wrong—a disfiguring microorganism was spreading over the paintings, and flakes of calcite appeared on the walls. Studies established that Lascaux was being doomed by its admirers, whose shoes carried soil and slime into the cave, and whose breath made a chemical alteration in the paintings. Lascaux has since been closed to the general public. The London *Times* found in the event proof that culture and art are "the first victims of the revolt of the masses," adding: "What better symbol than the survival of the handiwork of Upper Paleolithic Man through fifteen thousand undisturbed years, so that it might eventually be silently obliterated by the steady footfall and hushed breathing of his remote descendants."

This reproof is a trifle unfair since some of the most deplorable destruction of world art has occurred with the full knowledge and complicity of the patrician denizens of the museum and art world. What *The Times* failed to consider was that simple lack of information is often responsible for what it attributed to the revolt of the masses. A final illustration

121

may help make the point. Few people are aware that emissions of the carbon monoxide engine, in combination with those of industrial and home-heating furnaces, are doing incalculable damage to the outdoor carved-stone art of the world. The acids formed by these emissions have done more damage to outdoor monuments in the past twenty years than the ravages of time extending, in some cases, over more than two thousand years. The effects are irreversible, since the loss of a millimeter on a carved surface can render sculptured detail unrecognizable.

A scientist who is deeply concerned with the problem is Professor Seymour Z. Lewin, a chemist at New York University, whose specialty is the preservation of stone. In the past decade, he has traveled widely to study the diseases that afflict stone in Europe, Asia, and Africa, and in this hemisphere. His verdict is that the carved outdoor art of the world "is melting away like an ice-cream cone in the summer sun." Not only are cathedrals like Chartres imperiled, but even remote Buddhist sanctuaries, such as Borobudur in Indonesia, are visibly dwindling away. No foolproof protective film has yet been devised by chemists (though Dr. Lewin has invented a solution that he believes can save some monuments). What is lacking is the money. Dr. Lewin's estimate is that for $1 million—the price paid by the Metropolitan Museum for its great krater —mankind could perfect a formula that would save many of its greatest civilized treasures from civilization itself. The conclusion is irresistible: The past has no future unless we are willing to pay for it.

CHAPTER FOUR

THE SHERD TRADE

It is naught, it is naught, saith the buyer: but when he is gone his way, then he boasteth.

Proverbs XX. 14

1. The Selling of the Past

The sale of antiquities is a business unlike the others. In the sherd trade, most of the dealer's stock has been acquired, at one point or another, through a violation of law. The matter was stated plainly by John D. Cooney, curator of ancient art at the Cleveland Museum, who in March, 1972, told a reporter that ninety-five per cent of the ancient art material in the United States had been smuggled in. "Unless you're naïve or not very bright," Mr. Cooney went on, "you'd have to know that much ancient art is stolen." His frankness was upsetting to many in the museum field, one of whom—Dietrich von Bothmer of the Metropolitan—found the Cleveland scholar's statement "odd" and "crude."

Odd or not, Mr. Cooney was undeniably candid. There may be some dispute as to the exact proportion of stolen art, but no one who makes even a cursory inquiry can doubt that the great majority of antiquities offered for sale is indeed smuggled goods. It is true, as Dr. von Bothmer protested, that much of the material is described as coming from old collections and in some cases the assurances may be genuine. But as one Swiss museum curator remarked, "It's public knowledge that ninety per cent of the certificates of origin accompanying such works of art are totally unreliable." In this respect, the trade is also unusual: the falsification of papers is a routine business method, as generally accepted by the seller as by the knowledgeable buyer.

The exact size of the market can only be estimated. A published calculation is that $7 million worth of antiquities originates each year from the Mediterranean, with Italy alone accounting for $3 million of the total. If one adds in the art smuggled from Asia and Latin America, a worldwide total of $15 million to $20 million seems highly conservative. Most of the best work goes to a few thousand collectors and a few score of museums, and it is sold by a few hundred dealers. A far larger number of people is involved in getting the material out of the earth—a work force of perhaps several hundred thousand people. Taken together, the art market is a fascinating and infrequently explored subculture.

At the apex is the dealer. Speaking from experience, Bernard Berenson once remarked: "It would take a Balzac to describe the power and glory of gifted dealers and their influence for good and for evil over the public." The trade has yet to find its Balzac; surprisingly, there is not even a history of art dealing, but only a scattering of memoirs and biographies (of which S. N. Behrman's profile of Duveen remains the best). One consequence of this absence of information is that many are prepared to believe the worst of the dealer—he is in a secretive business, competing with ruthless and even unscrupulous rivals, and yet to succeed he must wear a mask of geniality. There is always the suspicion of sharp practices, of hypocrisy and meanness.

The preconception is not always fair. It is too easy to over-look the dedication of the serious dealer, his specialized scholar-ship and authentic commitment to art. Even if his motives are not disinterested, the dealer can play a creative role, drawing attention to an overlooked school of art or even propounding ideas that deserve attention. An example, in the antiquities field, is the work of Carlo T. E. Gay, an Italian-born dealer in New York whose specialty is the ancient art of Mexico. Mr. Gay, a soft-spoken, reflective man, has more than anyone else helped to identify and publicize a fascinating, little-known pre-Columbian cultural style, Xochipala.

In February, 1967, during a trip to Mexico, Mr. Gay was shown a few stone and ceramic artifacts that reportedly were found by a farmer in a small village called El Zacatoso, some six miles south of the town of Xochipala in the State of Guerrero. To Mr. Gay, the pieces had a special interest because the style seemed akin to that of the Olmecs, the mother civilization of Mesoamerica, whose origins were believed to be on the Gulf Coast. It had been his suspicion that the Olmecs in fact arose originally in the western state of Guerrero, and as he pursued his research he found other objects that seemed to support that view, all emanating from the area around Xochipala (pro-nounced sochi-pála). What to him was especially exciting was the aesthetic quality of the scultpure he saw—the figures were modeled in a lovingly realistic fashion, and faces were true por-traits and not rendered in the more stylized mode of other pre-Columbian pieces. As it happened, the same realistic modeling could be seen in a curious piece of unknown origins given to the Peabody Museum at Harvard in 1903 by an American explorer named William Niven, who had traveled in Guerrero in 1896–97.*

* Niven was an adventurer who subsequently was accused of selling fakes to the National Museum in Mexico; he is also the source of the 925 fake inscribed tablets, covered with a mysterious writing, which he claimed he found in 1923 near Amantla, Mexico. The supposed tablets were the prime

Xochipala is a little-visited mountain village of about five thousand inhabitants that overlooks deep ravines and the site of an ancient lake. It can be reached only by a steep and winding ten-mile dirt road, and its people are sustained mainly by corn grown in the valley, a dietary limitation that is possibly the source of a disease similar in symptoms to pellagra and known locally as *el botón* (the button). As elsewhere in Mexico, water is scarce, and one of the few springs—called Ojo de Agua (Eye of Water)—was most probably used in ancient times. The modern age has barely touched Xochipala, and it is deep in a state known for its rough terrain, its banditry, and its guerrillas. No archaeological excavations have been conducted in the area.

It thus required some intrepidity for Mr. Gay to carry out his inquiries, and in the course of several trips he found evidence of at least four burial sites from which had been unearthed sculptured figures that seemed to him proof of early Olmec occupation. On two of his visits, Mr. Gay was accompanied by Gillett G. Griffin, the curator of pre-Columbian and primitive art at the Princeton University Art Museum. This collaboration led to a path-breaking exhibition of Xochipala art held early in 1972 at the Princeton Museum. In the preface to the catalogue, whose text was written by Mr. Gay, the Princeton curator noted that for the first time the Xochipala culture was being shown as an entity of its own. "It is the initial portrait figures indelibly charged with an inner life that take the breath away," Mr. Griffin wrote. "It is miraculous that they have been waiting over 3000 years to be discovered. . . . Hopefully these notes may inspire careful scientific investigation."

In Mr. Gay's identification and preliminary investigation of the Xochipala culture, one sees the catalytic role that can be played by a serious dealer. Though scholars differ on the early date Mr. Gay has assigned to the Xochipala material, none of

source for a series of books written by James Churchward claiming that the New World was settled by the fleeing survivors of the Lost Continent of Mu. The Peabody piece, however, is of unquestioned authenticity.

126

which has been archaeologically excavated, there is no disagreement on the outstanding aesthetic quality of a hitherto unknown style. Let Mr. Gay's work stand as an instance of enterprise and scholarship in a calling more often associated with greed and chicanery.

Plainly the chicanery also exists. Even the casual inquirer will hear a dozen succulent stories of double-dealing. A good example is the tale told about the Basel dog; it is unverifiable but has an authentic ring. The Basel dog was for years a prize exhibit in that city's Museum of Art until its banishment as an alleged fake around 1966. A fierce-looking canine of indeterminate breed, the Basel dog is carved in white marble and at some point lost its lower limbs. Its age is also indeterminate, having been placed variously as fifth century B.C. Greek, Hadrianic Roman, and contemporary Italian.

At one point, the dog was either owned or purchased by an Italian collector whose wife had a strong preference for artistic depictions of dogs. The story told in Rome is that the dog was a spurious antiquity made to order by a forger, and that the lady died before the work could be delivered. This was in the late 1930s, and during World War II, it is said, the dog languished in one of the many antiquities shops on the Via del Babuino. After the war, the art market revived, and one day a foreign dealer was informed that a Greek masterpiece was available—one of the few classical canines to be found anywhere. The visiting dealer liked the dog, and the question then arose as to how it could be exported from Italy. "I have an idea," the dog's owner remarked. "Why don't I list the dog as a cheap modern copy on the export manifest? There'll be no problem with Italian customs. I'll give a receipt saying the dog is worth 16,000 lire, and then you can pick it up abroad with no trouble at all."

In due course, the dog left Italy and eventually came into the

127

hands of another dealer, the German-born Herbert A. Cahn, an authority on ancient coins and the proprietor of Münzen & Medaillen A.G. in Basel. Soon it was purchased at a modest price by the Friends of the Basel Art Museum and proudly placed on display. But there were scholarly doubts about the dog's pedigree. Some were unhappy with the dog's style, others felt the price was too low for a piece with unimpeachable lineage, but the more telling objection concerned the white marble from which the canine was carved. Tests showed that the stone was uncannily similar in composition to the marble found in a modern Italian quarry, which cast doubt on the dog's claim to Greek ancestry. By the mid-1960s, the dog had become a local joke in Basel, the subject for a derisive carnival song and for a terrible pun—a carnival float, bearing a model of the dog, had on it the sign "Cave Cahnem."

In the meantime, so the story goes, the dealer who had originally purchased the dog in Rome returned to the little shop on the Via del Babuino angrily to confront the beast's vendor. "I'm sorry, I don't understand what you're complaining about," the Roman antiquary is reported to have said. "Here is the original receipt—you paid 16,000 for a modern copy, which is precisely what you obtained." And what of the dog? In 1966, a splendid new antiquities museum opened in Basel, and the dog was conspicuously missing. Cornelius Vermeule of the Boston Museum, drawing on his curatorial sarcasm, put it this way in a review of the affair in 1968:

> Seemingly a vigorous fellow and well able to defend himself by administering a good bite or two, he had succumbed to a concerted series of attacks, some aimed at his qualities as a work of art, but others designed more to embarrass those who had sheltered the poor beast. . . . For the crime of seeming to exist under false pretenses, the animal was banished from the Basel Museums and, like so many refugees from persecution, he fled the Old World for

the New. At the time of writing, he is a resident, on a temporary visa, of the Museum of Fine Arts in Boston.

In Dr. Vermeule's judgment, the dog is neither fifth century B.C. Greek nor a modern forgery, but instead a Roman copy of a Greek original, probably made in the Trajanic or Hadrianic period. If so, possibly it was sold as an original to an eager Roman collector, who was given a certificate in Greek to prove that it had once been in the personal collection of Pericles.*

The antiquities dealer lives in a Darwinian world beset with perils; he must be constantly wary of being taken in by a fake or caught in a police scandal. Moreover, he depends on the whims of the rich, or near-rich, whose collecting interests can suddenly change or who can be wooed and won by a rival. He must search continually for fresh customers, using all his persuasiveness to stimulate interest. His market is so small and specialized that, as he knows all too well, a single big buyer can transform it.

An instance in the field of fine arts is the impact that Paul Mellon has had on the market for English paintings. The Pittsburgh multimillionaire has for some years been assembling one of the world's most comprehensive collections of English eighteenth- and nineteenth-century art. Mr. Mellon recently gave his collection to Yale University, where a new museum, designed by Louis I. Kahn, is being built to house it. In the past ten or fifteen years, he is said to have spent several hundred thousand dollars

---

* As Ogden Nash has put it in his poem "The Collector":
> I met a traveler from an antique show,
> His pockets empty, but his eyes aglow.
> Upon his back, and now his very own,
> He bore two vast and trunkless legs of stone.
> Amid the torrent of collector's jargon
> I gathered he had found himself a bargain,
> A permanent conversation piece post-prandial,
> Certified genuine Ozymandial
> And when I asked him how he could be sure,
> He showed me P. B. Shelley's signature.

a year on English masters, and is credited, by those in the field, with increasing by as much as a factor of ten auction prices of lesser-known English painters.

In the pre-Columbian field, a single wealthy buyer can have a similar impact. Few have heard the name William Palmer, who in the past decade has become a major collector of ancient American art, with a special interest in gold figures. Mr. Palmer lives reclusively in Maine, and according to scholars who have seen his collection, he has bought tens of thousands of pieces in a short time. His heavy buying is credited with doubling and even tripling price levels in certain categories of pre-Columbian art.

For a dealer, a great compensation is to see a casual customer turn into a serious collector, sometimes with a scholarly interest in his particular field. In conversation, dealers speak contemptuously of very wealthy buyers who accumulate magpie-fashion, relying on the advice of hired experts. The dealer prefers to talk about collectors of moderate means who choose with love and discernment. A name always mentioned with special respect is Leon Pomerance, a Brooklyn-born wholesale paper dealer who has become an acknowledged authority on ancient Mediterranean art as a result of his collecting.

The collection began as a result of a chance encounter. In 1951, Mr. Pomerance and his late wife Harriet were on an anniversary holiday in Europe, and while visiting Switzerland they first saw private collections of antiquities—though they had an interest in ancient art, they had not realized that such objects were openly for sale. Soon afterward, the couple was on a train from Florence to Rome, and shared a compartment with Dr. Elie Borowski, who, after earning his doctorate in art at the University of Toronto, was just beginning a new career as a dealer. The Polish-born Borowski was carrying with him some stock, including Sumerian seals which (as Mr. Pomerance later remembered) were "all stashed in those tin boxes that Gold

Flake cigarettes come in." After seeing the seals, the Pomerances stayed up until two in the morning making impressions of
them in plasticine; later, they bought two miniature bronzes
that were also in Dr. Borowski's Gold Flake tins. "From then on,
we never looked back," the New York businessman told the
journalist Joseph Alsop, who has described the encounter.

A few years passed, and the Pomerances visited Crete, where
they learned, in reading a museum catalogue, that major Minoan sites were still unexcavated. Mr. Pomerance promptly vol-
unteered to help finance a new dig, and as a result a series of
campaigns were undertaken, beginning in 1961, at the site of
the Palace of Kato Zakros in eastern Crete. Every summer the
couple went to Crete and looked on as major finds were unearthed, including a cache of tablets inscribed in the rare, still
undeciphered Linear A script. The couple's patronage was
wholly disinterested; all of the finds went to the Archaeological
Museum in Heraklion, which the excavator of the site, Dr. Nicholas Platon, had formerly directed. Mr. Pomerance, meanwhile,
developed an expertise in the recondite archaeological problems
of Bronze Age Greece. He presented papers at scholarly meetings on such questions as "The Final Collapse of Santorini
(Thera), 1450 B.C. or 1200 B.C.?," (his paper was later published by Göteborg University in Sweden). At the same time,
the Pomerance collection grew, and in 1966 the best pieces from
it were displayed at the Brooklyn Museum, whose catalogue
said: "Mr. and Mrs. Leon Pomerance have, in the short space
of twelve years, formed a remarkable collection and this they
have done in no haphazard way. They have not been interested
in merely assembling a number of objets d'art which have nothing in common but 'beauty'. . . . The collection was formed as
the result of much devoted study and appreciation of the arts
and the craftsmanship of ancient peoples."

In all of this, the Pomerances (Mrs. Pomerance died in
1972) showed a special attitude. Mr. Pomerance at no point

regarded himself as anything but a temporary custodian, saying of his objects: "How long does one have them? Thirty or forty years, perhaps—and these things may be three or four thousand years old. That is very sobering." The couple never sold a piece, though occasionally they made exchanges. They were devoted, in the very best sense, to the past. But the Pomerances are the uncommon collectors. To satisfy less fastidious appetites hundreds of thousands of tomb robbers ply their trade. From the dealer at the apex of the pyramid, we descend to its base.

2. *The Second-Oldest Profession*

In ancient Greece, they were called *tymborychoi*, in modern Italy they are known as *tombaroli*, in India their name is "idol-runners," in Guatemala it is *esteleros*, and in Peru *huaqueros*, but in all times and places the terms signify the same thing: those who plunder tombs and temples. It is assuredly the second-oldest profession, practiced as widely if not always as profitably as the first. Like the courtesan, the tomb robber knows there is money in beauty, and rarely a shortage of customers. Laws, moral constraints, and bodily hazards have had roughly the same deterrent effect on the one calling as on the other.

The Greeks, indeed, ascribed the origin of art to an act of larceny. In his dialogue, *Protagoras*, Plato asserts that Prometheus, in order to provide a means of salvation to newly created man ("naked, unshod, unbedded, and unarmed"), stole for him the gift of skill in the art, together with fire ("for without fire it was impossible for anyone to possess or use this skill"). With this stolen gift, man had a share in the traits of the gods, because he alone among living creatures believed in supernatural beings "and set to work to erect altars and images to them."

What began with theft continued in the same tradition. One

132

of the earliest Egyptian legal documents, known as the Amherst Papyrus and first published in 1873, tells of charges of tomb robbery brought against the mayor of Thebes in the reign of Ramses IX, around 1134–1117 B.C. The records are replete with intrigue; but one familiar point emerges. As the Egyptologist Barbara Mertz writes: "Recorded confessions of tomb robbers make it clear that part of the normal business expense in the trade was the bribery of officials."*

However ancient the trade, the literature on tomb robbing is scant. One of the few volumes dealing with the subject is by Dora Jane Hamblin and has the nice title *Pots and Robbers.* Miss Hamblin has for years lived in Rome, and wrote much about Italy for *Life* magazine; once, in the 1960s, a publisher asked her to do a book on any subject that interested her. "Well," replied Miss Hamblin, "I know a good deal about tomb robbing," and the illuminating and useful book was the result. As she points out, tomb robbing has been against the law in Italy since the time of the Emperor Vespasian, and in theory any antiquities a farmer finds must be sold to the state. Official penury makes the law an absurdity. Once in 1958 a farmer near the old Etruscan town of Orbetello found a lovely small bronze statue, for which a local dealer offered $16,000. Word of the discovery reached police, and the statue was confiscated. The farmer was paid $500, supposedly "twenty-five per cent of the value." As a result of such niggardliness, few Italian farmers would for a moment consider selling any finds to the state.

* The plunder of Egypt has continued ever since, though, to their credit, successive regimes in Cairo have made some provision for a legal trade in duplicates. Even Communists have joined, if one can believe Philippe Bernert, writing in the right-wing Paris newspaper *L'Aurore.* He reports (July 25, 1972) that Soviet technicians have been smuggling antiquities in diplomatically privileged luggage—the parting Russians, he writes, have been carrying *"des valises singuliérment lourdes."* On April 9, 1973, an Associated Press dispatch reported that in the first three months of 1973 thousands of ancient tombs have been rifled. Aside from statuary and painted walls, papyrus scrolls have been a prime target. One collection of scrolls, the dispatch said, was one of the largest known. Its owners are said to be asking for $1 million.

133

As Miss Hamblin learned, money is not the only motive for the *tombaroli*. In 1964, while having a picnic with friends in another old Etruscan town, Vulci, she encountered a tomb robber who gave his name as Pepe. This dialogue followed:

"Are you a *tombarolo*?"

"*Si, signore*. Eleven years now. . . . It is the most beautiful thing in life, finding these things. Until the end of the world, I will do this, because it is so beautiful."

"Have you ever been caught?"

"Sure. Twice. But it is nothing."

"Would anything make you stop?"

"No, *signore*, nothing. I love the digging, to find the tombs. I cannot stop. I don't even make any money on what I find, because I have to pay my fines when I am caught, and bribe the guards—"

"Bribe the guards?"

"*Si, signore,* guards don't make much money. For a few lire, they will look the other way."

For Pepe, the money is less important than the thrill of discovery, which he calls the *passione*, the "passion." He said: "You have worked so hard. Then you stand in front of the tomb and you are ready to open it. You do not know what is inside, and you must know. That is the moment. You would push away your father or your mother if they tried to stop you. . . ."

Pepe, who invited the group to his home, later said that he got the best prices from an American dealer living in Rome. "I get word to him, and he comes. Once I had two beautiful painted Greek vases. Fifth century B.C., I think. I got everything ready. I put them on the table—here, this table—and I covered them with a blanket, and I turned out the light. I brought my American in here, and I said 'wait,' and I took away the blanket and turned on the light, and he saw them. He gasped. He almost couldn't talk, they were so beautiful."

* * *

In the New World, one of the best descriptions of the tomb-robbing subculture is by a Brown University anthropologist, who became involved with the problem because he suffered from insomnia. From July, 1968, to June, 1969, Dwight Heath was a visiting professor of anthropology at the University of Costa Rica, under the auspices of the Fulbright-Hays program. A lean and restless man, Dr. Heath sometimes found it difficult to sleep, and he would walk long past midnight through the empty streets of San José. Near the main square he found an all-night café, the Esmerelda, a clean, well-lit place where one can always buy excellent coffee or the good local beer.

It chanced that the Esmerelda is also the favorite gathering place of the *huaqueros* (from the Inca word *huaco*, an ancient or sacred spot). The North American anthropologist befriended them and gradually won their confidence, while making it clear that he had done some archaeological work in the United States and deplored unsystematic excavations. He explained that he was interested in understanding their trade, and when the *huaqueros* became convinced he was neither an official spy nor a bargain hunter they came to look upon him, as one of them put it, as "a friend of both God and the devil."

Dr. Heath made a number of interesting discoveries, the first being the very size of the calling. Costa Rica is a small country with about 1.5 million inhabitants, and when he was told that there were from 3,000 to 5,000 *huaqueros*, he thought the figure was grossly exaggerated. However, Costa Rica until a few years ago had an unusual arrangement whereby the National Museum issued permits to treasure-hunting excavators. By consulting the museum files, the anthropologist learned that 693 persons had obtained such permits from 1954 to 1967, each permit being valid for three people. In his interviews, Dr. Heath determined that only twenty per cent of his informants had ever bothered to get a permit. He was thus able to make the reasonable calculation that around 4,330 persons were full- or part-time tomb robbers. By taking into account other people involved in the trade—shopkeepers, street vendors and specialists in restoration—Dr. Heath concluded that one per cent of the total economically active population was involved in the sale of pre-Columbian art. In other words, as he later reported: "It is altogether possible that there are more part-time commercial archaeologists in a country the size of West Virginia than there are academically trained (so-called 'professional') archaeologists in the entire world!"

As a meeting place of pre-Columbian cultures, the territory that is now Costa Rica has great interest for scholars, though little scientific exploration has been carried out. Costa Rican jade and gold have developed a collector market, but the pottery found in the country has not yet become fashionable. Nevertheless, Dr. Heath estimates that *huaquerismo* earns the country about $500,000 a year. There is a complex system of beliefs and behavior in the trade. Old *huaqueros* can analyze in detail the "family trees" of tomb robbers in various regions, and they make a careful distinction between the *ganchos*—old bums who hang around central markets and pretend to sell things they dug themselves—and skilled professionals. Those in the trade have their secrets. Some say that where there is a stone altar, there is gold underneath. Others believe that the neck of a large jar points in the direction of other large jars, and that in certain regions the richest burials are not at the center of a cemetery but at its "entry" or "exit" at the eastern and western extremes.

Every *huaquero* dreams of a great strike, of discovering El Dorado. Yet when a rich find is made, money is dispersed into a dozen hands. At one dig Dr. Heath learned about, everyone was getting a cut in a complicated system of payoffs. The organizer of the dig paid the foreman, an experienced *huaquero*, $83 weekly, while unskilled laborers got $2.35 a day, plus food and cigarettes. The landowner was paid up to $200 a month for the use of his property. Then came the special arrangements. The sponsor would tell some workmen to pocket any gold or jade they found so that the owner of the land and the foreman wouldn't know about it; later the sponsor would negotiate privately with the diggers for "premium stuff." At the same time, the sponsor had a similar deal with the dig foreman, paying a bonus for what he hid from both the landowner and the other workers. The landowner was also making his private deals. A regular cut went to the chief of the local police—$140 a month to look the other way, a few choice pieces on the side. All the finds eventually wound up by various routes in San José, the capital, with the art going to small antiquity shops or street salesmen. Some of the business was shared by "runners," who knew local collectors and who would get a ten per cent commission on the seller's minimum price. So swift was the commercial velocity that Dr. Heath, after a few months, gave up trying to record the multiplying transactions.

The money earned can be important to the *huaquero*. In Costa Rica, a family of five can live on $34 a month, and the highest-paid teacher that Dr. Heath knew of made only about $102 a month. At one rich cemetery, four men in twelve days found 226 pots that brought $5,330, or more than $265 a day. Another *huaquero* reported that he had found gold worth $12,400 in a single day. Dr. Heath was told about two men who took jade and gold to New York on consignment, staying thirty days and spending nearly $7,500; the pair paid $11,500 to the six *huaqueros* who had entrusted them with the goods, and still returned with a profit of $4,000 each. As everywhere, the forgery industry also prospers. Dr. Heath writes: "The traffic in fakes deserves a monograph in itself—for the moment, let me just mention one completely falsified pot that brought $2,400 from a North American; then, adding insult to injury, a copy of that fake brought $1,000 in Panama."

In December, 1971, I paid a visit to Costa Rica, in the course of which I sought out the *huaqueros*. They are easy to find, since tourist brochures at the hotels list all antiquities shops, at some of which pre-Columbian art can be charged on American Express. At the Café Esmerelda, the merest expression of interest brought a half-dozen Costa Ricans to my table, each with a shoebox filled with what were allegedly invaluable jades, gold pieces, and pottery. Shortly thereafter, I was led to the back of a shop where larger pieces were taken from a closet and proudly displayed on a workbench. I was allowed to photograph the objects, and while doing so asked if it would be illegal to export them. "If you want, we can get export permits," I was told. "We have a friend at the museum. But you can take them with you on the plane—nobody will look at your bags. Why should you worry? In New York, you can easily sell any of these pieces for much more than we are charging. Would you like to see a catalogue with some recent prices?"

In Costa Rica, the trade is so open as to be quasi-legal. Elsewhere in Latin America, particularly in countries whose pre-Columbian objects command higher world prices, the market is truly clandestine. Yet the pattern is almost always the same. A country with a rich and varied archaeological heritage is Colombia, where another scholar—Karen Olsen Bruhns, a lecturer in anthropology at San Jose College in California—found that tomb robbing was as ubiquitous as in Costa Rica.

Miss Bruhns, who has spent three field seasons in the Colombian Andes, has a special interest in the Quimbaya culture, an early Indian civilization known for its rich burials. Many Quimbaya tombs contain spectacular gold figurines. In an article published in 1972, she reported: "Today almost every male in the Central Cordillera, the area of the Quimbaya culture, is involved in illegally locating and opening ancient tombs. Until recently only precious metals or objects of exceptional beauty or interest were saved but the growing interest in Colombia for collecting antiquities, combined with the appearance of dealers on the international antiquities market, has given new impetus to *guaquería* [in Colombia, tomb robbers are known as *guaqueros*]."

In Colombia, the key implement is called *media caña*, a curved steel blade fastened to a long handle. This implement, held upright, is driven into the ground and brings up with it a core of earth. Mixed soil, the *guaqueros* say, is always the sign of a tomb, and once a shaft is opened other soundings will be taken to determine the size and shape of the burial. The tomb site is cleared with a machete and shovel, and a small coffee basket is lowered with ropes as a brigand empties the chamber. The main interest is in what is salable—broken pots, human remains, and objects without market value are left in the tomb. There are no records kept, and false information is deliberately given to protect the location of a rich site from "poachers." The shaft is then abandoned, and may remain as an open pit for years until the softer ground around it collapses, leaving a circular impression to mark its site. "The fields and orchards of central Colombia are riddled with such testimony to the activities of the *guaqueros*," writes Miss Bruhns.

For the robber, the easiest mark is the unguarded temple. This is true all over the world, and especially in India; everywhere in the subcontinent there are Hindu temples, many of them covered with rare and beautiful carvings. Until the 1950s, most were left unharmed, but as the prices of Indian art rose, a new calling evolved—that of the "idol runner." In 1971, more than one hundred sculptures were taken from the Khajuraho temples, the Chandigarh Museum was robbed at gunpoint, and a seventh century A.D. bronze of great historical importance was stripped from a temple in Himachal Pradesh. (The statue was later recovered in a Bombay warehouse.) As a correspondent for the *New York Times*, Sydney H. Schanberg reported: "It is no exaggeration to say that idol-running and antiques have become big business in India. Antique dealers have been kidnapped for ransom. In one recent case, in Gwalior, the ransom—which was paid—was $100,000. . . . Most of the smuggled art objects are sold in Western countries, particularly the United States, and many end up in museums."

Mr. Schanberg added that the problem is not that Indian laws are too loose, but that there is no effective machinery to enforce them. Corruption is pandemic. In a report on looting in India at a 1971 symposium, Professor Frederick Asher of the University of Minnesota noted that guards at Indian temples are paid less than fifty cents a day, low even by Indian standards. Customs officials offer little resistance to the export of stolen art. Dr. Asher declared: "In 1969, when my wife and I sent home our household goods from Calcutta—and really they were our household goods, nothing more—we received a bill from the shipping agent which included an item literally marked, 'fee for not to open boxes.' Upon inquiry, I was told that this was the bribe paid to customs officials so they would not open the boxes and would accept the contents as stated on the customs declaration forms."

Elsewhere in Asia, the situation is much the same. Wilhelm G. Solheim, professor of anthropology at the University of Hawaii, reporting at the same symposium, was particularly concerned with the problem in the Philippines, where an antiquities market developed in the late 1950s. There was a special demand for ceramics from ancient cemeteries south of Manila in Batangas Province. Dr. Solheim said:

> Unfortunately, the burials excavated had many associated whole Chinese, Annamese and Siamese bowls and plates which the public started to covet. Local collecting of these kinds of ceramics developed into a status matter within the Philippines, and to supply this market professional "diggers" started finding new burial sites and min-

140

ing them for whole ceramics, completely destroying them as far as any careful excavation was concerned.

In the 1960s, a series of burial sites were located near Laguna de Bay, just to the southeast of Manila. Here developed a do-it-yourself ceramics mining pastime. A number of antiquities shops developed in Manila in areas where tourists would see them and into these went the surplus of relatively common items while the more unusual and better items went into a number of remarkable collections, the owners of which had first choice from shipments brought into the field.

The University of Hawaii scholar, who has excavated in different Southeast Asian countries for twenty-two years, reported that in Thailand there is a double problem—plunder for the export market and a strong internal demand for Buddhist reliquaries, which are believed to possess great supernatural powers. In his work in Thailand, he was less concerned with finding gold (always an incitement to banditry) than with coming upon a reliquary deposit. As a result, army protection is needed for the excavation of Buddhist monuments, and in one case, during the 1960s, when a National Museum party felt that an army guard was no longer needed, looters armed with machine guns immediately turned up and plundered the site. The army had to be recalled to drive them away.

The Thais, it may be added, have an ingenious system for protecting their patrimony from covetous tourists. All objects more than fifty years old must have an export permit from the National Museum; objects less than that age also require an export permit, which costs twenty-five cents. The stamps are all written in Siamese, and eighty per cent of the objects in antiquity shops are new copies, each with a stamp. As Dr. Solheim explains: "The dealer does not tell the buyer he is buying a copy but tells him the object is Ayuthia or Khmer style, etc., in which he is telling the truth. The buyer thinks the National

141

Museum export permit is authenticating the item, which it is, as new. Everyone is happy."

In the plunder of Southeast Asia, there is a famous criminal case that has become a footnote to literary history. The accused was André Malraux, then at the beginning of his career, who was charged with stealing sculpture from the Khmer site of Banteay Srei, in Cambodia. The case became a cause célèbre in Paris, made Malraux briefly notorious, and contributed to his early political development. (The episode forms the core of Malraux's novel *The Royal Way*, published in 1930.) In what follows, I have relied on the careful reconstruction contained in *André Malraux: The Indochina Adventure* (1966), written by Walter G. Langlois, an American professor of French who has taught at the Lycée Sisowath in Phnom Penh.

While still a student in Paris, Malraux first became fascinated by Asian art and learned of the temple site of Banteay Srei. After a study of archaeological laws, he concluded that the temple was, technically speaking, abandoned property, and, in 1923, he decided to organize an expedition to take some pieces from it. He obtained the necessary permit from the Colonial Office. Langlois suspects that his motives may have been partly financial, though aesthetic considerations were surely paramount. In his earliest essay on art, written in 1922, the novelist had asserted: "We can feel only by comparison. . . . The Greek genius will be better understood through the contrast of a Greek statue with an Egyptian or Asian statue than by the examination of a hundred Greek statues."

In late 1923, Malraux arrived in Indochina and there he proceeded to get what he felt was a validation for his project from the Ecole Française d'Extreme Orient (EFEO), which had official jurisdiction over ancient remains. But in his initial encounter with colonial officialdom, his youth (he was twenty-three), his brashness, and his Bohemian ways made an unfavorable impression. The expedition was soon underway, and a little caravan of ox-drawn two-wheeled Cambodian carts moved through jungle trails. Once at the remote site, which was thickly overgrown with foliage, Malraux and his young companion, Louis Chevasson, carefully pried from the temple nearly a ton of material, including carvings of goddesses and figured roof ornaments. This was loaded on a riverboat, which was promptly intercepted by an EFEO official. Whatever Malraux's prior understanding, the carvings were impounded and the two Frenchmen arrested on charges of stealing antiquities.

A trial was held in Phnom Penh in July, 1924, and in a verdict that had personal and political overtones, Malraux was sentenced to three years in prison, and Chevasson to eighteen months. The novelist's wife, Clara, who had accompanied him to Indochina, returned to France to mobilize support for Malraux; a petition in support of Malraux had among its signers André Gide, Anatole France, Louis Aragon, Roger Martin du Gard, André Maurois, François Mauriac, and André Breton. Meanwhile, Malraux was making a memorable impression—a Saigon newspaper described him thus: "Swept-back blond hair, a pale complexion, eyes by turn flaming bright, then clouded with melancholy, perhaps also with regret." Ultimately, the case was appealed to a court of cassation in Paris, and the jail sentences were set aside, though Malraux—to his deep disappointment— was never able to establish his clear title to the ancient remains he had removed.

His taste of injustice at the hands of colonial authorities brought Malraux in contact with the nascent nationalist and revolutionary movements within Indochina, and with rare clarity he was able to see the contours of the vast tragedy that was to come. As he wrote in *Temptation of the West* (1926): "But it is not Europe or the past which is invading France as this century begins, it is the world which is invading Europe with all its present and its past, its heap of offerings of living and dead forms, its meditations. . . . This great troubled drama which is beginning, dear friend, is one of the temptations of the West." *

In extenuation of Malraux, it can be said that when he succumbed to the temptations of the Orient, prevailing standards were quite different. It is a trifle harder to make excuses for Norton Simon, the wealthy California collector, who, in 1972, paid a reported $1 million for an invaluable tenth century A.D. bronze statue of the Hindu deity Shiva that had been stolen from a village temple in Southern India.

The idol, which is four feet, six inches tall, was accidentally discovered in 1952 by a villager in Sivapuram, in the Tanjore district of Tamil Nadu, formerly the Indian state of Madras. Archaeologists acclaimed the Shiva as a unique work, and the Madras government was anxious to place the Nataraja—the name by which Shiva is known in his guise as Lord of the Cosmic Dance—in the Madras museum, but villagers protested. A district court decree enabled the villagers to keep the idol in the region in which it was found, though the Madras museum director warned, "This is invaluable. If you keep it in a place where there is no security, thieves may remove it and sell it abroad." Nevertheless, the bronze figure was placed in the unguarded Temple of Sivagurunathswamy and, in 1969, it was found that the Shiva had been replaced by a copy. The Nataraja made its way to New York and came into the hands of a dealer, Ben Heller, who advertised it for sale in a London newspaper for $1 million; he eventually found a buyer in Norton Simon.

* I have omitted Africa from this survey, but in that continent the problem also exists. Africa, with some exceptions, is not rich in archaeological sites but its primitive art has become a major prize for collectors. Auction prices have leaped for West African ethnographic material, and in 1953 a Benin bronze head sold in London for £21,000, setting a record. According to the International Council of Museums, there has been wholesale destruction in Mali of archaeological sites by looters seeking large terra-cotta figures, especially in the Gourma district near the Niger border.

The idiosyncratic West Coast collector had visited India in 1971 and had acquired a taste for Oriental art. In November or December, 1972, Mr. Simon bought the Shiva, which he described as the "greatest of masterpieces," adding: "I have clear title to the piece. It entered America legally."

After the story of the idol's history was broken by the New York *Post,* the *New York Times* had a reporter question Mr. Simon as to whether the bronze had been smuggled. The collector replied: "Hell, yes, it was smuggled. I spent between $15 million and $16 million over the last two years on Asian art, and most of it was smuggled." According to the *Times* account, Heller had acquired the sculpture in India for a reported $500,000 from a Mr. Behran who, in turn, had bought it from a certain Lance Dane. Asked if he would return the piece, Mr. Simon volunteered these thoughts:

> If it did some good, I would return it. If there were reason and plausibility that smuggling could be stopped, I would do it. . . . But often countries encourage smuggling. They make a lot of money out of it. They often scream a lot and yet allow the thievery to go on. They should start enforcing the law.

Mr. Simon said that he was discussing with the Metropolitan Museum the possibility of exhibiting his Asian works, including the bronze Shiva. The working title of the exhibition is "The Art of Greater Asia." Questioned by the New York *Post* about Mr. Simon's collection, Daryl Isley, curator of the Norton Simon collection in Los Angeles, said that recent acquisitions included Khmer sculpture in Cambodia, Thai works of the Mon-Dvaratic culture, and Asian stone sculpture dating from the first century B.C. through the twelfth century. Mr. Isley said of his patron: "He's acquired some fabulous pieces that were never before available that just suddenly became available. I'd say he got into the Far Eastern market at just the right time."

145

3. Middlemen and Police

At the pyramid's bottom are the tomb robbers, at its top are the major dealers, and in between are the middlemen. The middlemen, known as *mediatori* in Italian, are the indispensable joining links in the chain of antiquarian commerce. The robber has access to the arts, but rarely to the ultimate customer. He needs the middleman, who may have a stall in a bazaar, or operate out of his home, or have another innocuous calling in a provincial village. It is he who knows which police and politicians have to be bribed, how to smuggle out art, and what international dealers are interested in which kind of art.

What most middlemen have in common is their anonymity— their identity is one of the trade's better-kept secrets. If the tomb robber has his visions of El Dorado, the middleman, too, has a dream of riches: of being able to buy up at wholesale prices an entire cache that he can then parcel out to dealers. The dream was realized in Mexico by a middleman to whom I shall give the name Juan Epsilon, who was able to make perhaps as much as a million dollars because a peasant lost a milk can.

The peasant lived near Los Soldados in the State of Veracruz, not far from a stream known as Arroyo Pesquero. In searching for the milk can (the story may be apocryphal), the peasant came upon a milky-green jade mask. The river, in its meandering, had apparently washed away the earth covering a unique and extraordinary trove of Olmec tombs. When the site was finally depleted in 1969–70, it had yielded at least thirty-two Olmec jade masks, three mirrors, a yoke, seated and standing figurines, and more than a thousand jade celts, or polished edged implements, these being the estimates of a Yale archaeologist, David Joralemon, who has made a thorough study of the Arroyo Pesquero finds.

146

When peasants brought the first masks to Mexico City, dealers were suspicious because of their extraordinary quality—the faces in some cases had gracefully hooked noses and the cheeks were covered with a strange iconography. Some thought these were crude originals which had been "worked up" for the market. But not Epsilon, a middleman known for his caution (when he went on buying trips in western Mexico, he would carefully park his car on the outskirts of market towns, in order to prevent police from tracing his plates). Epsilon immediately saw the potential of Arroyo Pesquero, and he invested heavily in what he hoped would prove to be a grand slam. The pieces were shaped by the Olmecs, the earliest civilization of Mesoamerica, a people best known for the enormous heads they carved. The existence of the Olmecs (their true name is lost) was not confirmed until 1939–40, when the North American archaeologist Matthew Stirling first uncovered the site of Tres Zapotes in the humid jungles of southern Veracruz. Even then, some scholars refused to believe in the priority of the Olmecs, the apparent inventors of hieroglyphic notations and creators of the first monumental temples. Miguel Covarrubias, in a paper read in 1941, was among the first to see the importance of Stirling's discovery. Later, carbon dating conclusively established that Olmec civilization was already present on the Gulf Coast around 1200 B.C., a full millennium before the rise of Classic Maya.

By virtue of its intrinsic aesthetic quality and its historic importance, Olmec art quickly became a major prize for collectors. Hence Epsilon's excitement. He soon made his way to Arroyo Pesquero; at about the same time, reports of the find reached Jalapa, capital of Veracruz, and at the urgings of the local museum director an army unit was sent to the area of the discovery to prevent looting. The army unit found itself amid indignant peasants and a dealer with an open purse; according to one report, the army in effect went into the trade. In any event, Epsilon was able to return to Mexico City with a large share of the best pieces, though there were enough left to provide a sampling for the Jalapa Museum.

Photographs of the choicer masks then went to New York, and in due course there was a pilgrimage of major dealers to Epsilon's modest home. At least eleven of the finest masks were divided among four New York dealers, and in 1970 they appeared on the market, one of them with an asking price of $110,000. Mexican police became aware of the transaction, and Epsilon was briefly arrested; finally, for reasons of health, he went to Europe, where at last report he still is.

Arroyo Pesquero is regarded as the site of the greatest single find of Olmec jade, but there has been no archaeological excavation carried out in the area. The discovery is unknown even to some specialists in the field. In May, 1972, a conference on Olmec civilization was held at a North American university, at which slides were shown of a group of the masks. Among those present was Matthew Stirling, the first excavator of an Olmec site; another visitor was the Mexican scholar Marianne Cervantes, the Olmec specialist at the National Museum of Anthropology. An attractive and cheerful woman, Señora Cervantes had a fixed if polite smile as the slides of the masks were shown on the screen. It was the first time she had seen photographs of these important finds from her own country.

In the presumed collusion between Epsilon and the army unit at Arroyo Pesquero, one sees an important facet of the antiquities trade not only in Mexico but in all poor countries rich in art. Like other such nations, Mexico has enacted successively more stringent laws intended to protect ancient art, and, as in other countries, the laws have been a prime source of corruption. In 1972, Mexico strengthened its law to require registration of all pre-Columbian art in private collections. Soon thereafter, a Mexican collector was visited by a ragged peasant who was trying to sell a handsome piece. The collector, a bit suspicious, refused to buy, and as he was talking with the peasant, police swarmed around him to make an arrest. The collector's caution had saved him the cost of a bribe.

At the same time, two Mexicans appeared at the home of another collector, identifying themselves as agents of the procurator general. They said the collector would have to pay a hundred-peso registration fee for each piece he owned, and in his panic the collector gave the alleged officials 30,000 pesos, or about $2,500. He later learned he had been duped, and that no such agents existed.

Equally instructive was the experience of a European dealer, a youngish man who visited Mexico a few years ago and made enemies by too quickly dismissing some pieces he was shown as fakes. While in Mérida, he bought a number of Maya pieces, packing them in suitcases he purchased locally. On flying back to Mexico City, the dealer was startled by an airport announcement saying that all baggage would be subject to search—something that rarely happens on an internal flight. Leaving his new luggage, which he had not tagged, unclaimed on the rack, he headed directly to his hotel. In his room, the telephone rang. "We have your bags at the police station," an authoritative voice said. "Please come and claim them." At the police station, the European dealer was shown a book of Mexican laws and informed that he faced jail and disgrace. "But," an officer said, "for 50,000 pesos [about $4,100], we can forget about it." As the dealer reached for his checkbook, the officer went on, "And for another 50,000 pesos, you can have your bags back." The dealer left Mexico the following day.

Such episodes suggest why cynics believe that laws against the antiquities trade are designed to be violated rather than enforced. Since most Mexicans do not regard stealing antiquities as a heinous offense, periodic crackdowns have a ritual quality, and middlemen regard a short sentence as a routine occupational hazard. Occasionally, the consequences are more

149

serious, especially when a public official is accused of being implicated in the illicit market. An instance was the death of Miguel Malo Zozaya, an inspector of the National Museum of Anthropology and director of a cultural center in San Miguel de Allende. In May, 1972, five looters were arrested at the archaeological site of Moncada near Guanajuato, and they told police they were working for a group headed by the museum inspector. A state archaeologist promptly went to Malo Zozaya's home and asked to see the 270 pieces from official collections which he had been allowed to keep in his home. He could produce only seventy, saying, according to press accounts, that the rest were elsewhere in the house. He excused himself to get keys, and a few minutes later, a shot was heard as the compromised inspector put a bullet in his head. In a subsequent search, some 5,000 pieces were found in the house, many of them destroyed by Malo Zozaya after he learned of the accusation, in an apparent attempt to eliminate the evidence.

To be sure, not all police are dishonest and antiquities laws are sometimes properly enforced. But the scale of the enforcement effort is so modest that it is like countering a forest fire with a water pistol. In the words of an Interpol official, "We are in about the stage in countering the illicit traffic in art that we were twenty years ago when we first began to deal with the narcotics problem." The International Police Organization has its headquarters in Saint Cloud, on the outskirts of Paris, in a large and immaculate white building. Its small art thefts bureau is directed by a retired French police officer who explains that Interpol can act only at the express request of a member force, and that its chief function has been to circulate information on stolen works of art. In 1971, it sent out 110 notices, more than two-thirds of which listed art stolen in Italy. The recovery rate is about eight to ten per cent. Besides circulating fliers, Interpol maintains a file of known art thieves, and a small reference library. "We cannot do anything more," the assistant chief of Interpol told me, "until the governments of the world decide to do more."

On the national level, various police forces have established specialized squads to cope with mounting art thefts; such squads now exist in London, Paris, and New York. In Italy, there is a special carabinieri unit assigned to protect the national cultural patrimony. The unit's commander is Colonel Felice Mambor, a square, gruff, unsmiling man whose office is lined with art books and who presides over a small palazzo which contains something very like a war room. The room has a wall-sized map dotted with flags and symbols to denote archaeological sites and to locate recent robberies; there is a radio-communications system which enables the unit to dispatch carabinieri to the scenes of the now daily thefts.

A complicating factor is Colonel Mambor's feud with Rodolfo Siviero, who since shortly after the end of the war has headed Italy's Commission for the Recovery of Works of Art. In theory, Colonel Mambor is supposed to deal with internal thefts, while Signor Siviero, for his part, deals with art smuggled abroad, but since the market is international, the distinction is arbitrary. The two men dislike each other. When I saw Colonel Mambor, I erred by mentioning Signor Siviero's name. "What was that name you mentioned?" said the Colonel, squinting with annoyance. "I never heard that name before." Later, I saw Signor Siviero in Florence and I erred for the second time by mentioning that I had already interviewed Colonel Mambor. Why, my interpreter was subsequently asked, had I seen *that* man first?

The Ministry of Public Education has been publishing a directory of all important stolen art, dating from 1957 to the present, but, incredibly, the books are regarded as restricted documents and can be examined only with great difficulty. During an interview with an official of the Department of Fine

151

Arts, a division of the Ministry, I naïvely asked to see an annual report. With a smile, the official replied in English: "You will wait for such a report from here to eternity."

Still, there are successes in Italy, one of them owed to Signor Siviero, who, in a famous cops-and-robbers chase, recovered a statue known as the Ephebus of Selinunte. Originally, this three-foot-high bronze likeness of a youth had been found by a shepherd, in 1886, in a cemetery at the ancient site of Selinunte in southwest Sicily. The statue was dated to fifth century B.C. Greece and is ascribed by some scholars to the great sculptor Phidias. It was on proud display in the mayor's office in the town of Castelvetrano, from which it was stolen in October, 1962. An alarm went up, and Signor Siviero went to work. He learned that the Metropolitan Museum of Art had been offered the statue even before it had been stolen, and that a Philadelphia collector had also been approached, the asking price in his case being $500,000. The thieves could not find a buyer. In 1965, a Swiss dealer was sounded out and he turned it down, and later a reputable Florentine dealer informed Siviero that he had been called by a Sicilian who said the Ephebus was for sale. The Florentine expressed interest, but he said he was too old to make the inspection trip himself and would send his "nephew." Posing as that "nephew," Siviero, in early 1968, went to Agrigento in Sicily and made contact with the thieves, who by now were asking for the equivalent of $112,000. Signor Siviero responded with an offer of $32,000. The next day the asking price sank to $64,000, and the "nephew's" bid rose to $48,000. This price was agreed upon, and Siviero was told the statue would be delivered at Foligno, an industrial town northeast of Rome. The art policeman came with $48,000, and with a picked squad of police. The capture involved gunfire, rare in Italy; in the exchange of shots a robber was wounded, and all but one of the six-man gang was arrested. The Ephebus was then given a new home in a local museum, where it still is as of this writing.

The gunfire, it is worth noting, is a token of escalating violence in the theft of art. In 1968, three brigands made a *Topkapi*-style entry into the Izmir Fair Archaeological Museum, in Turkey, and pilfered a collection of antique jewelry, vases, and marbles. A watchman who tried to stop the theft was killed after his head was crushed with a stolen statue; the thieves, one of them a former German army sergeant, were later caught and convicted.* More recently, in May, 1972, thieves entered the Art Museum in Worcester, Massachusetts, and one of the robbers shot an unarmed guard who tried to block their escape. Paintings valued at more than $1 million were stolen— including works by Rembrandt, Gauguin, and Picasso—but were recovered a few months later by police. The guard survived; the thieves were arrested; and the case is still before the courts.

One is often struck by the contrast between the shadow of official good intentions and the substance of official neglect. Guatemala has on its statute books laws enacted in 1947 and modified in 1966 which, as elsewhere in Latin America, specify that all monuments, archaeological objects, and cultural relics are national treasures under state protection. Successive articles declare that the destruction or movement of any part of this patrimony is forbidden without express permission, that the export of all such properties is also forbidden, that express authorization is required for any explorations or excavations, that a register of the national patrimony shall be compiled, and

---

* The German was later sentenced to twenty-four years in prison by an Izmir court; a Turkish companion was sentenced to nine years, while another defendant, who had fled to Yugoslavia, was given eight years in absentia.

that violations of the law shall be punishable by up to four years in prison.

As elsewhere in Latin America, however, there is a gap between lofty assertions of national policy and the resources committed to the job. Antiquities are under the official supervision of the Institute of Anthropology and History, whose budget in 1971 was $167,381. With this money, the institute operates four museums in Guatemala City, four in Antigua, and three others elsewhere; the total payroll is about seventy persons. The highest salary is $350 a month, the sum paid the director of the institute, Lic. Luis Luján Muñoz; guards get paid $60 a month. The total expense allowance for the National Museum is $63 a month, which represents all the money available after salaries and electric bills are paid.

In practice, this means the museum has no funds for improved display, and none for acquisitions. The museum is housed in a decrepit building which was badly damaged by a hurricane in 1972 and has since been closed indefinitely. The museum charges no admission, even to tourists, nor is there an admission fee at Guatemala's premiere archaeological site, Tikal. Under existing laws, if an entrance fee were charged, the revenue would go into general funds and could not directly benefit the institute. The institute, finally, has little independent authority but is a stepchild of the Ministry of Public Education.

This lack of authority has engendered a stoic passivity among institute directors. A decade or so ago, a North American archaeologist vigorously protested the wanton demolition of Kaminaljuyú, a major early Maya site within the boundaries of Guatemala City. The then director shrugged unhappily and replied, *"Que podemos hacer?"* ("What can we do?") As a consequence, this fascinating site within the capital city itself has been all but obliterated by developers.

There is a modest effort at reform; a report has been prepared recommending that the institute be given more authority.

Yet change takes time in Guatemala, and one cannot be optimistic. A similar nonchalance can be found at the Foreign Ministry. When I asked a senior official—who himself has been directly concerned with countering the antiquities traffic—why there was not a single sign in the country's principal airport reminding tourists of prohibitions against export, the official amiably replied: "I suppose you're right, we should do something about that, but we haven't."

In the Department of El Petén, there are only a hundred police and at best they can give perfunctory attention to unguarded Maya sites. No official list of looted sites has yet been compiled.

Yet, in fairness, this negative account must be qualified. Guatemala has had major political and economic distractions in the past generation; since 1956, the country has operated under three different constitutions. Given the problems of political unrest and widespread poverty, archaeology has necessarily been low on the national agenda. Nor can it be forgotten that of Guatemala's 5.4 million people (as of 1970), some forty-five per cent are full-blooded Indians in twenty-one different language and cultural groups.

As elsewhere in Latin America, the political life of Guatemala is overwhelmingly concentrated in the capital, and in that life a numerically small, well-educated minority exercise an influence out of all proportion to its size. In Guatemala, a portion of the elite has become seriously concerned with the preservation of Maya sites, following the founding, in 1964, of the Tikal Association. A voluntary group of several hundred influential members, the association has undertaken a number of creditable projects. One of them is "Operacion Rescate," begun in 1970 with the cooperation of the government and of the Institute of Anthropology and History, which has as its express aim the saving of imperiled antiquities. With a small budget, some public assistance, and a few modest grants, Operacion

155

Rescate has already succeeded in moving a score or so stelae from vulnerable sites and is paying the salary of two guards at the threatened site of Yaxhá. In Guatemala, as elsewhere, the best hope of countering the destructive trade may well lie in the efforts of voluntary groups like the Tikal Association.

4. The Web of Influence

The illicit traffic in antiquities is unique in the breadth of the social spectrum it comprehends, a spectrum extending from illiterate peasants to cultivated and wealthy collectors. One can sensibly speak of the trade as a democratic demimonde, since rich and poor, highborn and lowborn, are all citizens within it. This patronage by the well-placed also gives the trade a certain immunity. Occasionally major dealers and important middlemen are arrested, but seldom for long, and shops briefly closed are soon open again.

In 1957, the Italian police thought they had finally put a well-known dealer out of business. The dealer was Franz Renn Rain, an Austrian who since 1939 had had a shop near the Spanish Steps with a sign at the entrance saying, "F. Renn Rain, Unique and Worldwide Famous." Though he was watched by police, no identifiable stolen goods could be found in his shop. Eventually it was discovered that his real place of business was in a dilapidated palazzo not far away, to which favored customers were taken. In the courtyard of the palazzo, police discovered some 15,000 items, of which 4,000 were classified as rare museum pieces with an estimated value of $1 million. The art was confiscated, but within days Renn Rain was back in business at his "Unique and Worldwide Famous" shop.

However the Austrian dealer managed it, the explanation in most such cases is influence. Those in the trade have important allies, among them diplomats, wealthy collectors, financiers, and in some instances, it may be surmised, intelligence services. The diplomat is an old and familiar friend; in the past, envoys were themselves frequently involved in archaeology or antiquities, as was the case with Sir Henry Layard, John Lloyd Stephens, Lord Elgin, and General Luigi Palma di Cesnola. Diplomats are often collectors, and sometimes they help other collectors or dealers by making accessible that invaluable privilege, the untouchable diplomatic pouch.

Early in this century, an enterprising Yankee named Edward Herbert Thompson was appointed United States consul in the Yucatán, and shortly after his arrival he acquired the land which encloses the great Maya site of Chichén Itzá. Thompson was fascinated by a story told by early Spanish chroniclers— that the Maya had flung rare jewelry and sacrificial virgins into the Sacred Well, or Cenote, at the site. He learned the skills of diving, and plumbed the Cenote, exhuming hundreds of offerings, some of them gold, as well as bones of some of the victims. The gold and bones were sent via diplomatic pouch to the Peabody Museum at Harvard, but the consul did not trouble to notify Mexican authorities. During the 1920s there was a scandal, and as a result of it Thompson was forced to leave the Yucatán. (Years later, in a becoming gesture, the Peabody Museum returned a selection of the gold to Mexico.)

In Thompson's case, there was no thought of gain, and his offense was deception, not greed. In other cases, the use of the pouch has not been so innocent. In Rome, it had long been known that an ambassador from one of the Low Countries had been making his diplomatic seals available to favored collectors and dealers. A police inquiry was underway when, before charges could be pressed, the ambassador died.

In Panama, government privilege has taken a special form. The Canal Zone, which bisects the republic, is under the sovereign control of the United States as a consequence of a treaty deeding the United States the land in perpetuity. Pot hunting has long been a hobby of some United States citizens who work in the Zone; highly salable antiquities can be found in Panama (especially beautiful Coclé gold). In 1958, the Zonians organized the Archaeological Society of Panama, which published a journal and sponsored some of the digs. What marred an otherwise laudable enterprise was the fact that some of the Society members were active in the antiquities trade. This led to a protest from the government of Panama, to which the governor of the Canal Zone replied that he would not interfere with the leisure-time activities of Zone personnel. In 1967, after persistent protests, the Society was disbanded, and unofficial pot hunting was finally forbidden.

If the diplomat is an important friend, the collector is an equally influential ally. When the collector has wealth and social standing, as he often does, he is able to make his influence felt when a dealer gets in legal trouble. In some cases, the collector is a dealer, too. In one Central American country, the most important dealer is also one of the country's major collectors. He has financed clandestine digs in neighboring countries and has gathered tens of thousands of pre-Columbian pieces over the past few decades. He is also a member of a politically influential family. In March, 1972, I visited his home and talked with the collector, who showed me through room after room in an old-fashioned house filled with both bric-a-brac and extraordinary artifacts. At one point he paused, singling out a good Maya pot, and asked how much I thought it was worth. "I like to sell to people who appreciate art," he explained as he politely offered to part with the piece.

An early prototype of the collector-dealer was a North American named William Spratling, a native of Sonyea, New York, a professor of architecture in New Orleans, and an expatriate resident of Taxco, Mexico, from 1929 until his death

158

in an automobile accident in 1967. Spratling is remembered for founding the modern silver trade in Taxco, and for being a pioneer aficionado of pre-Columbian Mexican art. He was an inspired promoter. He built a showplace ranch midway on the highway between Taxco and Iguala, and formed a private museum of pre-Columbian art. He had a serious interest in archaeological finds and sold only to friends, among whom he counted the leading artists and writers in Mexico. Spratling was intrigued by the illicit trade, and provides in his autobiography vivid portraits of the native sellers of antiquities in Iguala, the dusty market town that is the center of the illicit traffic in western Mexico. His words, written in 1967, have documentary value:

> . . . In Mexico, where ten years ago there were perhaps less than a hundred collectors, today there must be more than ten thousand in Mexico City alone; also, whereas a few years ago, there were only four or five little dealers, or "runners," today these number in the hundreds and have been classified by the government, in its publicity, as gangsters. . . . There are all types of dealers, and among them a very few have criteria. The poor Indians who find things in caves or plow them up in their fields have no criteria or knowledge.
>
> But they have heard that something old was sold for a very high price, and they conclude that any piece, just because it is ancient, must be worth thousands. . . . I know of certain villages where they will let a planting season go by without planting corn because they have discovered a few small tombs. . . . They are unconscious of committing an act of vandalism. But real vandalism occurs when, from the higher echelons among the dealers, true gangsters who are criminals will advance money and implements to bring out pieces.

Of the dealers, an Indian woman especially interested Spratling. She was wise in the ways of the world and of the police in her native Iguala. Spratling reports that when an Indian digger refused to sell to her at her usual low prices, she permitted him to go to the town square to think it over. There, he was picked up by the police, who confiscated his contraband art. The police then promptly sold it to the woman for a moderate sum.

Spratling left his collection to the town of Taxco and to the National University of Mexico; his ranch passed into the hands of a European motorcycle racer whom I visited in 1972. The new owner told me that even though Spratling had left his valuable library to the university, it had never been claimed and had been under lock and key for years. Eventually, the European protested, and he had finally been given a key only the week before I arrived. We went together into the musty library, the books being covered by every variety of Mexican fecal material; all else was as it had been the night of Spratling's death. A decanter of whiskey—still half-full—was on the sideboard. Volumes that were collector's items were destroyed by mold. It was a cinematic montage, a sad image of the decline and fall of the pre-Columbian past.

A new entry in the antiquities trade is the financier. As the prices of antiquities have mounted, ancient art has become a fresh field for speculative money. A dozen or so art investment firms have been founded in the past decade, but few have realized the promises in their glossy brochures. An exception is the Artemis Fund, incorporated in Luxembourg in 1970 for the purpose of trading in works of art. The fund is owned by two of Europe's richer bankers, Baron Léon Lambert, senior partner in the Banque Lambert in Brussels, and his cousin in Paris, Baron Elie de Rothschild.

Artemis has as its chief advisor on purchases David Carritt, formerly with Christie's auction house in London, and is also assisted by a distinguished group of art experts. Although the

160

commercial focus of Artemis has been on Old Masters and contemporary art, the fund has recently become interested in antiquities. In March, 1973, the *New York Times* reported that Artemis had put up the purchase money for an extraordinary Greek bronze reputedly executed by the great sculptor Lysippus. A Munich dealer named Hans Herzer reportedly acquired the masterpiece for Artemis, which was said to have paid $700,000 for it.* The piece has been offered to J. Paul Getty, who according to one report decided to buy it but then changed his mind: it has been on the market for an asking price of as much as $4.5 million—reputedly Norton Simon is interested in the precious bronze.

The story illustrates again the secrecy that can envelop a truly major work of art. Museum curators had been aware for several years that the unique bronze was for sale, but until the story appeared in the *Times* there was no public knowledge of its existence. There are varying accounts of the statue's origin. Some say it was found in the sea near Turkey; others say it was discovered in a classical shipwreck in the offshore waters near Naples, or in the Straits of Messina; still another version is that the statue was netted by Italian fishermen in extraterritorial waters. All versions are in accord on one point: that the purported Lysippus was found in the sea.

Skin diving for antiquities has become a specialized branch of the sherd trade. In the Mediterranean, classical wrecks have been the prime target; and in the Caribbean, the prizes are Spanish caravels laden with doubloons. Several commercial operations in the United States cater to would-be undersea archaeologists. One of them is the Under Sea Academy, a regular advertiser in the *New York Times*, which mails inquirers

* According to some informants, the bronze statue has also been responsibly attributed to Phidias by an outstanding English scholar.

161

a brochure giving the price lists for artifacts and coins recovered from previous expeditions. The brochure explains:

Collecting archaeological treasures will give you profit and inflation protection. Now, more than ever before, there's an urgent need for investments that are enduring. *Investments that are tangible,* not stock certificates or Federal Reserve Notes, churned off the presses by the millions. . . . Things that are war-proof, recession-proof, inflation-proof and crash-proof. One of the foremost authorities at the Parke-Bernet Art Galleries says *artifacts and coins are in a diminishing supply* . . . The Times-Sotheby Index (the Dow-Jones of the art and antiques world) has risen *continuously and steadily.*

TAX BENEFITS UNDER OUR TAX SHELTERED PROGRAM: You can own any of these archaeological treasures and deduct 100 per cent of the cost from your taxable income. When you decide to sell, you are eligible for capital gains treatment. To assist you in building your personal collection, we have two tax-sheltered plans: Thirty-Day Plan and Time-Payment Plan. . . . If you wish to inquire about our tax-sheltered plan for any of the pieces in our current acquisition list, use the space provided on the front of our order form.

Sometimes, the undersea explorers come upon a major find which they·have difficulty marketing. In November, 1970, I received from an undersea operator based in Florida the following letter:

Dear Mr. Meyer:

I read with interest your recent piece in *Life,* exploring the possibilities of a pre-Columbian melting pot. Your approach to the subject prompts the assumption that your research may have exposed you to sources of possible interest in a most unique collection of gold artifacts dating from this approximate period.

This collection was put together by illegal means, but I am informed reliably that it now satisfies all requirements for a public sale, although the offering is private. It is presently in a bank vault, and could be made available for firsthand inspection on reasonable notice. The asking price is $500,000 U.S., and I am told that the gold content alone is worth a six figure sum. I am in a position to provide photographs of reasonable quality as a preliminary for any party seriously interested.

Though I replied promptly asking for photographs, the vendor plainly had second thoughts; I did not receive them.*

In examining the web of influence, another thread is the relationship of the art dealer to intelligence services. Those who know the art market well in the Mediterranean have been struck by the number of persons involved in it who served in Western intelligence during World War II. There appears to be something like an "old boy" network among former intelligence operators now in the art market. Dikran A. Sarrafian, the Lebanese coin dealer who allegedly was the original owner of the Metropolitan Museum's Euphronios krater, was a British intelligence operative in wartime Yugoslavia; a prominent dealer in Rome has the police nickname of "La Spia" because of a belief that he owes his legal immunity to his past or present services as an agent. Another specimen is a Yugoslav named Ante Topic-Mimara, a dealer whose wartime role is especially

---

* Another underwater outfit, Fathom Expeditions, of Venice, California, has sent out a flier saying, "The purpose of this expedition is the excavation and recovery of pre-Columbian artifacts from various sites in Costa Rica. We will be dealing directly with the Indians, purchasing and excavating pottery, stone, gold and jade artifacts. Previous recoveries from the area are now on display in the Los Angeles County Museum. . . . We have all the necessary permits for exportation of all finds. Our last expedition netted us almost 2,000 pieces of this rare and valuable material."

163

mysterious. Immediately after the war, Mr. Topic-Mimara turned up in Western Europe with a truckload of art, including the extraordinary Bury St. Edmunds Cross. This small but exquisite medieval ivory was purchased in 1963 at a still undisclosed price by the Metropolitan Museum, upon the urgent recommendation of Thomas P. F. Hoving, then the curator of the museum's collection at the Cloisters.

But where did Mr. Topic-Mimara acquire the Cross? Originally, the British Museum had an option on its purchase but allowed the option to drop, in part because there was a question about Mr. Topic-Mimara's clear title to the piece. When the British Museum telephoned its decision to Zurich, where the owner kept the Cross in a bank vault, the option was immediately picked up by the Metropolitan, and the sale was later concluded—one condition being that the price was to remain secret. Years later, a biography of the German Nazi and Western superspy General Reinhard Gehlen referred ambiguously to Mr. Topic-Mimara as head of the Yugoslav spy apparatus in Germany in the 1940s. He clearly had been in both the art and intelligence trades during that time. Somehow, somewhere, he had acquired a magnificent ivory that escaped both the pillage of the English Reformation and the holocaust of World War II. The story of its survival has yet to be told.

5. The End of the Game?

In March, 1973, a gallery in Houston, Texas, invited its customers to an opening of a new exhibition of pre-Columbian art. The invitation noted: "Because of recent legal restriction in this country and in Latin America, our fifteenth annual Latin American exhibition will be our last. Hereafter, we will continue to assemble in our gallery the most interesting examples of available world art." The announcement is one of a number of indications that the halcyon years of the antiquities market are coming to an end, though some great sales may yet be made in the next few years.

"It's been fun while it lasted, but it's over," a prominent Midwestern museum curator remarked to me. A number of dealers are either retiring (like J. J. Klejman, who sold the Metropolitan its Lydian hoard) or are switching to other collector fields, such as ornamental rocks or contemporary art. A Philadelphia dealer is now concentrating on rare books, and a woman who operated a successful pre-Columbian gallery went out of the business because she could no longer reconcile herself to its ethical ambiguities. There is a valedictory air in the conversation of the major dealers in Switzerland, who talk of making a few final big sales and retiring to publish scholarly monographs. A number of factors account for this mood: the increasing difficulty of obtaining antiquities, a fear of scandal among customers, and the gradual change in public attitudes and government policies.

The supply of antiquities is finite, and some much-plundered sites are nearly exhausted. Plainly in countries like Turkey there is still a vast underground Louvre, which can be rifled for years to come. But even where supplies remain ample, the market for such smuggled art is constricting. Both collectors and museums are likely to be increasingly wary of "hot" art, in part because of growing scrupulousness and in part because of changing laws and public attitudes.* The more reflective

---

* There is also a palpable air of greater defensiveness among big dealers in answering queries about the possible legality of their operations. I sent a dozen letters to various major international dealers asking, in the guise of a potential customer, whether my pieces would be subject to seizure or whether their purchase would contribute to the destruction of antiquities. Spink & Son of London replied: "The ratification by the United States of the UNESCO treaty concerning stolen works of art would not, I hope, affect any pieces that we sold as we do not acquire pieces on which there is any question as to their origin. We buy exclusively from private collections and reliable dealers." A Philadelphia dealer, Hesperia Art, replied: "As far as

curators realize that unless museums show more sensitivity to the ethical issues involved, politicians may impose upon them drastic and perhaps unwise restrictions—in New York, during the tempest over the Metropolitan's "de-accessioning" process, several politicians proposed that all such acquisition and sales decisions be subject to review by the city's Board of Estimate. After the Euphronios affair, State Senator William T. Conklin of Brooklyn, the Republican deputy majority leader, introduced a bill intended to prevent any museum in New York State from "illicitly" acquiring, selling, or trading cultural property.

A much simpler and potentially more effective reform has been suggested by Paul Bator, a professor of law at Harvard. Mr. Bator is a specialist in constitutional law with a lively appreciation of political realities (his brother, Francis, was a White House aide to President Lyndon B. Johnson). In 1969, Professor Bator carried out a special study on the law of art for the Panel on the International Movement of Art Treasures sponsored by the American Society of International Law. His assignment was to analyze and gather information on existing policies concerning the export of cultural properties. He reported that, as a newcomer to the field, he found it striking "how hard it is to find any thoughtful analysis of or information about just how great the jeopardy is to what values." He added: "As far as I know, nobody has even an approximate idea of what the total volume [of art exports] from any country is, either in terms of value or number of objects. Nor is there

---

I know, there is no plan to return art which came out of any country. The major museums of this country would fight such a proposal since it would empty their cases. . . . If the countries that complain had ever wanted to pay the going price for objects dug up, they could have everything." Hartwell J. Kennard, of McAllen, Texas, replied: "As far as excessive looting is concerned, I am sure some of it is happening much to the dismay of those interested in the art of these primitive peoples. Since the archaeological significance has already been recorded from the type of tomb from which my pieces come, their value as a piece of primitive art becomes paramount. Our Constitution guarantees that there shall be no *ex post facto* laws, and any piece you purchase now would not be subject to seizure."

more than the most impressionistic knowledge about what might be called the structure of the trade."

Mr. Bator learned more about the problem as a member of the six-man United States delegation to the UNESCO meeting in Paris, in April, 1970, at which a convention was drafted on the Means of Prohibiting and Preventing the Illicit Import, Export and Transfer of Ownership of Cultural Property. The chairman of the delegation was a shrewd State Department counselor, Mark B. Feldman (who, a few years later, negotiated an agreement with Cuba aimed at deterring skyjacking). The American delegation succeeded in working out a compromise that led to a draft convention which Mr. Feldman believed the United States Congress would approve and implement. In the process, it became apparent to Americans on the delegation that the campaign to end the illicit trade would be a long and hard one, and the problem not subject to simple cure. (For all its merits, the UNESCO convention has been fully ratified only by a handful of countries, including Ecuador and Honduras; the British and Swiss did not even bother to attend the UNESCO meeting in Paris.)

At Harvard, Mr. Bator continued his work in the field by serving on the committee that drafted the new restrictions on acquisition policy that now apply to all the university's museums. Still, he was troubled by the failure of the great art museums in the United States to follow suit. Always there was the problem of lack of information. In April, 1973, Mr. Bator came to New York to attend a meeting sponsored by the City Bar Association on the topic "Art, Museums and the Public."*

During the meeting, a dealer favorably contrasted the art market with Wall Street, saying that art dealers were, after all,

---

* The speakers were Ashton Hawkins, the secretary of the Metropolitan Museum; John Hess, a reporter for the *New York Times*; Palmer B. Wald, an Assistant Attorney General of New York who has been directing an inquiry into the Metropolitan Museum; and André Emmerich, a dealer in pre-Columbian and contemporary art and president of the Art Dealers' Association.

concerned with beauty as well as profits. Mr. Bator was sitting in the audience, and this observation troubled him. In the question period, he noted that there were rules of disclosure that applied to Wall Street but that did not apply to museum acquisition. Why shouldn't museums divulge the full provenance of any new work of art, including the name of the dealer and the price paid for it? His question was asked, but not really answered. If museums themselves will not adopt a policy of full disclosure, legislatures can reasonably impose this requirement on what are quasi-public institutions.

Still, one cannot be foolishly optimistic about the effect of any unilateral steps taken by, or in, the United States. The matter has been concisely put by the distinguished columnist, Joseph Alsop. In a friendly letter to the author, Mr. Alsop writes:

> I must tell you that mere American self-restraint will do no good in this area. In many sectors of the art market, the Japanese are already spending more than American collectors. And before much time has passed, this will be true of *every* sector of the art market. In addition, pre-Columbian objects also command very high prices in Europe, especially in Germany and Switzerland. Unless a self-denying ordinance is truly international, in fact, it will merely have the effect of denying the United States what other people will then snap up.

Some would use this argument as an excuse for total inaction. Clearly (as I replied to Mr. Alsop), any attack on the illicit trade to be effective must also be international. Yet, in the absence of such a concerted effort, the United States is still responsible for what its citizens and museums do, and is not responsible for the Japanese or Europeans. Since the American government offers a uniquely generous tax benefit to collectors, it has a special reason for taking a unilateral lead—and the force of the American example cannot wholly be ignored.

This prompted a further rejoinder from Mr. Alsop:

> I do not agree with you that there may be some force in the American example. If you examine the art market's history, you will find it has always amounted to an enormous world-eddy, rather frequently clandestine or illegal, in which new centers of wealth and power have always exerted enough magnetic force to attract the great prizes of the period.
>
> In our own art tradition, the first attempt to prevent loss of works of art was made by one of the fifteenth century Popes; and there is a surviving letter from Isabella d'Este, indicating how the Pope's regulations could be circumvented. It has always been that way. . . . At the moment, the Japanese dealers and collectors are going through the art market like voracious, but undiscriminating vacuum cleaners. But they have always been fast learners. And you will soon enough see them going for the real prizes that are still available.

The argument is a powerful one. If there is any hope of saving the imperiled past it may require not only new laws, but an entirely new attitude, and it is to this problem that we finally turn.

CHAPTER FIVE

WHOSE PAST?

Far-stretching, endless Time
Brings forth all hidden things,
And buries that which once did shine.
The firm resolve falters, the sacred oath is shattered;
And let none say, "It cannot happen here."

SOPHOCLES, Ajax

1. Lord Byron's Curse

One scandal involving antiquities that nearly everybody has heard about is the unending controversy over the Elgin Marbles. Every few years there is a fresh Greek demand for the return of the Parthenon carvings, and this is usually followed by a debate in the British Parliament and a flurry of letters in the London *Times*. As with so much that originates in Greece, the dispute has its mythic overtones, and encompasses within it many of the themes touched upon elsewhere in this book. Three of its original protagonists—Elgin, Byron, and Haydon—anticipated attitudes found everywhere today in the art world. Old as the controversy may seem, it deserves a fresh analysis be-

170

cause it opens up the most fundamental question of all: Who really owns the past?

The pitch of emotion the Elgin Marbles can arouse is suggested by an episode in the life of the late Sir Harold Nicolson. In 1924, the British author was serving as a junior clerk in the Foreign Office, and his special field was supposed to be Greece. He had traveled to that country the previous year and had visited, among other places, Missolonghi, where Lord Byron had died in the Greek War of Independence. A date caught Nicolson's attention. The centenary of Byron's death would fall on April 19, 1924, and it occurred to him that Anglo-Greek relations might benefit from a symbolic anniversary gesture, such as the return to Athens of the famous Caryatid in the British Museum. The Caryatid, a pillar carved in the likeness of a handsome woman, was part of the large collection removed from the Acropolis a century before by Lord Elgin. Its place on the Erechtheum, the small Ionic temple near the Parthenon, was later filled by a terra-cotta copy, which sticks out like a fake tooth.

Interest was expressed in Nicolson's idea, and he was asked to draw up a memorandum, which he did—a very sober, schematic document, he later recalled, with austerely numbered subparagraphs. Fully aware of the strong feelings about the Marbles, Nicolson expected nothing more to happen and was agreeably surprised when he was summoned for an interview with his chief, Ramsay MacDonald, at the time serving as both prime minister and foreign secretary in Britain's first Labour Government. One can imagine the interview: Nicolson, then thirty-seven, seated in a deep leather chair amid ticking antique clocks while MacDonald solemnly studied the memorandum. In due course, the Prime Minister said that if the Caryatid was returned, then the case for retaining the other Marbles would be prejudiced. Nicolson replied, with some warmth, that no justification had ever existed for retaining the carvings in the first

171

place. "You forget," MacDonald rejoined, "that had not these lovely things been preserved in England, they would have been destroyed in the Greek War of Independence." With that, Nicolson's idea died, and the Caryatid has ever since remained firmly in British hands.

Was the Prime Minister right? If so, does the preservation of the Marbles justify their permanent retention by Britain? The questions cannot be answered without considering how and why the Attic sculpture came to London in the first place. Thomas Bruce, the seventh Earl of Elgin and twelfth Earl of Kincardine, was a Scottish peer born in 1766 who, after attending Harrow and Winchester, made diplomacy his vocation. In 1799, he was named British ambassador to the Ottoman Empire, and seemed destined for a notable official career. In fact, the appointment was a disaster for Elgin; in its course, he lost his fortune, his reputation, his wife, and the lower half of his nose, while the one great prize he did obtain, the Marbles, has forever shadowed his memory.

At the outset, the Scotsman never intended to remove the Phidian ornaments from the Acropolis. The event had its innocent inception when a friend suggested that Elgin could greatly benefit British art by securing plaster casts and competent drawings of the Parthenon sculptures. The envoy-designate enthusiastically agreed, and on the way to Constantinople he stopped in Sicily to recruit a team of artists and architects to carry out the project. As happens in politics, the ardor of his subordinates led to an expansion of the original scheme.

The ambassador's team arrived in Athens in 1800. Its members were dismayed by what seemed to them the appalling Turkish neglect of the Acropolis monuments. Greece was then part of the Ottoman Empire, and Turks tended to regard classical ruins as infidel relics; for a small bribe, tourists could carry away fragments of the Parthenon. A bold suggestion arose: Why shouldn't Elgin ask permission to remove the or-

172

naments? The suggestion was sent to Constantinople, and Elgin liked it. The timing was propitious. The Empire was then at war with its old ally France, whose forces had recently conquered Egypt, then nominally an Ottoman province. Britain was the new ally; the sultan was jubilant when the British in 1801 drove the French from Egypt as Nelson's warships harassed Napoleon's Mediterranean fleet.

As a result, the British ambassador received all possible honors—an aigrette from the sultan's turban, the Order of the Crescent, caparisoned horses, and fireworks displays. It was at this moment that Elgin made his unusual request, and in due course he received a *firman,* or permit, enabling him in his capacity as ambassador to carry out excavations on the Acropolis. Unfortunately, the Turkish original of the document was lost, and the only surviving copy is an Italian translation in which the key words are ambiguous. The *firman,* in this version, said that the envoy's team could without hindrance take away *"qualche pezzi di pietra con inscrizioni e figure,"* which in the British Museum booklet about the Elgin Marbles is translated as "any pieces of stone with inscriptions or figures." Among those who differ with this rendering is Harold Nicolson, who translates *qualche* as "some" rather than "any," adding this comment: "Even a most free and lavish translation of the Italian tongue cannot twist these words into meaning a whole shipload of sculptures, columns and caryatids."

At any rate, Elgin's agents stretched the *firman* to its permissive limit.* Over a period of years more than three hun-

---

* Credit, or blame, for first proposing the removal of the Marbles belongs to Dr. Philip Hunt, the British Embassy chaplain, who attached himself to Elgin's team in Athens. Dr. Hunt knew how to get things done; when the *firman* arrived, he tested its powers by proposing removal of an important metope. Adolf Michaelis writes: "The elastic final clause of this memorable permit was so luminously expounded by Hunt to the Governor of Athens, the interpretation being backed by an appropriate present of brilliant cutglass, lustres, firearms, and other articles of English manufacture, that the Governor at once gave leave for the metope to leave the Parthenon." (Michaelis, 1882, p. 135.)

dred workmen were employed in dismantling and packing the Marbles. By one count, Elgin acquired seventeen figures from the Parthenon pediments, fifteen metopes, and fifty-six slabs of the temple's friezes. He also got the Caryatid column, four pieces of the Temple of Victory, thirteen marble heads, and a large assortment of carved fragments, painted vases, sepulchral pillars, and inscribed albas. The shipment alone was a major logistic task—at one point, part of the collection was lost in a wreck and had to be retrieved by divers, an operation taking four years. All expenses (save for the use of naval vessels) were borne by the ambassador himself.

As the work proceeded, the ambassador's original ideas about improving British taste took on a new dimension. Elgin had recently married a vivacious heiress and was planning a new mansion at Broomhall, his family seat in Scotland. It occurred to him that the Marbles might make a decorative feature. As he wrote to Giovanni Battista Lusieri, the Neapolitan artist who was supervising the removal of the Marbles:

> [T]he plans for my house in Scotland should be known to you. The building is a subject that occupies me greatly, and offers me the means of placing, in a useful, distinguished and agreeable way, the various things that you may perhaps be able to procure for me . . . the Hall is intended to be adorned with columns, the cellars underneath are vaulted expressly for this . . . In either case I should wish to collect as much marble as possible. I have other places in my house which need it, and besides, one can easily multiply ornaments of beautiful marble without overdoing it, and nothing, truly, is so beautiful and also independent of changes in fashion. . . . You do not need prompting from me to know the value that is attached to a sculptured marble, or historic piece. . . .

In this mingling of motives, this blend of disinterest and

174

avarice, we find the outlook of the archtypal collector, which in some ways Elgin surely was. But as it turned out, the Marbles never did go to Scotland because in the next few years every conceivable calamity overwhelmed the Scottish peer.

The first was disease. In 1802, Elgin contracted a skin disorder in Constantinople which afflicted his face and ultimately ate away the lower part of his nose, disfiguring him for life. Then there was a professional disaster. Napoleon took a personal dislike to Elgin, whom the French blamed for their diplomatic reverses with the Sublime Porte, as the sultanate was known. Chance then put Elgin at Napoleon's mercy. There was a brief interlude of peace between France and England in 1802 and early the following year the ambassador, his tour over, made his way home by way of Rome and Paris. While he was in France, war again broke out and Elgin was taken prisoner and held as a hostage for three years. He was finally released in 1806, but under a crippling parole imposed by Talleyrand which effectively ended his diplomatic career. There was a further misfortune; his wife Mary had preceded him to Britain by nine months, and when Elgin returned he discovered she was living adulterously with a Scottish neighbor, one Robert Ferguson of Raith. An ugly and bitter divorce trial followed. On top of all this, in 1807 Elgin lost his seat as one of sixteen representative Scottish peers in the House of Lords.

Then there were the Marbles, for which the seventh Earl had sacrificed so much. Successive shipments of the Greek carvings had arrived in London while Elgin was still a French prisoner, and on his return he promptly arranged for their public display in an improvised shed on Park Lane. Regrettably for him, the Marbles, too, became the focus for a controversy in which he wound up the loser. First, there was the question of their true worth. Even before their display, the Marbles were attacked as mere copies by Richard Payne Knight, an influential classical scholar, who had met Elgin in France in 1806 and had

175

told him over a dinner table, "You have lost your labor, my Lord Elgin. Your marbles are overrated: they are not Greek: they are Roman of the time of Hadrian." Until his death, eighteen years later, Payne Knight stuck to that opinion.

On the opposing side was the artist and diarist Benjamin Robert Haydon, who was to become the leading British champion of the Elgin Marbles. He was among the first visitors who saw them in 1808, leaving this vivid record in his memoirs:

> To Park Lane then we went, and after passing through the hall and thence into an open yard, entered a damp, dirty penthouse where lay the marbles within sight and reach. The first thing I fixed my eyes on was the wrist of a figure in one of the female groups, in which were visible, though in feminine form, the radius and ulna. I was astonished, for I had never seen them in any female wrist in the antique.
>
> I darted my eyes to the elbow, and saw the outer condyne visible, affecting the shape as in nature. I saw that the arm was in repose and an idea which I had felt so wanting for high art was here displayed to midday conviction. My heart beat! If I had seen nothing else I had beheld sufficient to keep me in nature for the rest of my life.

Haydon felt as if a "divine truth had blazed inwardly upon my mind" and he knew the Marbles "would at last rouse the art of Europe from its slumber in darkness." In his rapture, he all but dragged a friend—the Swiss-born artist Henry Fuseli —to Park Lane, giving us this pleasant description:

> I drove off to Fuseli, and fired him to such a degree that he ran upstairs, put on his coat, and away we sailed. I remember that first a coal-cart with eight horses stopped us as it struggled up one of the lanes of the Strand; then a flock of sheep blocked us up; Fuseli, in a fury of haste

and rage, burst into the middle of them, and they got between his little legs and jostled him so much that I
screamed with laughter in spite of my excitement . . . .

At last we came to Park Lane. Never shall I forget his
uncompromising enthusiasm. He strode about saying, "De
Greeks were godes! de Greeks were godes!" We went back
to his house, where I dined with him, and we passed the
evening in looking over Quintilian and Pliny. Immortal
period of my sanguine life! To look back on those hours
has been the solace of my bitterest afflictions.

In Haydon's ecstasy, we encounter the curatorial view of the
past. It never occurred to the artist to inquire how or why the
carvings had reached England; their aesthetic revelation was
to him transcendent. In the arguments that followed over
the purchase of the Marbles by the British Government, Haydon was a principal advocate for their merit, furiously opposing
the querulous doubts of Payne Knight. A special Committee
of the House of Commons weighed their purchase from Elgin
—who by now was close to bankruptcy—and in 1815 the Committee found that Elgin had full authority for acquiring the
Marbles, that he had got them in his private capacity, though
only an ambassador could have obtained such liberal rights,
and that the carvings were "in the very first class of ancient art."
The Committee felt that £35,000 was adequate compensation to
Elgin, and though he was deeply disappointed by this figure, the
seventh Earl in the end accepted it, and thus the Marbles became the property of the British nation.

There was, however, another view about the matter—the ro-
mantic nationalist view—as expressed by Lord Byron. The poet
happened to arrive in Athens during the Christmas holidays in
1809, and among his new friends was Lusieri, Elgin's agent.
Byron toured the Acropolis, with the Neapolitan artist as his

guide, and saw the fresh gashes in the Parthenon, which Lusieri, with sly mischief, pointed out. Byron's reaction was as vehement as Haydon's, but of a distinctly different sort. He was moved when he heard that some Greek workmen had abruptly thrown down a case of sculptures when, they said, the statues shrieked in protest. In the arguments over the merits of Elgin's deed, when it was put to the poet that the Marbles might be better preserved in Britain, and indeed have an elevating effect on British art, he replied that the carvings were Greek property. "I opposed, and will ever oppose," he later wrote, "the robbery of ruins from Athens, to instruct the English in sculpture (who are as capable of sculpture as the Egyptians are of skating) . . . ."

Legend has it that Byron carved into the Acropolis the lines "Quod Non Fecerunt Gothi, Fecerunt Scoti" ("What the Goths spared, the Scots have destroyed"). His other observations on Elgin are more abundantly documented. In a poem entitled "The Curse of Minerva," Byron's rage spread over eighteen stanzas, this being the message:

> Daughter of Jove! In Britain's injur'd name,
> A true-born Briton may the deed disclaim,
> Frown not on England—England owns him not;
> Athena! No— the plunderer was a Scot.

Elsewhere Byron (whose mother was Scottish) likened Elgin to a jackal, an idiot, and the greedy keeper of a "stone shop." In "Childe Harold," he wrote:

> But most the modern Pict's ignoble boast,
> To rive what Goth, and Turk and Time hath spared:
> Cold as the crags upon his native coast,
> His mind as barren and his heart as hard,
> Is he who conceived, whose hand prepared,
> Aught to displace Athena's poor remains:
> Her sons too weak the sacred shrine to guard,

Yet felt some portion of their mother's pains,
And never knew till then the weight of Despot's chains.

Whatever else may be said about Byron's view, which was
more felt than reasoned, he anticipated the emotions of na-
tionalists everywhere about what they have come to regard as
European and American exploitation. The point has been fairly
made by Colonel C. M. Woodhouse, who commanded the Allied
Military Mission to the Greek guerrillas during the Nazi occupation and who served as Conservative Member of Parliament
for Oxford from 1959 to 1966. In his book *The Philhellenes,*
Woodhouse remarks: "Elgin suffered bitterly for his pains and
was subjected to many infamous and irrelevant attacks. But
these are not to the present point. The point is that it never
occurred to anybody, before Byron, that the removal of the
Elgin Marbles might be seen as an act depriving the Greeks of
their historic heritage. Nobody thought it in the least odd that
the Greeks were allowed no say whatever in the matter."

Thus the controversy over the Elgin Marbles can be seen as
embodying three distinct views of the human past. There is
first the collector's view, that of Lord Elgin, who saw himself as
a savior of antiquity while at the same time having an eye to
future market values. Next is the curator's view, as embodied
in Haydon, in which the end—the enrichment of national sensibility—is seen as justifying any doubtful means of acquisition. Finally, there is the Byronic attitude, which regards ancient
monuments as indissoluble parts of the national patrimony.

These attitudes continue to collide in the increasingly im-
passioned debate over the human past, and each has its legitimate claims. But where does this leave the Parthenon? While
the arguments rage, the great temple is dwindling away. Georges
Dontas, the director of the Acropolis, has said that the Parthenon is seriously imperiled by internal structural decay, by
the vibrations of jet aircraft, the ceaseless shuffle of shoes, and

179

—most ominous of all—by the aerial assault of rock-eating fumes emitted by smokestacks and automobiles. In 1687, a major disaster befell the monument when, during a Venetian siege of Athens, a shell landed in the temple, exploding a powder magazine within it. The explosion left fissures in the marble, and into these crevices water infiltrates. In the winter cold, the water freezes and expands, splitting the stone. Writes Mr. Dontas: "On the morning after such freezing spells our people go around picking up the fragments of marble, carefully noting the precise spot where they belonged, or where they fell." The director of the Acropolis is even more concerned with the heavy calcification of the marble which has been aggravated by industrial and automotive fumes. Experiments have been made with chemical coatings, but, as Mr. Dontas remarks, "I regret to say, no miracle substance has been found that offers full protection and no drawbacks."

Whether the Elgin Marbles would have been damaged during the Greek War of Independence is a matter of dispute. But surely it is inarguably true that if the carvings had not been taken from the temple, modern pollution would have disfigured them. In this sense, the seventh Earl was indeed a conservator of antiquity. Thus the Elgin controversy does give us a fresh perspective for examining the question of who owns the past. What is really at stake is not so much ownership but preservation—and this, surely, is the more fundamental point which gets lost in the cacophony of voices.

2. *The Nationalist Past*

Of these voices, perhaps the loudest is that of the nationalist, Byron's heir. The birth of archaeology in Europe is linked to the rise of nationalism, beginning with the appointment of an

Antiquary of the Realm by Henry VIII in Reformation England. (A prize discovered by the Antiquary was the supposed original Round Table of King Arthur and his knights, which the Tudor monarch proudly displayed to Charles V during that emperor's visit in 1552; the table now hangs in Winchester Castle.) At the heart of the nationalist interest in archaeology is a wish to demonstrate a continuous identity between land and people. In many cases, as in Greece, the continuing link is plainly there and a source of evident pride, all the more so since archaeologists have now shown that even in Minoan Crete the Greek language was used in royal archives written in Linear B.

In other cases, a past can be invented to give a pedigree to nationalist claims. Something like this occurred in Turkey as part of the revolution led by Mustafa Kemal Atatürk, the great soldier-statesman. After the fall of the sultanate in 1920, Kemal presided over a decade of fundamental change; he created a secular republic, moved the capital, banished the fez and veil, launched public schools, transformed the alphabet and calendar, and changed the very names of his people (before Kemal, most Turks had no patronym). At the same time, Atatürk strove to create a fresh sense of national identity in which the old ties to an Asiatic past and an Islamic "fatherland" would be minimized. In the end, he helped invent a new past for a new republic.

The Father of the Turks was deeply absorbed, in his later years, in history, linguistics, and archaeology. The accepted view is that the Ottoman Turks were originally a warrior people from Central Asia who first entered Anatolia around the eleventh century A.D. Kemal came to believe in a different theory—that the Turks were an Aryan people speaking an ancient Sun Language who had first entered the Near East long before and who were somehow linked with the Sumerians and Hittites. He was certain that corroborating evidence could be found in the soil,

181

and under his personal patronage a Turkish Historical Society was established in the new capital of Ankara, as was a Hittite Museum. Archaeology became a benign national obsession. Bronze stags unearthed near Ankara by the Society became popular emblems (one appeared on a Turkish stamp issued in 1937, the year before Kemal's death). Banks were named after the Sumerians and Hittites, and even new surnames had archaeological overtones—the German-trained Hittite scholar Ekrem Akurgal took a last name which in Sumerian means "mountain water." If archaeology has not proved the nationalist case, it has surely benefited from political interest.

In few countries has the spade been given a more forceful political assist than in Israel. As Amos Elon writes in *The Israelis: Founders and Sons:*

> The millennia-spanning mixture of ancient and modern history, coupled with notions of "controversial" legitimacy, combine to produce this peculiar Israeli syndrome. Archaeological finds have inspired nearly all Israeli national symbols, from the State Seal, to emblems, coins, medals and postage stamps. . . . Israeli archaeologists, professionals and amateurs, are not merely digging for knowledge and objects, but for the reassurance of roots, which they find in ancient Israelite remains scattered through the country.

This need for reassurance, wholly understandable in a country whose very right to existence is under continuing challenge, has nurtured a *bulmus* for archaeology, a Hebrew word denoting a ravenous hunger, a mania, a faintness resulting from long fasting. Israel is possibly the only country in which army recruits are routinely given a short course in archaeology—General Moshe Dayan is only the most famous of archaeologically obsessed officers.* Specific sites, such as Masada, have acquired

* General Dayan was seriously hurt in 1968 when earth collapsed on him while digging at a site, breaking his ribs and injuring his spine. A few

182

an intense patriotic significance. Masada was excavated by a team of volunteers directed by the soldier-archaeologist Yigael Yadin, the Chief of Operations in the 1948 War of Independence. Poignant relics were found attesting to the courage of Jewish rebels who, on this great rock-fortress near the Dead Sea, made their last stand against Rome in 72 A.D. New recruits in the armored units of the Israeli Army take their oath of allegiance atop Masada, and at one such ceremony Professor Yadin declared: "When Napoleon stood among his men, against the background of the Pyramids of Egypt, he declared, 'Four thousand years of human history look down upon you!' But what would he not have given to be able to say to his men, 'Four thousand years of *your own* history look down upon you!' "

Even more hallowed than Masada are the Dead Sea Scrolls, which, it has been remarked, are regarded by some Israelis virtually as titles of real estate, or deeds of possession of a contested country. The Scrolls are preserved in the Shrine of the Book in Jerusalem, a building whose very design—a spotless white dome entered through a long tunnel—seems a fusion of past and present in a talisman of fertility. In nationalist countries otherwise quite different from Israel, one also finds a political accent in museum architecture. This is manifestly so in Mexico City, where the National Museum of Anthropology is also a token of reborn pride in a magnificent past. Built in the short period of twenty months and opened in 1964, the museum is set handsomely in Chapultepec Park and has displays of almost theatrical impact. Its theme is proclaimed by the Spanish inscription over its portals: "Mexicans, look at yourselves in the mirror of this splendor; stranger, know also the unity of human destiny. Civilizations pass, but man has always within

---

years later, his hobby involved him in an angry dispute when a Tel Aviv lawyer charged that he was exporting antiquities without a license. Israel's Attorney General investigated the charge and ruled that Dayan had broken no laws in occasionally selling pieces to finance new purchases. (See Jerusalem *Post*, December 1, 1972.)

him the glory of those who struggled to bring him into being."

Everywhere in Mexico the visitor encounters the political use of archaeology for the entirely creditable purpose of giving a people who are part European, part Indian, a common national pride. "Every time an archaeological discovery is made," remarks Victor Alba in *The Mexicans*, "each time some scholar declares that an artifact dates back ten, fifteen or twenty centuries, the press treats the news as a matter as important as politics or sports." In the terse words of the poet Octavio Paz, "The history of Mexico is the history of man seeking his parentage, his origins." But sometimes this laudable impulse yields strange results, as in the angry dispute that followed the discovery in 1949 of the supposed bones of Cuauhtémoc, the last Aztec emperor and nephew of Moctezuma. Cuauhtémoc, through the alchemy of time, has become a national symbol of resistance to European imperialism, and it was a major news event when his alleged remains were found in a church crypt at Ixcateopan, a small village near the Pacific Coast. The controversy over the authenticity of the bones was a political as well as scholarly dispute. Two successive commissions were appointed by the government to examine the remains, and both failed to support what was already the popular verdict. "When our report was made public," said the president of the second commission, "the hostility of certain journalists was vociferous. They described us a gang of traitors, and in several periodicals they went to the extreme of demanding that we be shot."

In the event, none of the scholars was shot, but the episode suggests the intensity of emotions over archaeological finds in many nationalist countries. New nations, it has been remarked, can resemble senile old men in their insistent search for a fountain of youth in a mythic past. In Ghana, for example, children have been taught that their ancestors invented the alphabet and the steam engine, and examples of other claims could be endlessly multiplied. But as the British historian J. H. Plumb points out, there is no warrant for laughter and none for sneers because "all white pasts have made assumptions equally outrageous for the same purpose—to create confidence and a sense of special virtue." Indeed, he adds, "is it less arrogant to claim the steam engine and alphabet than 'freedom' and 'liberty' in a society in which there were slave markets?"

The outlook symbolized by Byron has undeniably benefited scholarship by increasing popular interest—and consequently popular support for—archaeology. Still, the nationalist champions of archaeology focus their interest on what is politically useful or blatantly showy. Byron himself was more interested in ruins as symbols than as subjects for scholarly inquiry. He thought nothing of carving his name in huge letters on a column of Sounion and disdainfully dismissed what he called "antiquarian twaddle." When he was once invited to inspect some ruins, he replied, "Do I look like one of those emasculated fogies?" and proposed a swim instead.

This trait persists. In Mexico, which is no longer among the poorest of developing countries, politicians volubly celebrate the national patrimony while at the same time keeping the National Institute of Anthropology and History on a starvation budget. Though Mexico has some 11,000 registered sites, the institute at best can carry out six or seven campaigns a year with the funds allotted to it. (In 1971, because of a shortage of pesos, the institute undertook no excavations whatever.) Everyone involved in Mexican archaeology is notoriously underpaid—an archaeologist with a graduate degree is lucky to make the equivalent of $240 a month.

There is a further negative aspect in the nationalist concept of the past—a tendency to regard foreigners per se as villains and to enact dogmatic laws forbidding not only the export but (as in Guatemala) even the loan of antiquities for any reasonable period to foreign museums. As we have seen, these laws can create a cynical complicity between politicians, police, and the illicit vendors of antiquities. Archaeologists assert that in any given dig some ninety per cent of all objects unearthed can be classified as duplicates. Much of this material could be legally sold, satisfying at least the collecting appetites of those with a moderate income, with the money used to support excavations. Though proposals of this kind have been repeatedly advanced, in most cases they have been doomed by nationalist passion. At one point a few years ago, an advisory commission was appointed in Mexico, its members consisting of leading scholars and collectors. The commission suggested that all antiquities in private hands in Mexico be divided into categories —first, pieces of such outstanding importance that they should be acquired at a fair price by museums; second, objects of such interest that they should not be permitted to leave the country though they could be privately held; third, pieces that should be deemed freely salable duplicates; and finally, copies and fakes. This sensible notion got absolutely nowhere.

Others have collided against the same stone wall. In May, 1970, Froelich Rainey, the director of the University Museum of the University of Pennsylvania, proposed that an international conference under UNESCO auspices be called to suggest a uniform antiquities law for all nations belonging to UNESCO. Such a model law, Dr. Rainey contended, could make provisions for a legal trade in archaeological objects. "Our object should be the preservation of sites which still exist," he wrote in a letter to the International Council of Museums. "It is unrealistic to expect to stop all trade in archaeological objects and in fact a *legal* trade should help to stop the illicit trade." Not a single member-nation of UNESCO has seconded Dr. Rainey's appeal. While it is true that some countries rich in antiquities —notably Iran, Israel, and Egypt—have made some provision for a legal trade, the prevailing dogma is that the past is indivisible national property. This impulse springs in part from

186

the memory of past exploitation. But it also indicates the one-eyed limitation of the nationalist outlook.

3. The Collector's Past

In opposition to the nationalist view is that of the collector. What the nationalist sees as untouchable and public, the collector sees as portable and private, and his passions are often equal to those of Byron's heirs. The great collector has a sense of destiny, a feeling that he is mankind's agent in gathering and preserving what otherwise might be heedlessly dispersed. And the collector is capable of collecting anything—one has a complete cabinet of all varieties of Coca-Cola bottles, while another displays an array of Ford radiators (to his distress, two years are missing: 1906 and 1908).

What the rest of us may regard as trash can be prized by a collector. In September, 1972, six hundred beer-can collectors met in Lake Geneva, Wisconsin, to gossip, swap, and haggle in their own specialized jargon. "You must be kidding," a collector was overheard saying. "One current can for an obsolete? I can get three for this one easily." Plans are underway for publication of a complete listing of all 12,000 types of American beer cans, including such forgotten labels as Jaguar, Buccaneer, Bullfrog, and Old Frothinglosh. Other enthusiasts accumulate barbed-wire prongs, cheese labels, silver ingots, cigar bands, and even plaster casts of the phalluses of pop stars. La Bruyère has said of collecting: "It is not a pastime but a passion and often so violent that it is inferior to love or ambition only in the pettiness of its aims."

One can intelligibly speak of a collector's neurosis. Maurice Rheims, the Paris auctioneer who knows collectors well, has said in his book *The Strange Life of Objects*, "For many people, the process of collecting generates a clandestine atmosphere of intrigue and deceit, rather as if they were having an illicit love affair." He tells of a French coin collector who for years lied to his wife about his health in order to covertly spend money supposedly used for medicine on his collection. Only when the man died did the widow discover that he had hidden away a large coin collection valued at three hundred million francs (in the 1961 valuation of French currency). Collectors are often aware of their own infirmity. The novelist Henri de Montherlant, a great collector of antiques, once confessed: "I lower my eyes when I walk past an antique shop, like a seminarian passing a nightclub."

Though the condition is prevalent, the psychiatric literature on collecting is scant. A pioneering medical thesis on collecting was written in 1921 by the Frenchman Dr. Henri Codet, who concluded that there were four underlying motives: the need for possession, the need for spontaneous activity, the impulse to self-advancement, and the tendency to classify things. Another French analyst, René Brimo, took, in 1938, a more sympathetic view by stressing also the love of beauty; he treated the collector as an artist, if of a special kind. Princess Marie Bonaparte, a disciple of Freud's, linked collectors to anal eroticism. Still, anyone reviewing the literature must conclude that the collecting syndrome has yet to be explained.

How can one account, for example, for Homer and Langley Collyer, the sons of a well-known New York physician who lived in a decaying town house on upper Fifth Avenue? In 1909, the brothers shut themselves up from the world, boarding over the windows of their three-story house. Decades passed, and in 1947 the New York police were anonymously informed that there was a dead man in the Collyer house. When the police chopped open the front door, they encountered a solid mass of newspapers and junk, and in order to enter the house they had to climb through a second-story window. In a cave-like

188

burrow within the rubbish they found Homer dead, naked except for a bathrobe, his long white hair flowing to his shoulders. In a ghoulish excavation, the police then dug into rooms packed with junk, including thousands of books, heaps of newspapers, obscene photographs, a dismantled Model T Ford, fourteen pianos, innumerable childhood toys, and the remains of everything else the Collyers had ever bought. Ultimately they found Langley, his body partly devoured by rats. He had been crushed under a pile of newspapers, apparently caught in one of the burglar traps the brothers had contrived to protect their invaluable collection.

The Collyer brothers recall a character in fiction—a landowner named Plyushkin in Gogol's *Dead Souls,* who was an avid accumulator of everything: bits of string, bird feathers, scraps of paper, old bills, sealing wax. Amid his pile of junk, Gogol writes, Plyushkin in the end became "a kind of gaping hole in humankind."

Yet if the collecting impulse mingles the childish and the sublime, its fruits can be unique and delectable. Culture creates collections, and collections create culture, Dillon Ripley, the secretary of the Smithsonian Institution, has observed. Museums would not be possible without an instinct whose roots are obscure but whose results are benign. The ancestor of the museum is the collector's cabinet of curiosities; what otherwise might have been irrevocably lost or dispersed is now visible to all. In the case of collecting, private greed can become a public blessing.

The collector, then, is a friend of the past. But he can be a difficult friend. If there is any common trait in all collectors it is the wish to please himself, to create a unique world of objects over which he reigns. In 1970, I entered one such world, a realm of fantasy shaped and ruled by the artist Eugene Berman, whose best work was for the theater and opera. Mr. Berman (who

died in 1972) had transformed a magnificent apartment in the
Palazzo Doria in Rome into a pleasure dome for the eye. Here,
in cunning juxtaposition, were arrayed Etruscan figurines and
pre-Columbian pottery; a Cycladic idol would be in a niche
with a Gothic icon; folk art mingled with high art, ancient with
modern, and even the contrived with the natural, for as a com-
plement to his collection, Mr. Berman had a shelf lined with
minerals. But for all its enchantment, his collection was of
negligible scholarly value, because the criterion for his choice
was simply what gave him pleasure. This is not said in condem-
nation, but rather in order to explain why the eclectic style, so
prevalent among collectors, limits the value of what is accumulated.

By contrast, some collectors develop a rigorous scholarly
interest in their objects. Norbert Schimmel, a New York businessman, has in a few decades gathered a superb collection of
classical, Egyptian, and Near Eastern art, including an exceptional group of reliefs in the style associated with Tell el-
Amarna, capital of the heretic Pharaoh Ikhnaton. Mr. Schimmel
has over the years consulted with leading scholars, and he talks
about his holdings with a quiet authority. On several occasions,
he has purchased antiquities at the request of museums, to prevent their disappearance or dispersal. (Mr. Schimmel has always made his collection available to qualified experts, and a
catalogue is presently being prepared by a group of scholars
under the editorship of Oscar Muscarella of the Metropolitan
Museum.) Yet, like other serious collectors, Mr. Schimmel is
troubled by the ethical implications of purchasing illicitly excavated art.

"It's very much like the disarmament problem," he said to
me. "It's no good if one nation stops buying arms if everyone
else continues. If I don't buy a piece, someone else will." The
argument is logically unanswerable. Until something like a
collective sense of scruple develops among collectors of antiqui-

ties, they will continue to support a traffic many of them otherwise deplore. For his part, Mr. Schimmel came to a decision after much soul-searching; he recently told a friend he was no longer in the market for new, undocumented acquisitions.

4. *The Museum Past*

For obvious reasons, the museum is in close association with the collector. More than eighty per cent of the works the Metropolitan Museum owns, for example, have come to it as gifts or bequests. Every collector is a potential donor, and those with outstanding pieces are courted with unashamed flattery by curators. Further than that, the museum staff will frequently assist the collector, guiding his purchases and providing invaluable expertise.

But the curator's commitment is to the public, his public, and to the institution for which he often selflessly works. Frequently, the curator is himself a frustrated collector, with the appetite for acquisition but without the means to satisfy it. The point was made by John Walker, the former director of the National Gallery of Art in Washington, in a 1972 article entitled "Secrets of a Museum Director." Mr. Walker wrote:

> Addiction to collecting is as hard to break as addiction to drugs, and I have been addicted. The rise in prices, however, has made the acquisition of great works of art virtually impossible, except for the colossally rich and for museum directors or curators using Other People's Money. The use of O.P.M. I found one of the great charms of a museum career.
>
> Without it, I could never have satisfied my cravings to

191

collect paintings and sculpture of supreme quality. Then there is the excitement of the quest, the safari through the jungle of dealers in New York, London, Paris, Zurich and elsewhere, with the constant danger of pitfalls and traps. Or need I mention that most fascinating occupation—wheedling treasures from private collectors when one's colleagues constitute the determined and often unscrupulous competition?

This competitive zeal can make the curator and director more ruthless than the collector, since the museum worker has a larger sense of virtue, a feeling that what he is doing is for the public and the cause of art. There is a parallel in the competition among monks and priests in the Middle Ages, who contended, often unscrupulously, for the relics of saints and of the Savior Himself, the pious end always justifying dubious means. So deeply felt is that dedication that museum workers sometimes die prematurely or suffer from insomnia or alcoholism. In 1967, Thomas P. F. Hoving of the Metropolitan told an interviewer: "When I learned the other day that the National Gallery had bought that Leonardo—the *Ginevra de' Benci*—for six million dollars, I couldn't sleep all night. We should have reached for it. The reputation of the Metropolitan has always been based on its power to acquire things without reserve. . . . If you lose that one day of going for a great thing, you can lose a decade. Any trustee should be able to write a check for at least three million dollars and not even feel it."

For Mr. Hoving, and for many traditional-minded museum workers, the getting is paramount. When the Metropolitan director learned in 1968 that Egypt had offered the United States the Temple of Dendur in gratitude for American help in the Nubian rescue campaign, he raced to Washington to see that the little temple did not go to a rival institution, the Smith-

192

sonian. He secured the prize, and later shrugged it off, saying: "The quality of the Temple of Dendur isn't high, but don't knock it. Its impact is extraordinary. It's an environment, something you can walk into . . . any work of architectural sculpture I can get my hand on, I'll buy."

When so powerful an acquisitive drive is joined to the vast resources of a museum like the Metropolitan, the temptation is strong to shrug off other nations' laws as a mere inconvenience. As Mr. Hoving remarked to an interviewer in 1967: "The museum has never done anything illegal. You had better believe that. We are no more illegal in anything we have done than Napoleon was when he brought all the treasures to the Louvre." This attitude, expressed with such unembarrassed forthrightness, explains why the American art museum can be seen as the last bastion in the world of self-confessed imperialism. As the writer Eleanor C. Munro commented during the Euphronios controversy: "Just as in the nineteenth century some Americans believed that, because of their superior mentality and mechanics, they had a mandate to possess the West and the Philippines and sectors of China, so today it is felt by some trustees that they have a mandate to possess and trade art, the last transferable national entity, now that people cannot any more be colonized or countries concessionized."

The outlook can be viewed not only as imperial, but also as an expression of retarded Victorianism. The very architecture of the art museum proclaims its nostalgia for the Victorian past—the columned entrance, the vast galleries with their surfeit of marble, and the reverential atmosphere, so like that of a central bank or a cathedral. An early American critic of the art museum was John Cotton Dana, the director of the Newark Museum, who in 1917 published a pithy paper entitled "The Gloom of the Museum." Mr. Dana found it a "grotesquery" that such reverential attention was paid to objects that are (1) old, (2) rare, and (3) high in price. He went so far as to argue that the value of objects in art museums was "largely fictitious," born of the rivalry of rich collectors "and even of rich museums." Surely, he said:

> a function of a public art museum is the making of life more interesting, joyful and wholesome; and surely a museum can not very well exercise that function unless it relates itself quite closely to the life it should be influencing, and surely it can not thus relate itself unless it comes in close contact with the material adornments of that life— its applied arts.

A lone voice in 1917, Mr. Dana would find ample company today.* One particularly searching critic is Dillon Ripley, who as secretary of the Smithsonian Institution presides over museums and research facilities prodigious in their variety. In a book entitled *The Sacred Grove,* Mr. Ripley observes that art museums in America embarked on a course that tended to ally them with the dominant forces in the community: the civic boosters and the wealthy philanthropists. As a result of this too exclusive alliance, he argues, museums have also tended to alienate themselves from three important groups—the art historians, the artists, and the poor. "If the wonders of a fantastic collection like that of the Metropolitan Museum in New York," he writes, ". . . cannot somehow be brought to the humblest among us, then the purposes of the organizing committee of the Metropolitan in 1870 have not been served."

Indeed, it can be further maintained that when museums like the Metropolitan seek to interest a mass audience it is through

* Mr. Dana's Newark Museum, though small, has been beset by a familiar problem. In 1970, the museum paid about $10,000 for a fourth-century Roman mosaic, depicting two Amazons on horseback. The mosaic originally had been discovered in 1967 by Belgian archaeologists digging at the ancient site of Apamea, in western Syria. When the museum learned that its mosaic had probably been stolen, its response was prompt and virtuous— the Newark trustees, in April, 1973, ordered the return of the mosaic to Syria.

the one activity that the museum's wealthy trustees overwhelmingly support—the acquisition of masterpieces. And in the focus on masterpieces, there is still another distortion. Hugues de Varine-Bohan, director of the International Council of Musuems and an archaeologist, put it this way in a recent speech:

> I believe the root of the problem lies in [a] false conception of a museum. An object of scientific interest should not be considered primarily as an art work. Yet museums, which are supposed to educate the public, often contribute to the idea that such and such a culture is represented only by uniquely beautiful objects. . . . In fact, the picture the public builds of ancient cultures can be permanently distorted when the past is consistently presented as a kaleidoscope of masterpieces.
>
> Tourists and collectors, art dealers and museum curators, become obsessed in this quest for the unique work. And this "Mona Lisa complex," as I call it, can give rise to an illegal market, leading in turn to looting and the destruction of monuments.

The supreme example of the Mona Lisa complex is the purchase of the Euphronios krater by the Metropolitan Museum. Few better expressions exist of the traditional curatorial view than a defense of that purchase made by Dietrich von Bothmer, who said of the vase: "I want to know where it was made, who did it, and when. I want to know if it is genuine or fake. Its intermediate history is not important to archaeology. Why can't people look at it simply as archaeologists do, as an art object?" Archaeologists instantly protested that Dr. von Bothmer was looking at the vase not as an archaeologist but as a museum curator—that, indeed, the vase's intermediate history was of some importance to scholarship. One critic recalled a trenchant remark by the renowned Egyptologist Flinders Petrie, who once described museums as "charnel houses of murdered evidence."*

In fairness, it must be added that the traditional museum outlook has enriched our collective sensibility, and that American museums—whatever their faults—remain a source of envy and surprise among foreign visitors. Those who press for reform do not want to repudiate the museum tradition, but to build something new onto it. Even those who uphold the orthodox outlook sense that there are tides of change at work. There was almost a valedictory note in an interview that Thomas P. F. Hoving gave to *Newsweek* during what he described as the "kefluffle" over the Euphronios krater. Mr. Hoving asserted:

> I began as a collector, and my instincts are still there. When I see something I want, I do everything I can to get it. I've bought $300 million worth of stuff since I've been here, and I've never made a mistake. What other museum, what other city in the world has gotten these things? I'm

* The controversy prompted Felicia Lamport to parody Keats in *The New York Times Magazine*, a few months after that publication put the vase on its cover. Her "Ode to a Grecian Urn" was deft:

> Thou krater by the Hoving eye transfixed
> And bought with numismatic revenues
> Thou mayest prove a blessing not unmixed—
> The latest form of Irving versus Hughes.
> What legendary provenance thou hast
> That mak'st thy unearthed worth a million cool!
> Wert sold to hectored Hecht? If so, by whom?
> A Lebanese collector or a ghoul?
> Whence came'st thou to New York? How hast thou passed
> These fifty years? In hatbox or in tomb?
>
> O Attic shape! that strik'st curator dumb
> And shatterest museum etiquette
> So gravely that thou threaten'st to become
> A pox von Bothmer houses at the Met:
> Dost realize thous't flung the golden ball
> That causeth antiquarians to spar
> About good faith and sum of *quid pro quo*?
> What price such small details with *objets d'art*?
> Money is truth, truth money—that is all
> The public knows and all it needs to know.

proud that I've gotten the greatest objects in the world, in my time here. . . . I'm a breed that won't happen again, not because of genius, but because of treaties and other complications. . . . They thought I was the beginning of something new. They were wrong. I'm the last of something old.

The glory of the "something old" is that it acquired so much that was in private hands for the public. But the shame of the tradition is that the focus was invariably on the old, the unique, and the high-priced. In the process, much else was overlooked—such as, in the United States, the remains of the American Indian past.

5. *The Devouring Bulldozer*

Even more than the tomb robber, the bulldozer imperils our archaeological heritage. The problem is universal, and as yet unsolved. Civilization spreads with rapacious speed, and consumes much that is precious as it does so. In poorer countries, economic necessity is an overriding circumstance which explains, if it does not justify, the destruction of the past. Yet if anything, the problem is more serious in wealthier countries, precisely because wealth generates the development that menaces everything hidden in the soil.

Recently Tom King, the president of the Society for California Archaeology, called attention to the wanton destruction in his state of the remains of the prehistoric past. "Not content to destroy Indian culture as viable living units," he said in a report to members, "we are now bulldozing out the tattered physical remains of their one-time existence." The American Indians are being twice destroyed, though, ironically, the second catastrophe is occurring at the very moment when all things Indian are in fashion in the United States. California affords a sobering case study. When the first explorers reached the state, there were as many as 75,000 archaeological sites, of which only a fraction remain because of land development, with wholesale devastation concentrated in the past thirty or forty years.

As an example, the archaeologist Michael J. Moratto cites a survey in 1908 that located about 450 Indian mounds in the San Francisco Bay area; today archaeologists can identify only forty. Of these, a half-dozen have escaped all damage; the rest are only battered remains. In the Los Angeles region, the devastation has been more serious—Mr. Moratto estimates that less than five per cent of all archaeological sites are still intact. He reports that real estate developers use Indian associations to increase sale price of houses, while making scant provision for any scientific study of what the bulldozer decimates. In 1969, an enterprising firm bought a full-page color advertisement in a northern California newspaper which advocated "Indian relic collecting" by the "kiddies" while dad and mom were inspecting real estate. In California, as elsewhere in the United States—and indeed, as elsewhere in the world—there is no local authority responsible for archaeology. As Mr. Moratto summarizes the situation:

> The California situation is critical; only a small portion of the state has been searched for prehistoric remains; urban sprawl, water resource development programs, highways and vandalism have obliterated thousands of important sites; existing governmental agencies are inadequately funded and improperly structured to accommodate archaeological programs on a significant scale; the California Indians have no voice in the management of their prehistoric heritage; and, above all, at least one thousand prehistoric sites are being destroyed every year.

In the course of my research, I wrote to the responsible state archaeologist in each of the fifty American states. The majority of replies were variations on the same theme. In excerpt form, here are some of the responses:

Connecticut: "A large chunk of the archaeology of Connecticut (I wouldn't venture to estimate what fraction) was probably gone by 1900, but the increase of heavy construction activities and population expansion in the last twenty years is posing a serious threat to the remainder."

Illinois: "The biggest problem now affecting archaeologists in this state as well as throughout the nation is that we need political assistance. We simply are inadequately prepared to deal with problems of archaeological destruction at our level."

Idaho: "Building construction, especially those funded by the Corps of Engineers and the Board of Reclamation, have been highly destructive. These projects, though federally funded, seldom include sufficient funds for archaeological salvage. In fact, if I had to point to a single agency other than pot hunters, I would say that the federal government more than anyone else has been responsible for the greatest amount of damage to archaeological sites in Idaho."

Louisiana: "I think that in the last decade the most earth-effacing device that has appeared in the Mississippi Valley is the land-plane. . . . The land-plane simply levels off the field, and any slight bump that might have had archaeological significance is completely eliminated."

Maryland: "Our greatest losses are due to various types of construction and erosion along the shores of the Chesapeake Bay. We have found contractors, landowners and government agencies cooperative, but we lack the manpower and funds to do an adequate job."

Minnesota: "Our major problem is that of the presence of archaeological sites on private land. . . . I would judge that the vast majority of sites that do disappear these days, do so

199

because of lack of information and knowledge on the part of the private citizen. We are continuing to develop an active educational program through elementary and secondary schools and into the adult community, but it is a long, slow fight, and I am not sure that we are going to win."

Missouri: "Our greatest problem consists of the various projects that are funded, supported or authorized by federal agencies that alter the terrain daily. . . . In spite of the fine cooperation of members of the Missouri Archaeological Society, we are losing more of our past than we are recording. It's almost as if we were attempting to climb an ice-clad mountain, sliding back ten steps for every one that we gain."

Mississippi: "Across the Gulf Coast, there is tremendous destruction of archaeological sites for both private industry and residential expansion. I was told, within the last two weeks, that in Jackson County alone three houses are completed per day. This gives you a pretty good idea of the increase in population and development in the area. Those three Gulf Coast counties are extremely crucial areas because the archaeological cultures are quite unique and quite different from those of in-state Mississippi."

Oregon: "Two major problems face archaeology in Oregon, aside from construction and development. . . . First, the archaeological materials are of such quality that they are valued by collectors. Projectile points made of opal, carnelian, bloodstone, onyx and other semiprecious stones are fairly common. . . . A second problem is that archaeological research is not supported directly by the state of Oregon. . . . Some money has been available for summer field schools at the University of Oregon, but none is available for excavations, investigations or surveys."

Alaska: "Within the past couple of years, archaeological specimens from St. Lawrence Island have been bought by state-affiliated museums in Alaska. This notwithstanding the fact that the State Antiquities Act contains a clause outlawing the possession of illegally acquired specimens. The prices paid have been quite high: $1,000 for a small ivory figurine of the Okvik culture. . . . You will undoubtedly be wondering why, if these activities are fairly common knowledge, nothing has been done about them. The answer to that is dismayingly simple. Who will bother to enforce laws dealing with misdemeanors? The enforcers are concerned with bigger things."

This small sample is entirely representative, and the complete record of my correspondence will be made available to anyone with a serious interest in the problem. A fair conclusion is that between the bulldozer and the pot hunter, little will be left of the American Indian past by the year 2000, barring a change in official attitude. Change *is* possible, as evidenced by the experience of Charles R. McGimsey III, the director of the Arkansas Archaeological Survey. In a path-breaking book, *Public Archaeology,* published in 1972, Dr. McGimsey reported on the grim realities in his own state—from 1960 through 1964, an estimated 703,000 acres in Arkansas were newly cleared, usually with such archaeologically destructive techniques as chisel plowing, subsoiling, and land leveling. The United States Soil Conservation Service has forecast that within twenty-five years all levelable land in Arkansas will have been leveled, with the result that ninety per cent of archaeological information will have been destroyed. As Dr. McGimsey writes: "The next fifty years—some would say twenty-five—are going to be critical in the history of American archaeology. What is recovered, what is preserved, and how these goals are accomplished, during this period will largely determine *for all time* the knowledge available to subsequent generations of Americans concerning their heritage from the past."

A scholar of energy and intelligence, Dr. McGimsey undertook a survey of all state laws, and found that in twenty-four out of fifty states little or no provision was made for salvage archaeology, and that only six states—Arkansas, Delaware, Florida, Hawaii, Missouri, and Texas—had laws he found adequate. The fact that Arkansas is on the list is due in no small part to McGimsey himself, since he became a one-man lobbyist for the past. In 1967, the legislature appropriated $125,000 for a state survey, with a further $215,000 earmarked for the second year of a survey of all Arkansas archaeological sites. In the process, many people became concerned for the first time with the vanishing past of Arkansas.

The political problem has been competently expressed by Francis A. Riddell, supervisor of the Cultural Resources Section of California's Department of Parks and Recreation, who writes: "Before anyone gets overly excited about the rotten state of affairs in archaeology in state government, it might be well to analyze the situation. The lack of any great concern for archaeological resources is nothing more than a mirror image of the lack of concern for it by the taxpayer. Everyone, or nearly everyone, is captivated by archaeology—until it comes time to pay for it."

In the United States, the principal federal law affecting archaeology is the Antiquities Act of 1906, a law that has become the model for many state measures—and it provides protection only for sites on public land. A later federal law, enacted in 1935, makes it national policy to designate and protect places of national significance, and a third measure, adopted in 1966, calls for a National Register of important sites and establishes a program of matching grants for specific programs at the state level. Other federal laws provide funds for salvage archaeology when sites are destroyed as a result of dam building or highway construction, but not enough money is available to keep pace with development.

The bulldozer cannot be stopped. All that the archaeologist can reasonably expect is that provisions will be made for salvage work on sites due to be destroyed, so that some record may exist. Such salvage can be undertaken when enough people are aware of what is being irrevocably lost—and an example of what can be done took place in Marin County, California. There, when urban sprawl menaced Indian sites, two teachers at Sonoma State College recruited forty high-school students and trained them in the exacting skills of excavation. For two years, the teen-age archaeologists dug in an Indian site scheduled for demolition, and later published a thoroughly professional report on their findings. In a letter to *Science*, the journal of the American Association for the Advancement of Science, one of the volunteers, Terrence Jay O'Neil, wrote of his experience: "For high school students, two years of weekends and summer days, rain or shine, might seem an impossible price to pay for a little 'adventure in time.' And yet, without receiving academic credit, and without pilfering for personal collections, the students joyfully worked on, with occasional professional monitoring. It did not stop there. The case for a Marin County antiquities ordinance was carried by the group, both students and faculty, to the county Board of Supervisors. The Supervisors passed the ordinance, to their unending credit."

6. A Danger List

The nationalist, the collector, and the curator all have made a claim upon the past, and each in his own way has made a contribution. But each looks upon the past as a piece of property. Another approach is possible—to see our collective cultural remains as a resource whose title is vested in all humanity. It is a nonrenewable resource; once exhausted, it cannot be replaced. And in our lifetime we may see it dwindle meaninglessly away, not so much because anyone has willed it, but because not enough people are aware that the problem exists, as the destruction of American Indian sites all too clearly suggests.

In 1968, UNESCO published a sadly revealing technical book, *The Conservation of Cultural Property*, in which the various plagues that afflict the past were appraised. The plagues range from climate and vegetation to insects and pollution, and the volume drew on the expertise of UNESCO scientists who had gone into the field to help member-countries preserve their imperiled heritage. One of the experts, the late Paul Coremans, listed major monuments whose future is uncertain. In updated form, here are some of his findings:

Borobudur, Indonesia. A Buddhist sanctuary built around the ninth century A.D. and abandoned in the sixteenth century. The outstanding monument of its kind in Indonesia, it is built on a man-made mound that is slowly collapsing, pitching walls at perilous angles. Its terraces, lined with 2,460 carved panels, are being chewed away by vegetative growth and eroded by seeping water. Looters are decapitating its idols. A UNESCO mission has proposed a $7.75-million salvage program that would involve replacing the sanctuary's infirm central core with absorbent gravel. Indonesia has agreed to contribute, and preliminary work is underway, but sufficient funds are lacking.

Pagan, Burma. The ancient capital of Burma is about 250 miles north of Rangoon and is the most important site in the country. Its monuments date from the eleventh to the thirteenth century A.D., and after the city's fall thousands of its buildings were mutilated and left to decay until the twentieth century. Heavy rains in the monsoon season have been largely responsible for the continuous destruction of once vivid mural paintings.in its pagodas. Dr. Coremans commented: "The preservation of Pagan will only be possible when the Archaeological Survey has the means to cope, first, with the structural problems of the ancient buildings, and then with the preservation of the mural paintings within them." The funds are lacking.

Ayudhya, Thailand. The capital of Thailand from the four-teenth century to 1767, Ayudhya is perhaps the most important Thai site. Most of its buildings are in ruins, and most of its murals have been lost. Heat, rain, and vegetative growth have caused extensive damage. Dr. Coremans remarked: "No hope of real preservation work at Ayudhya and other sites unless a specialized technical division is set up within the Department of Fine Arts." The money is lacking.

Persepolis, Iran. This great Achaemenian capital, founded about 500 B.C. and destroyed in 330 B.C., is the most important site in Iran. Its beautiful and extensive architectural and sculptural remains have been under excavation since 1931. A survey in 1960 found that twenty-nine years after the first excavations the uncovered sculpture had lost much of its sharper detail mainly due to erosion caused by sandstorms and wide variations of temperature. Conservation requires the overhead and side screening of the carvings and the moving of irreplaceable works of art to the local museum. Little has been done because of lack of money.

Hatra, Iraq. A group of monumental ruins in the desert some thirty-five miles southwest of Mosul, Hatra dates to the second century A.D. and is one of the most important ancient sites in Iraq. It offers a unique example of Parthian civilization, blending Greek and Mesopotamian influences. Frost and earthquakes have caused extensive damage, and though restoration work began in 1963, progress has been hampered by political unrest and lack of funds.

Chan-Chan, Peru. The former capital of the Chimu kingdom, Chan-Chan is on the Pacific coast some three hundred miles north of Lima. An enormous site, covering about six square miles, Chan-Chan consists of hundreds of adobe buildings grouped around ten major plazas and dates to 1300–1440 A.D. The city has never been adequately excavated or thoroughly mapped, and the opportunity to do so may be lost as incessant weather-

205

ing and extensive pillaging slowly destroy the site. Dr. Coremans said: "The establishment of a national laboratory and a national historical monuments service is considered essential; preservation of monuments and sites is a matter for organization at national level." Thus far funds have been lacking.

Bonampak, Mexico. This small but important Maya site is in the State of Chiapas, near the Guatemalan border, and contains the most extensive murals of the Classic Maya period yet found. The paintings date to the seventh century A.D.; the site was abandoned a few centuries later and was rediscovered in 1946. In the brief time since its discovery, Bonampak has become a target for the adventurous tourist willing to make a special flight to its remote jungle locale. Guides have been known to wipe the paintings with an oil-soaked rag "to bring out the colors." Through natural and human causes, deterioration has been considerable. UNESCO has proposed restoring the temples and air-conditioning the room with the murals, but so far funds have not been available for these steps.

To these examples listed by Paul Coremans, others can be added. In Turkey, there is the important site of Çatal Hüyük, one of man's earliest urban settlements, dating to 7000 B.C. and excavated in 1961–63 by Dr. James Mellaart. Paintings and plaster reliefs are especially difficult to protect from weathering, and though a protective shed has been placed over the unearthed buildings, wind and moisture have already eroded details of unique Neolithic art. New forms of preservative are urgently needed, but funds for research have not been available.

In Afghanistan, the two Giant Buddhas of Bamian are probably the largest human likenesses ever carved. The taller idol, a man 173 feet high, is nearly three times the height of the presidential heads carved on South Dakota's Mount Rushmore. Both colossi are imperiled by constant water seepage; there are fears that a rock slide could bring down on the shrine a huge slab weighing three thousand tons. A UNESCO mission in 1962 proposed a seven-step preservation project, which has not been carried out for lack of funds. The great figures, which date to the seventh century A.D., could be rubble by the end of this century.

Mohenjo-Daro in the Indus Valley of Pakistan is another of man's earliest cities; the name, which means Mound of the Dead, was given the site at the time of its discovery and excavation by the British in the 1920s. The 4,000-year-old city is in the middle of a rich rice-growing area, and the irrigation of the fields has raised the water level in the ruin, soaking and destroying its bricks. A UNESCO team in 1964 proposed major remedial measures, but funds have not been available to undertake them. In India, scores of great temples are menaced by infiltrating water, stone diseases, vegetation, and illicit looting. A notable example is the richly carved temple city of Sri Ranganatha-swami in Sirangam. Built by the Dravidian peoples in what is now Madras State in the eleventh century A.D., the temple complex is approaching terminal decay. A UNESCO mission in 1966 proposed conservation steps, but, as elsewhere in India, funds are lacking to carry them out.

Angkor Wat, in Cambodia, is a special case. It has been visited by another plague, war, and since May, 1970, this world-famous Khmer site has been a battleground. UNESCO attempted without success to make the site a neutral zone in conformity with the Convention on the Protection of Cultural Property in the Event of Armed Conflict, which was adopted at The Hague in 1954. Of the belligerents, only Cambodia had ratified the convention. Built between the ninth and the thirteenth centuries A.D., Angkor Wat is the most elaborately carved temple in an archaeological area spread over several hundred square miles and encompassing hundreds of ruins. For a period, Bernard-Philippe Groslier, the monument's chief conservator, was able to cross military lines and confer with Angkor's Communist-led occupiers, but this arrangement ended in January,

1972. Though the temple was struck by a few mortar shells, the more serious problem has been its neglect during its occupation. It is being nibbled by weather and jungle rot, and in the absence of prompt remedial steps the damage could be irreversible.

A last example is the city of Venice. A UNESCO expert has estimated that Venice contains 10,000 masterpieces, and that every year it is losing six per cent of its marble works, five per cent of its frescoes, three per cent of its canvas paintings, and two per cent of its wood paintings. "This is an enormous proportion," asserts Louis Frédéric, who made these calculations. "At this rate, in thirty years there will remain barely half of what makes present-day Venice a 'peerless gem.' " Several plagues afflict the city—rising waters that soak the stone and polluted air emitted by home and industrial smokestacks. Restoration money, some of it raised through an international appeal, is available but has not been spent partly because of an internal political quarrel.

7. *Humanity's Past*

To be sure, the world will not end if Venice ceases to be Queen of the Adriatic, just as mankind will endure the degradation of the Parthenon or the bulldozing of thousands of American Indian sites. One must be hard-headed. In the world's cost accounting, the past is a small item; it makes a negligible contribution to the Gross National Product; its preservation is scarcely a central concern of the modern state. But one can manifestly contend that if the remains of the past should disappear, our lives will be poorer in ways that the statistician can never measure—we will live in a drabber world, and will have squandered a resource that enlivens our existence, offers a key to our nature, and, not least, acts as a psychic ballast as we venture into a scary future.

What difference will it make if the jungles, the looters, and the tractor devastate ancient Maya sites? One can as well ask what difference it will make if the whale, and other endangered species, vanish from the planet. The whale is no longer of economic importance, and—in the absence of effective international controls—it is being relentlessly slaughtered, just as, for lack of comparable controls, the remains of the past are being eradicated. There will always be photographs of the whale, and a few stuffed specimens will be visible in natural history museums. When the last harpoon slays the last titan of the seas, life will go on. But it will be a different kind of life, because we will have lost the chance to study a unique creature whose habits are still obscure, whose songs can now be heard but not yet understood, and whose very image pervades our literature and folklore.

Just as the whale suggests an extreme limit of zoological development, so the evidence of archaeology attests to the variety of our cultural development. That the Classic Maya were able to create so original a civilization, in so unpromising an environment, is an exhilarating instance. In jungles hostile to settled life, the Maya created temples whose baroque luxuriance resembles the foliage that has since engulfed them. Long before the astronauts and cosmonauts, the Maya had their eyes on the stars and planets, charting their course with cunning accuracy. They learned to write, and left us inscriptions that may yet tell us how they mastered the rain forest and why they watched the sky. To say that this knowledge would be insignificant is to say that human behavior is a worthless subject for study.

In March, 1972, I was fortunate enough to visit the Petén, and to see firsthand four remarkable Maya sites, Tikal, Yaxhá, Aguateca, and Seibal. My guide was Amilcar Guzmán de la Cruz, the young Guatemalan who is administrator of Tikal National Park, and who has an impressive knowledge of the obscure corners of the humid Petén. To get to Aguateca and Seibal, we undertook a journey of Conradian intensity, chugging up the blue waters of the Río de la Pasión in a hollowed-out log powered with a motor. Innumerable birds flitted over the river; a species that delighted me was known as *golondrina*, a tiny black and white bird, glinting like a jewel in the crystal light. The jungle around us was still inviolable, surreal in its scale and variety, and in its heart we came upon beautifully carved and unguarded stelae, and upon vast temples subdued by foliage. By insensible degrees, I felt an increasing pride in the strange genius of the human species. There is evidence enough of our calamitous failings; here one saw evidence of success, of an inspiring ability to overwhelm every obstacle. This is a point often, and easily, lost in the dry treatises of archaeology, which tell more about the shape of pots than of the inner universe of the imagination.

Judged by any reasonable standard, the Petén, with its human and natural marvels, does not belong simply to Guatemala. Nor does it belong to the rich collector or the curator. Instead it is as much our common property as the oceans or the air. Yet its future is in doubt. Between the looter and the bulldozer, the Petén is being inexorably, and planlessly, transformed, and its wildlife as well as its archaeology is in jeopardy. One cannot judge Guatemala harshly, since the same problem presents itself in so many other countries. It is a collective failing, with roots in archaic notions of sovereignty and property; like peace the past is truly indivisible. If it is being destroyed piecemeal, it is because of our inability to view its preservation in larger terms. Before that outlook can be changed, enough people must have enough information to know that a problem exists. In 1972, an international conference was held in Stockholm to debate the deterioration of our environment, and if the meeting failed to produce facile solutions, it did at least succeed in placing an international problem at the center of an international stage. Without being unrealistically sanguine, I would hope that a similar international conference, with representation at a similarly august level, may yet be called to discuss the use and abuse of the human past—that is, while there is still something left of that past to discuss.

APPENDIX A

1. LOOTED SITES IN EL PETÉN, GUATEMALA

Site	Date	Comment
1. Aguas Calientes [Sayaxché]	1967	Stela 1 stolen.
2. Amelia, La [Sayaxché]	Before 1965	Stela 1 sawed apart, lower panel shown in Paris exhibition; New York dealer has jaguar base. Hieroglyphic step missing.
3. Anonal, El [Sayaxché]	c.1971	Fragments of architecture looted.
4. Cancuén [Sayaxché]	1971	Stela 1 stolen, bottom half recovered in Cobán when delivery attempted; thief arrested. Stela 2, front sawed off.
5. Caribe, El [Sayaxché]	1960s	Stela 1 in Isaac Delgado Museum, New Orleans. Two New York dealers have one stela each.
6. Cedral, El [just south of Seibal]	c.1965	Sculptured panel taken.
7. Chochkitam [Melchor de Mencos]	1961	Stela taken.
8. Dos Pilas [Sayaxché]	1960s 1964 1971	Glyphs sawed off stela 8; "Prisoner Step" stolen; stela 17 seized in crate addressed to Hahn Brothers, New York warehouse.

213

Site	Date	Comment
9. Encanto, El [within northern section of Tikal Park]	1969	Attempted robbery stopped by park employees.
10. Florida, La	1965	Stelae 7 and 9 smashed into pieces, and parts removed.
11. Itzimté [La Libertad]	1969	Stela 4 taken, but later recovered; now in Flores.
12. Ixkún [Dolores]	1972	Stela 5 destroyed.
13. Jimbal [just north of Tikal Park]	1970	Top of stela sawed off.
14. Machaquilá [Poptún]	1971	Stela 2 seized in Los Angeles area by FBI; stela 5 seized by FBI in Little Rock, Ark.
15. Mirador [San Andres]	1970	Destruction of architectural fragments; extensive looting.
16. Motul de San José [Flores]	1971	Stela 1, top partially sawed off.
17. Nakum [Flores]	c.1970	Destruction of monuments.
18. Naranjo [Melchoir]	1960s	Stela 30 shipped to Houston and seized; stela 8 on loan by Morton D. May to St. Louis City Art Museum; stela 19 in St. Thomas University Museum, Houston. Stelae 6, 8, 19, 21, and 24 smuggled to Belize and seized; stelae 2, 3, 7, 23 partly destroyed. Three heads recently taken from hieroglyphic stairway.
19. Naya, La	1971	Site looted, Guatemalan guide murdered. Stelae from site reported on American market.
20. Pasadita, La [San Andres]	1960s	Lintels stolen, frescos ruined.

Site	Date	Comment
21. Piedras Negras [San Andres]	Early 1960s	Stela 5 sold to N.Y. Museum of Primitive Art; stela 3 sold to Brooklyn Museum. Stela 35 in Rautenstrauch Joest Museum, Cologne. Stela 11 in Houston Museum of Fine Arts. Stela 34 exhibited by Paris dealer. Stela 2 in Minneapolis Institute of Arts.
22. Polol [La Libertad]	1969	Stela taken but later recovered.
23. Peru, El [San Andres]	c.1970	Several stelae smashed and parts removed.
24. Seibal [Sayaxché]	1968	Attempted theft of stela thwarted when dog began barking.
25. Uolantún [within Tikal Park]	1970	Fire used to shatter stela 1.
26. Yaxhá [Flores]	1969–71	Stelae 1 and 12 stolen; stela 3 shattered; stela 6 mutilated. Extensive tomb robbing.
27. Yaltitud [Dolores]	1960s	Stela 1 hacked apart, fragments now in Guatemala museum.
28. Zapote, El [Flores]	1970	Stela 1 shattered; fragments later recovered in Guatemala City.

Name in brackets is that of closest town.

SOURCES: Luis Luján Muñoz, director, Institute of Anthropology and History; Rafael Morales Fernández, director, National Museum of Anthropology and Ethnology; Ian Graham, Research Fellow, Peabody Museum; Amilcar Guzmán de la Cruz, administrator, Tikal National Park; Miss Joya Hairs; Clemency Coggins, Fogg Museum, Harvard; Nicholas M. Hellmuth, director, Yaxhá excavations.

2. PILLAGED MAYA SITES IN MEXICO

Site	Object	Comment
Calakmul, Campeche	Stela 53	Exhibited Delgado Museum, New Orleans, 1968. Shown by European dealer, 1970.
	Stela 65	Shown by European dealer, 1970.
	Stela 89	Rautenstrauch Joest Museum, Cologne.
	Mask panel from temple	Removed and partly destroyed, taken to New York, offered to Metropolitan Museum and later returned to Mexico.
Dzibilnocac, Campeche	Painted capstone	Rautenstrauch Joest Museum, Cologne.
El Cayo, Chiapas	Lintel 1	Exhibited by Paris dealer, 1966.
El Chicozapote, Chiapas	Lintel 2	Shown by European dealer, 1970.
El Tortuguero, Tabasco	Stela 6	In three pieces, one in Museum of Primitive Art, New York, others in Tabasco Museum, Villahermosa.
La Mar, Chiapas	Stela 1	In Hirshhorn Collection, New York, 1958.
	Stela 2	In private Mexican collection, c.1960.
	Stela 3	George Kennedy Collection, Los Angeles.
	Stela 7	European dealer, 1970.
Lacanjá, Chiapas	Stela 7	Paris Dealer, 1966.

Site	Object	Comment
	Lintel 1	Dumbarton Oaks, Washington, D.C., 1966.
Oxkintok, Yucatán	Stela 9	Bottom register, Rochester Memorial Art Gallery.
	Stela 14	Paris dealer, 1966.
	Stela ?	Yale University Art Gallery.
Palenque, Chiapas	Relief panels in style of Palenque	Dumbarton Oaks, 1966; Virginia Museum of Fine Arts, Richmond.
Pasión de Cristo, Campeche	Stela 2	Front partially sawed off.
Pomona, Tabasco	"Tablero Rojizo"	Houston Museum of Fine Arts.
Yaxchilan area, Chiapas	Lintels in style of Yaxchilan	Leyden, National Museum of Ethnology; Berlin, Völkerkunde Museum; Munich dealer, 1970; Hirshhorn Collection, New York; Museum of Primitive Art, New York.
Xcalumkin, Campeche	Door jambs, North building	Paris dealer, 1966.
Yucatán peninsula	Sculpture of unknown provenance	Column, Berlin, Völkerkunde Museum.
		Column, Worcester Art Museum.
		Column, Museum of Primitive Art.
		Standing stone figure, Reitberg Museum, Zurich.
		Standing stone figure, Metropolitan Museum of Art.
		Stela with masked figure, St. Louis City Art Museum.

Site	Object	Comment
Usumacinta region, Mexico and Guatemala	Sculpture of unknown provenance	Stela with female figure and dwarf, Cleveland Museum of Art.
		Relief panel, Cleveland Museum of Art.
		Lintel, Nelson Gallery, Kansas City, Mo.
		Stela, Freiburg Museum, West Germany.
		Stela, Reitberg Museum, Zurich.
		Relief panel, Reitberg Museum, Zurich.
		Stela, female figure, Dallas Museum of Fine Arts.
		Reclining figure step, New York collection.
		Ball player panel, Chicago Art Institute.
		Ball player panel, Museum of the American Indian, New York.
		Glyph panel, Miles J. Lourie Collection, New York.
		Glyphic fragments, Thomas Ford Gallery, Boston.
		Stela, Francis Crane Collection, Marathon, Florida.
		Stela fragment, Philadelphia Museum of Art.
		Wall panel, Delgado Museum, New Orleans.
		Wall panel, Dumbarton Oaks, Washington, D.C.

SOURCE: Clemency Coggins, "Displaced Maya Sculpture," *Estudios de Cultura Maya*, Vol. VIII, Mexico, 1970.

3. MAJOR ART THEFTS, 1911–1972

This table prepared with the assistance of Bonnie Bonham Flam, of the International Council of Museums.

Date	Place	Works Stolen	Comment*
1911	Louvre, Paris	"Mona Lisa"	Stolen by Italian nationalist who wanted to return it to Florence.
1930s	Private residence, Madrid, during Spanish civil war	Mondello of "Immaculate Conception" by El Greco	Recovered July, 1971, in the hands of a New York jeweler who was trying to sell it secretly.
1934	Ghent	Just Judges panel of Van Eyck altarpiece of the Mystical Lamb	Never recovered—replaced by a copy.
1939	Louvre, Paris	Fragonard, "L'Indifférent"	Stolen by art student who removed the varnish and returned it.

* Note: Absence of comment indicates lack of further information.

219

Date	Place	Works Stolen	Comment
1953	Victoria and Albert Museum, London	Rodin bronze	Stolen and returned by a student who wanted to "live with it."
1959			
January, 1959	Austrian Applied Arts Museum, Vienna	3 Oriental carpets—17th century	Anonymous letter claimed they were "borrowed" to make copies and denounced the museum for its thoughtless guard. The carpets were later recovered from Athens, Beirut, and Ankara.
November, 1959	Les Aubrais, Paris	Daumier painting on wood, insured at 100,000 francs	In suitcase pocket which was stolen on train. Not recovered.
December, 1959	U.C.L.A. exhibition	Klee, "Panel of Young Tree"	Stolen by student, sold eventually to Berlin-Dahlem State Museum. Returned and resold to Zurich dealer.
December, 1959	Berlin-Dahlem State Museum	Unframed head of Christ, oil on wood.	Inventory number 1048 on back.

Date	Location	Item(s)	Outcome
December, 1959	Frankfurt Art Institute	"Venus" by Cranach, signed	Found in September, 1960, in Munich train station locker after anonymous call.
1960			
April, 1960	Colombe d'Or Restaurant, St.-Paul de Vence, France	20 paintings valued at 1,949,000 francs by modern masters (Miró, Picasso, Buffet, Bonnard, Villon, Modigliani, Rouault, Léger, Braque)	Burglars arrested and all but 1 abstract painting recovered.
1961			
1961	Lord Chamberlain's office, St. James Palace, London	6 paintings	Recognized at Christie's by Royal collection marks.
July, 1961	Gallery Art de France, Cannes	Series of paintings with a Vlaminck worth 70,000 francs	Found in a truck parked in Cannes.
July, 1961	Musée de l'Annonciade, St.-Tropez	57 Impressionist and modern paintings, value 6–7 million francs	Found in unused barn near Fontainebleau 16 months later after anonymous letter.
August, 1961	Museum, Aix-en-Provence	8 Cézannes—value $2 million	Guard was sleeping in next room; found in abandoned car.

221

Date	Place	Works Stolen	Comment
August, 1961	Archaeological Museum, Nalanda, India	Bronze Buddhist statues	Interpol lists them among most wanted objects in 1973.
August, 1961	National Gallery, London	Goya, "Duke of Wellington," valued at £140,000	Found in Birmingham station four years later after anonymous letter; thief, an unemployed truck driver, was convicted.
December, 1962	Pordenone, Duomo	Painting by Pordenone, valued at 50 million lire	Abandoned by thieves.
1962	Castelvetrano, Sicily	Ephebus of Selinunte	Recovered by Italian special minister.
May, 1963	Private home, Florence	44 paintings (ancient and Impressionist) valued at 70 million lire	Few photos.
December, 1963	Calenzano, Italy, near Florence	Fresco, around 1400, by Paulo Schiaro	From unused church: thieves coated fresco with glue, applied canvas to whole surface, removed when dry.

1964

1964	Fine Arts Museum, Brussels	Rubens, "Head of a Negro"	Recovered after anonymous call.
March, 1964	Pitti Palace, Florence	Giorgio Morandi painting	Replaced in frame by a copy.
May–Aug., 1964	Villa, Florence	Fresco—Head and Shoulders of a Woman by Ghirlandaio or Pollaiuolo, value at 50 million lire	Had been detached for restoration and put into frame.
1964	Near Rome	"Madonna di Cossito," 13th-century panel valued at $1 million	Sold disguised in Swiss auction; recovered when offered for sale in New York by Uruguayan owner.

1965

1965	Ambrosian Library, Milan	Brueghel oil on copper; page from Leonard *Codex Atlanticus*	Stolen by young seminarian. First returned from New York, second from Switzerland.
June, 1965	Bonnat Museum, Bayonne, France	Corneille de Lyon, "Portrait of Cardinal de Lenoncourt de Lyon"	Among Interpol's Most Wanted.

1966

June, 1966	Panama City National Museum	Large collection pre-Columbian jewelry, worth $75,000 in gold weight alone	Never recovered.

Date	Place	Works Stolen	Comment
December, 1966	Dulwich College Gallery, England	Paintings worth $7 million	$250,000 ransom demanded. College refused to pay, and the paintings were eventually recovered after anonymous tip.
1967			
December, 1967–January, 1968	Rumania-Hungary	1 Magritte, 1 Alechinsky, worth 680,000 Belgian francs	Disappeared in transit. The paintings were on loan from the Fine Arts Museum of Ostend, Belgium.
1968			
January, 1968	Trèves Museum	12 Old Master paintings and 1 statuette	Fingerprints found but crime never traced.
April, 1968	Paris: On 6 November 1967, 38 paintings were seized at the Wildenstein Foundation by judicial order and left there under guard; on 8 April one was discovered missing; the circumstances surrounding its disappearance are undetermined. The painting was a landscape by Renoir.		
August, 1968	Private apartment, Bruges region	Modern painting collection including paintings by Ensor, Klee, Costeau, Cocteau, Magritte, Dufy, Rouault, Picabia, Rubens—valued at 8,400,000 Belgian	An Italian national was charged with the theft.

Date	Location	Object	Notes
September, 1968	Private house, London	8 paintings by Pissarro, Renoir, van Steenwyck	Access by scaffolding used for painting the house. An old typewriter was also stolen. The paintings were recovered in England.
November, 1968	Zurich Art Patrons Association	Salvador Dali, "Woman with Head of Roses," valued at 90,000 Swiss francs	Recovered at the opening of a Paris gallery in 1971.
November, 1968	Home of Luis Mailhos, Montevideo, Uruguay	12 paintings by Utrillo, Gainesborough, Derain, Vlaminck, Léger, Lebrun, Brueghel	
December, 1968	Museum of Modern Art, Kyoto, Japan	Toulouse-Lautrec, "Marcelle," insured at 500,000 francs	On loan from the Musée d'Albi, France. Frame recovered in Kyoto. Among Interpol's Most Wanted.
Before 1969	Village temple in Sivapuram, Southern India	Tenth-century bronze statue of Shiva, discovered in 1952	Original replaced by fake before 1969. Statue smuggled abroad and sold in 1972 for reported $1 million to Norton Simon, California collector.

Date	Place	Works Stolen	Comment
1969			
January, 1969	Singer Museum, Larens, Netherlands	Panel attributed to Rubens, valued at 250,000 francs	Found in Brighton in March, 1969.
April, 1969	Flat of Sir Roland Penrose, London	25 modern paintings worth £350,000	Recovered in London in July, 1969.
July, 1969	Dijon Museum, France	Van der Weyden, "Head of St. John the Baptist," valued at 100,-000–200,000 francs	
July, 1969	Izmir Archaeological Museum, Turkey	Large group of ancient gold and jewelry	Museum guard killed, thieves later arrested.
July, 1969	Pesaro, Italy	15th-century "Madonna of the Goldfinch," attributed to Perugino	Stolen during the night, found nearby.
August, 1969	Private home, Paris	27 paintings, 18th–20th century, including Delacroix, Chardin, Pissarro, Monet, Dufy, Jongkind	
October, 1969	Church of S. Lorenzo, Palermo, Sicily	Caravaggio, "Nativity"	Stolen during the night. Unrecovered.

May, 1970	Gasteinerhof Hotel, Salzburg	Ribera, "St. Paul," valued at 400,000 shillings	Stolen during morning hours.
May, 1970	Malaspina Museum, Pavia, Italy	3 Italian 15–16th-century paintings valued at 300 million lire: Antonello, "Portrait of a Man," Bellini, "Madonna and Child," Correggio, "Holy Family"	Broken into at night; theft still unsolved.
July, 1970	Chandigarh Museum, Punjab, India	102 rare antique Indian miniatures	Returned anonymously to the curator in August, 1972.
July, 1970	S. Mario del Popolo, Rome	13th-century Madonna	Recovered one month later in the Netherlands after a middleman was bribed.
July, 1970	Apartment, Paris	17 19th-century paintings	Attempt made to gain ransom. Later paintings were found in unused Metro station after anonymous tip.

Date	Place	Works Stolen	Comment
August, 1970	Jewelry store, Phoenix, Arizona	Renoir, "Young Girl Reading," valued at $80,000	Never recovered; rumored to be in private collection.
October, 1970	Jalapa City University Museum, Mexico	Jade sculpture of priest from "Las Limas"—55 cm. high, weighs 132 lbs.	
October, 1970	Private apartment, Palermo	Guardi, St. Mark's Scene	Among Interpol's Most Wanted objects.
October, 1970	Avenue Foch private apartment, Paris	9 modern and Impressionist paintings, value 850,000 francs	Recovered in Montparnasse station locker after payment of ransom by insurance company.
November, 1970	O'Hara Museum, Okayama, Japan	5 modern and Impressionist paintings	Breaking and entering; never solved.
November, 1970	Church of S. Dominico, Chioggia (Venice), Italy	Carpaccio, "S. Paulo"	Found in Italy in March, 1971.
December, 1970	Private apartment, Milan	Tintoretto, "Virgin and Child," Correggio, "Bearing of the Cross"	Tintoretto recovered, Correggio still missing.

December, 1970	Guggenheim Museum, New York	2 Picassos—a watercolor and a drawing—valued at $110,000	Returned within 48 hours by mail.
December, 1970	Private apartment, Courtrai, Belgium	8 paintings and a number of African, Eskimo, and Japanese figurines	Most of the objects recovered, none of the paintings.
December, 1970	Montepulciano Museum, Italy	Raphael, "Portrait of a Lady"; "Old Woman" attrib. to Caravaggio; 14th-century Siennese triptych; Sodoma, "Holy Family"; Van Dyck, "Portrait"	Triptych recovered from gangsters in Rome when it was thrown from the window of a pursued car. Other paintings among Interpol's Most Wanted.
1971			
January, 1971	Vernet-les-Bains, France	Several paintings by Courbet, Ingres, and Lebrun	
March, 1971	Bonnat Museum, Bayonne, France	3 Rembrandts	2 recovered in Hamburg, third in Frankfurt. Thieves had tried to resell it to the French state. Sentenced to 6 months and 1 year imprisonment.

Date	Place	Works Stolen	Comment
March, 1971	Palazzo Vecchio, Florence	Masaccio, "Virgin and Child," and Memling, "Portrait of a Gentleman"	Room had been closed to the public for several months. Recovered in July, 1973, in Florence.
March, 1971	Cerveteri Museum, Italy	15th-century Flemish triptych, "Adoration of the Magi"	Recovered in Cerveteri after anonymous tip.
May, 1971	Terrace of Museum of Modern Art, Paris	Sculpture by Tine	
May, 1971	Art Dealer, Old Masters, S.A., Chiasso, Switzerland	11 Old Master paintings, including a Filippino Lippi triptych	All recovered except one painting by Pellegrini; Lippi from a bank in Lausanne, other paintings in Turin.
May, 1971	Rome	Seizure of 29 paintings during search by police	
June, 1971	Stolen from transport company premises, Paris	Fragonard, "La Liseuse," (Girl Reading)	Recovered from St. Lazare station locker in November, 1971.

Date	Location	Description	Notes
June, 1971	Home of Denise Rolin, Knokke-Heist, Belgium	5 paintings and 2 statues valued at 5,700,000 Belgian francs	Frames abandoned on premises. Paintings on Interpol's Most Wanted list.
June, 1971	Prado Museum, Madrid, Spain	Oil painting on copper by Jan van Kessel, valued as priceless	Exhibited in a corridor leading to the cafeteria of the museum.
June, 1971	Brescia, Italy	Polyptych of 7 panels by Paolo Veneziano, "Virgin and Child with Six Saints," valued at 15 million lire	Recovered in October, 1972, in Brescia.
July, 1971	Apartment of Robert Frenkel, Paris	17 paintings by Vlaminck, Van Dongen, Renoir, Buffet, Pissarro, Chagall, valued at $140,000	Recovered with apprehension of 5 bank robbers in the apartment of one of the five (he was not the thief, as he had been in prison at the time of the art theft).
July, 1971	Munchenstein, Switzerland	Paintings worth 1,120,000 Swiss francs by Gauguin, Chasseriau, Rubens, Paul Bril	Stolen from premises of Dreispitz Transport Co.; a Gauguin sculpture seized in Paris is thought to be part of this lot.

Date	Place	Works Stolen	Comment
July, 1971	Galerie Le Nouvel Essor, Paris	69 engravings by 19th-century masters	
August, 1971	Art dealer, London	8th-century Pallava-style head of Devi, offered for sale, is contested by Thai government	Recovered by Thailand.
August, 1971	Church of SS. Giovanni e Paulo, Venice	Giovanni Bellini paintings and Vivarini triptych	Recovered locally after payment of an $8,000 ransom; thieves apprehended.
August, 1971	Pieve di Cadove (near Padua)	Titian, "Holy Conversation"	Recovered after dramatic car chase in Padua. Thieves also stole 13 other paintings and drank communion wine.
September, 1971	Village church in vicinity of Padua	Tintoretto painting	Recovered locally by police.
September, 1971	Apartment of Boris Christoff, Rome	Icons, and Renaissance and Baroque paintings	

September, 1971	Fine Arts Museum, Brussels	Vermeer, "The Love Letter"	Cut out of frame. Ransom of 20 million francs demanded for Bengali refugees. Recovered in damaged state.
September, 1971	Church St.-Nicolas des Champs, Paris	14th-century Italian polyptych consisting of 20 small paintings on wood panels	A painting by Le Sueur was stolen from the same church three months earlier.
September, 1971	Florence	Attic, Corinthian, and Etruscan vases	Seized by police at antique dealers' Biennale; products of illicit excavation.
September, 1971	Abomey, Dahomey	Gold treasures of the kings of Dahomey	Frenchman arrested at border to Ivory Coast; suspected because of strange comportment.
September, 1971	Private apartment, The Hague	7 paintings valued at $1 million; among them a Rembrandt, P. Potter, J. Steen	Apartment was vacant during vacation months.
September, 1971	Art gallery, Zagreb, Yugoslavia	7 paintings, including a Rembrandt and an El Greco, a Pourbus and 4 Italian primitives	Found in Yugoslavia in December, 1971; offender arrested.

Date	Place	Works Stolen	Comment
September, 1971	S.-Jean de Malines, Belgium	9 paintings, including Rubens' "Christ on Cross" and Jordaens painting	Stolen from church.
September, 1971	Hasselt, Belgium	24 Old Master paintings valued at $50,000	Stolen from converted church after special guard was removed; were to be sold the next day.
October, 1971	Sinai Peninsula Church	13th-century painting on wood depicting one of the early fathers of the church; very great value	Thought stolen and exported by a tourist.
October, 1971	B.A.S. art gallery, Amsterdam	61 icons, value of each between 1,000 and 12,000 florins	All were marked with labels and inventory numbers.
November, 1971	Montréal, France	4 alabaster altarpiece panels (14th-century)	
November, 1971	Galerie Knoedler, Paris	Picasso, "Tête d'Harlequin"	Recovered and offenders arrested.
November, 1971	Vernon Collegiale Church, France	Alabaster bas-relief of Tree of Jesse; six 17th-century Flemish tapestries of the Virtues	Classified as French Historic Monuments.

	Denis (Burgundy), France		
December, 1971	Hamburg Museum	Delacroix and Corot paintings	One Delacroix recovered in Mulhouse, France; offenders arrested.
December, 1971	Villa of Mrs. Peggy Guggenheim, Venice	17 surrealist paintings valued at 500 million lire	Recovered by police in Mestre, near Venice.
December, 1971	Municipal Museum, Tours, France	Paintings by Rembrandt and Van Goyen	Recovered in Berlin in the hands of a dealer; Van Goyen had been resold to a collector.
December, 1971	Private collection, Naples, Italy	Sculptured objects and paintings by Luini, Fra Angelico, M. Preti, L. Giordano, and others	Found in Naples in Oct., 1972.
1971	Nigerian museums	3 folk objects—an Ibo mask; a statuette of the idol Esu; and a statuette of the goddess Jebba	Smuggled to Paris, New York, and the Netherlands.
1972			
1968–1972	Northeastern U.S.	Invaluable graphic works returned to museums and libraries anonymously, through the mail	Connected with a New York lawyer arrested for thefts from the Metropolitan Museum print room.

Date	Place	Works Stolen	Comment
Early 1972	Sun Temple, Katarmal, India	Statue of a devotee, reported stolen in 1972	Bought by a New York collector, now in private collection.
January, 1972	Church of St.-Gervais, Paris	Vignon, "Beheading of John the Baptist"	Recovered in damaged condition; recovered 48 hours later in the hands of a middleman.
January, 1972	Church of St.-Martin, Colmar, France	Schoengauer, "Virgin with Rosebush," valued at $1,000,000	Church broken into during the night; security device under construction.
January, 1972	Capucine convent, Cortona/Arezzo, Italy	13th-century Tuscan Virgin and Child valued at 15 million lire	
January, 1972	Grobet and Labardie Museum, Marseilles	8 paintings by Delacroix, Ingres, Fragonard, Gericault	
January, 1972	Painting belonging to a Milan private collector in Mestre (near Venice), Italy	Guido Reni, "Assumption of the Virgin," valued at 200 million lire	Disappeared during transport from railway station.
January, 1972	Studio of Sergio Bonfantini, Novare, Italy	36 signed paintings valued at 20 million lire	

Date	Location	Item	Notes
January, 1972	Gemona del Friuli near Udine, Italy	Painting by Cima da Conigliano	Church broken into during night.
February, 1972	Museum, Düsseldorf	Three 17th-century paintings by Rembrandt, Hals, and del Mazo, value 1,040,000 DM	Interpol's Most Wanted list.
March, 1972	Konstgalleriet, Stockholm	Aquatints and lithographs by Joan Miró and Wolfgang Schulze-Wols, valued at 209,000 Sw. kronor	
March, 1972	Museum of Berthoud Castle, Berne	Four 18th-century portraits	Interpol's Most Wanted list.
April, 1972	Apartment of M. Lespinasse, Paris	31 paintings by modern (19th–20th c.) masters—Dufy, Marquet, Bonnard, Boudin, Monet, Renoir, Utrillo, Sisley, Van Dongen, Rouault, Vlaminck	Bandits gained entry through service entrance, overpowered servants. Fifteen of the 31 paintings recovered in June, 1973, from a Paris dealer.
May, 1972	Deerfield Academy library, Deerfield, Mass.	7 paintings by Diaz, Gros, Pissarro, Copley, valued at $80,000	Marked with inventory numbers.

Date	Place	Works Stolen	Comment
May, 1972	Worcester, Mass. Art Museum	4 paintings by Rembrandt, Gauguin, Picasso, worth more than $1 million	2 armed robbers burst into museum, shot guard; paintings recovered in June and offenders arrested.
September, 1972	Museum of Fine Arts, Montreal, Canada	18 oil paintings (including Rembrandt, Corot, Courbet) valued at $2 million, plus antique jewelry	Masked offenders, armed with sawed-off shotguns, broke in through skylight; guards bound and gagged.
September, 1972	Villa of artist Compigli, St. Tropez	Paintings by Compigli	Recovered in state of total deterioration after payment of 18 million lire ransom.
October, 1972	Caramoor, Katonah, N.Y.	12 works valued at $500,000, including Cranach portrait, Cellini bronzes	Works recovered in November following negotiations with thieves.
October, 1972	National Gallery, Prague	3 paintings by Hals (a portrait) and El Greco	

November, 1972	Town hall housing important modern collection, Bagnols-sur-Ceze, France	15 Impressionist and modern paintings	Two other burglary attempts have been made recently.
December, 1972	Castelfranco, Italy	Giorgione, "Castelfranco Madonna"	Recovered 11 days later at Swiss border after bizarre car chase. Motive considered to be extortion.
December, 1972	Local church, Uncastillo (Zaragoza), Spain	Polychrome Virgin and Child, value 400,000 pesetas	
December, 1972	Lyons, France	16 paintings	Recovered in breakup of smuggling operation from France to Italy.
1973			
January, 1973	London	Picasso, "Self-Portrait," value £80,000 (offered for sale)	Suspected to have been stolen from West Germany two years ago.

APPENDIX B

TABLE OF NATIONAL PROTECTIVE LAWS

Prepared with the assistance of Bonnie Bonham Flam, of the International Council of Museums.

Country	Date and Type of Legislation	Scope	Permitted Exports	Penalties	Remarks
Algeria	Ordinance regarding Protection of Monuments and Sites, 1967	All cultural property and natural monuments	Salable and exportable objects are registered; export of classified objects prohibited.	Fine of 500–2000 DA ($100–400); imprisonment of 2 months–6 years	Dealers are licensed

Country	Law	Ownership	Export	Penalty	Notes
Austria	Federal Monuments Law, 1923; export and sale laws, 1918; modified 1923 and 1958	All publicly or collectively owned monuments and objects protected by declaration	Technically all export of cultural property except contemporary works of art is forbidden.	Fine twice the value of the object for illicit purchase or sale	An efficient classification system protects important objects and allows others to be sold and exported.
Bolivia	National Monuments Law, 1927; decrees and ministerial resolutions, 1961 and 1967	All cultural properties are the ultimate property of the state	All export prohibited, including export by diplomatic means.	Application of Penal Code and fine. Fine is doubled or tripled if offense is repeated.	Import of cultural property is free; Bolivia has ratified the UNESCO Convention, 1970.
Brazil	Law of 1937—Protection of Cultural Property; Law of 1965—export control	All cultural property belongs ultimately to the state.	Export of objects produced before 1889 is prohibited.	Fine of 1,000–20,000 cruzeiros ($166–3,300.)	Foreign works may be imported free.
British Honduras	Ancient Monuments Ordinance, 1971	All antiquities are the property of the state.	Government license required for export or import of antiquities	Fine of US $6,650 or imprisonment 12 months–5 years	The government may search any premises or vehicles suspected of containing illicit antiquities.

Author's Note: From January through June, 1973, there were at least 15 additional major thefts in 7 countries, involving 298 paintings and a multitude of antiquities. It was not feasible to extend this listing, but a detailed supplement will be sent to those interested by Atheneum Publishers, 122 East 42nd Street, New York, New York 10017.

Country	Date and Type of Legislation	Scope	Permitted Exports	Penalties	Remarks
Cambodia	Legislative texts (1924) referring originally to French colonies	Registered monuments are protected; state may expropriate other objects.	Certificate of nonclassifcation required for export of pre-19th-century objects	Decided in court; unauthorized sale is void, first seller is responsible.	New law in preparation; UNESCO convention of 1970 ratified
Canada	Provincial laws between 1953 and 1964	Protection of archaeological objects and archives	Transfer outside of province is usually prohibited.	Varies to maximum of $500 fine in British Columbia and 6 months' imprisonment	A national law is being prepared regarding export control and internal registration of important objects.
China, Nationalist	Constitutional provisions and acts passed 1928–1938	All cultural property classified according to three classes	Export of cultural property prohibited except for loans not exceeding two years	Maximum penalty under criminal code	New law being considered to update existing legislation
China, People's Republic	Provisional measures, 1950	All cultural property	Export is prohibited; significant cultural property deemed an exception must be inspected.	No information	No important objects have been exported since 1950.

Country	Law	Protection	Export	Penalties	Remarks
Colombia	Laws of 1959 and decrees of 1963 and 1967	All cultural properties under protection of the state	Export prohibited except for temporary exhibition purposes	No enforced penalties	New law being drafted
Costa Rica	Law of 1938: Control of Commerce and Export in Archaeological Relics	Monuments are nationalized; other objects, except privately owned, are registered.	Export permitted of objects of a type represented in national collections (with permit)	Fine of 50–1000 pesos (maximum about $125)	Dealers must be licensed.
Cyprus	Antiquities Law, 1959	State protects all antiquities from destruction or unauthorized sale.	Export permit required; state may exercise embargo. Dealers licensed; dealers and collectors maintain inventory.	£50 or 6 months' imprisonment for concealing antiquities; £100 or 1-year imprisonment for illicit export	Internal political strife makes law difficult to enforce.
Ecuador	Law of Artistic Patrimony, 1945; Emergency Decree, 1971	All cultural property protected and registered by the state	Only temporary export and official exchange of objects are permitted.	Fine of 1,000–10,000 sucres ($40–400); confiscation of objects exported through diplomatic channels	Field research products must remain in country; a new draft law allows inspection of diplomatic valises and regulates commerce.

Country	Date and Type of Legislation	Scope	Permitted Exports	Penalties	Remarks
El Salvador	Law for Protection of Archaeology, etc., 1903	All cultural property belongs ultimately to the state.	Only duplicates of objects in national collections may be exported.	C3000 ($1,200) maximum fine or fine of value of objects	
France	Monuments Law, 1913, modified occasionally; Export Law, 1941	All publicly owned objects and ecclesiastic monuments	All works dating before 1900 must be authorized for export. Classified objects may not be exported.	Fine up to twice the value of objects involved, imprisonment up to 3 months	The state may acquire works whose export is sought within 6 months.
Germany, West	Law of Protection of German Cultural Property, 1955 (adopted by ratification in each *Land*)	Protected objects, monuments and archives are registered locally on an inventory	Permit required for export of registered objects; properties inventoried on federal inventory may be exported only if declassified		The government may exercise an export embargo and the owner must maintain the object within the country or sell it.

244

Greece	Antiquities Law, 1932	All cultural property is ultimate property of the state, including maritime finds.	Export permit required. Export tax is ½ value of object. Duplicate antiquities sold by national museum may be exported with 5% tax.	Fine of up to 25,000 dr. ($830), imprisonment 1 month–2 years	Collectors and dealers must be registered and maintain inventory and catalogue.
Guatemala	Decree for the Protection of Monuments, 1947; modified 1966	All cultural property is protected by the state.	No permanent exports are allowed (except field-research products).	Fine the value of the objects or 4 years' imprisonment	Unauthorized possession of cultural property is considered an offense.
Honduras	Law of 1955; Constitutional provision, 1936	All cultural property is protected by the state and may be expropriated.	Export of classified objects is prohibited, except for duplicate objects which may be ceded to foreign museums.	Application of Penal Code	

Country	Date and Type of Legislation	Scope	Permitted Exports	Penalties	Remarks
India	Monuments and Remains Acts of 1904, 1958 and 1959; Antiquities Act of 1972	State maintains right of protection and guardianship over all monuments and antiquities.	Antiquities may be exported only by central government or by authorized agencies.	Imprisonment of 6 months–3 years and fine (unspecified)	Eventually the state will take over control of all antiquities dealerships.
Indonesia	Monuments Ordinance, 1931	Registered and unregistered goods over 50 years old protected by the state	Permit required for export of registered or tentatively registered goods, or any pre-Mohammedan object	Fine of 500 rupiah (about $1.25) or imprisonment of 3 months	Smuggling of pre-Mohammedan goods is a considerable problem.
Iran	Law of 1930: preservation of Persian antiquities	All antiquities are controlled by the state; excavation is controlled on inventoried land.	Dealers are licensed and a permit is required for the export of antiquities.	Fine of 20–200 Tomfavis	The state may inspect the dealer's place of business but not his residence. Much dealing is done in the merchant's home.
Iraq	Antiquities Law, 1936	All antiquities are common property of the state.	A permit is required for the export of antiquities; the state may exercise embargo or preemption.	Fine of 500 dinars ($1,500) (double for dealers); 3 years imprisonment	Dealings in unregistered antiquities or forgery are offenses.

246

Country	Law	Description	Penalty	Notes
Israel	Law of 1929: antiquities ordinance	Antiquities discovered in Israel must be offered to the state for acquisition.	A license required for the export of antiquities, and payment of a 10% fee.	Fine of £1,000 (about $250) or imprisonment up to 6 months	95% of export applications are granted; the state occasionally sells duplicate antiquities.
Italy	Law of 1939 for the Protection of Artistic Patrimony	All cultural property more than 50 years old, including collections	Objects may be exported only if the state has refused its option to acquire them (2-month option).	Fine of 1,000 to 100,000 lire (maximum $200) plus confiscation of objects	Administrative processes for granting licenses can be cumbersome.
Japan	Law for the Protection of Cultural Properties, 1950	All cultural properties under protection of the state; national treasures are inventoried.	Export of national treasures prohibited, except temporarily. Other elements may be exported with permit.	Fine up to 100,000 yen ($350) or imprisonment up to 5 years.	Objects not desired by the government may be exported freely.

Country	Date and Type of Legislation	Scope	Permitted Exports	Penalties	Remarks
Jordan	Antiquities Law, 1968	All antiquities, including undiscovered ones, are the property of the state.	A permit is required for the export of cultural property; dealers are licensed.	Fine of 100–300 dinars ($280–$840) or 3 months to 3 years imprisonment; fine of 50 dinars for deceiving a purchaser	Dealers may operate only on premises indicated by license.
Lebanon	Antiquities Regulations, 1933	All antiquities dating before 1700 A.D. are the property of state.	A permit required for export; the exporter is subject to payment of a tax.	Fine of LL 50–500; informers and apprehenders are awarded 25–50%.	No import of antiquities from Iraq, Syria, or Jordan without permit
Libya	Antiquities Law, 1953	Antiquities over 100 years old and biological remains dating before 600 A.D.	A permit is required for the export of any antiquity.	Fine of £500 or imprisonment up to 1 year	Dealers are licensed and must maintain a register.
Mexico	Federal Monuments Law, 1972	All cultural property is protected and registered on inventory.	Export of pre-Columbian objects is prohibited, except temporarily. Other objects may be exported with permit.	Varying fines up to 50,000 pesos ($400); and 2–12 years' imprisonment	Dealers officially required to register objects with the state; export permits difficult to obtain

Country	Law	Protection	Export	Penalties	Notes
Nigeria	Antiquities ordinance, 1953; and export regulations, 1957	Antiquities and archaeological objects (including craftworks dating before 1918) belong ultimately to the state.	A permit is required, issued 3 months before export. The government may refuse permission.	Fine of N100 or imprisonment up to 6 months	The 3-month clause is almost always waived.
Pakistan	Antiquities Act, 1968	Antiquities, objects, and monuments dating before 1857 are protected and inventoried.	Permits granted for exchange of duplicates, temporary exhibitions, and objects awarded to excavators	Imprisonment of one year, fine, and confiscation of objects	Forgery is an offense; a license is required for copying antiquities for commercial reasons.
Panama	Law of 1946, creating National Monuments Commission	Historic monuments belong to the state.	Duplicate of objects in national collections may be exported with a permit.	Fine of 500 balboas ($500)	Exploration and commerce by inexpert and unauthorized individuals are prohibited.

Country	Date and Type of Legislation	Scope	Permitted Exports	Penalties	Remarks
Peru	Law of 1929—monuments; Law of 1958—export	Pre-Columbian antiquities are protected by the state and registered on inventory.	Export of classified material prohibited, except temporarily; permit required for other exports	Fine of 1,000–10,000 soles ($22.50–225) goes to Dept. of Museums. A 50% reward may be given to the discoverer of illicit operations.	Temporary loan of classified objects is prohibited, and requires the Supreme Resolution of the government.
Philippines	Cultural Property Protection Act, 1966	Cultural property over 100 years old protected and inventoried by state	Inventoried cultural treasures may not be exported; other objects may be exported with permit.	Fine of 10,000 pesos ($1,400) or imprisonment up to 2 years	
Spain	National Artistic Patrimony Law, 1933; export and commerce decrees 1953, 1960, 1961, and 1969	Objects over 200 years old are protected and registered by the state.	Export of nationally registered antiquities is prohibited. Otherwise a permit is required. There is an export tax.	Fine 3 times value of object, or 4 times if it is registered.	Loans forbidden from the Prado. Objects of value of more than 1 million pesetas must be bought at public auction to be exported.

Switzerland	Federal Law concerning the Conservation of Monuments, 1958	Swiss monuments and antiquities are officially protected in that the state appropriates sums for their purchase and maintenance.	Cantonal authorities may require export permission. There is no regulation of imports or of reexport of imported antiquities.	None	Because of absence of controls, Switzerland is leading international center for legal sale of major items of smuggled antiquities.
Syria	Antiquities Regime, 1963	Objects over 200 years old are protected and registered by the state.	Export and internal transfer must be approved. Antiquities must be approved by the state for sale.	Fine of LS25 to LS-10,000 (max. $2,200) or imprisonment of 1 month–3 years	Dealers must be licensed.
Thailand	Ancient Monuments Act, 1961; export and internal transfer ban, 1972	All registered antiquities and ancient monuments	Objects for sale to foreigners must be approved in advance.	Fine of 4,000 baht ($200) for illicit traffic; 10,000 baht or 2 years' imprisonment for destruction of monuments	The new law is intended to protect objects found fortuitously or through illicit research.
Tunisia	No real laws are in force. Two projects establishing protected historical zones are being considered.				

Country	Date and Type of Legislation	Scope	Permitted Exports	Penalties	Remarks
Turkey	Antiquities Regulations, 1907	All cultural property found on Turkish soil or in territorial waters is property of state.	Export prohibited	Application of Penal Code	Certain objects may be rewarded to directors of field research missions, and may be exported.
U.S.S.R.	Law of 1918 for the classification of cultural property	All monuments, art objects, and collections are nationalized.	No export without permission of the Dept. of Museums.	Reclusion	The state controls antiquity shops; objects bought in shops are exportable.
U.A.R.	Law on Protection of Antiquities, 1953 and 1965	All movable and immovable objects produced before the end of the reign of Ismail	Export certificate must be issued 20 days in advance.	Fine of £50–200 ($75–300), imprisonment of 3 months– 2 years	A significant number of exports are approved.
U.S.A.	Public Act, 1906, Preservation of American Antiquities	Only monuments and antiquities on public land	Import and export of antiquities are free	Fine of $500 for offenses on govt. land; $2,000 for falsifying Indian products	The 1970 Mexico–US treaty permits the return of illicitly exported archaeological material to the country of origin.

Vietnam, Republic of	Monuments decree, 1924; exportation decree, 1959	All objects and monuments, known or concealed	Classified objects may not be exported; permits are required for others.	Fine up to 7,500 fr. (1925) and imprisonment up to 3 months	Wartime conditions make protection of cultural property and particularly of objects in private collections impossible.
Yugoslavia	Fundamental Law for the Protection of Monuments, 1965	All cultural monuments are considered public property.	Important cultural monuments are not exportable. Artistic objects may be exported with permission.	Forced labor up to 5 years	

APPENDIX C

1. THE PENNSYLVANIA DECLARATION
DECISION OF CURATORS OF THE UNIVERSITY MUSEUM
UNIVERSITY OF PENNSYLVANIA, APRIL 1, 1970

The curatorial faculty of The University Museum today reached the unanimous conclusion that they would purchase no more art objects or antiquities for the Museum unless the objects are accompanied by a pedigree—that is, information about the different owners of the objects, place of origin, legality of export, and other data useful in each individual case. The information will be made public. This decision was recommended by the Director of the Museum, Froelich Rainey, and also by the Chairman of the Board of Managers, Howard C. Petersen.

The action of The University staff is the result of an increasing illicit trade in cultural objects, particularly antiquities, which is causing major destruction of archaeological sites in many countries throughout the world. Practically all countries now have strict controls on the export of antiquities but it is clear that such controls do not stop the looting and destruction of archaeological sites, probably because high prices paid for antiquities in the international market make it impossible for the countries of origin to stop the movement across their borders.

The United Nations Organization, through UNESCO, is now discussing an international convention which proposes, among other things, that the major importing countries for these objects, such as the United States, West Germany, France and England, should introduce more rigid import controls in order to restrict the trade and

254

protect the archaeological sites in countries such as Turkey, Iran, and Italy.

It is the considered opinion of The University Museum group of archaeologists and anthropologists who work in many countries throughout the world, that import controls in the importing countries will be no more effective than the export controls in the exporting countries. Probably the only effective way to stop this wholesale destruction of archaeological sites is to regulate the trade in cultural objects within each country just as most countries in the world today regulate domestic trade in foodstuffs, drugs, securities, and other commodities. The looting of sites is naturally done by the nationals of each country and the illicit trade is carried out by them and by the nationals of many countries. Hence the preservation of the cultural heritage for mankind as a whole is, in fact, a domestic problem for all nations.

The staff of The University Museum hopes that their action taken today will encourage other museums not only in the United States but in other nations to follow a similar procedure in the purchase of significant art objects, at least until the United Nations succeeds in establishing an effective convention to control this destructive trade.

2. THE HARVARD REPORT
ADOPTED NOVEMBER, 1971

On November 29, 1971, the President and Fellows adopted as official policy of the University the report of the Committee on the Acquisition of Works of Art and Antiquities.

The text of the report:

The collections in the museums and libraries of Harvard University have been formed and are augmented and maintained primarily to promote teaching and research. In recent years a flourishing international black market has grown up in the kinds of objects that are the proper concern of our collections, and this threatens the work of the University in various ways. For example, sites have been ravaged by thieves and vandals, to the irreparable damage and even total loss of important objects, while persons involved in this traffic either carelessly lose or deliberately conceal information about the precise origins of objects, often rendering them valueless for scientific study.

In response to this situation many countries have developed legislation designed to regulate the collection and export of antiquities, art objects, and natural specimens found within their borders. But without the cooperation of the ultimate consumer—the collecting institution or individual—such legislation has often proved inadequate to control abuses.

More and more countries attempt to regulate these matters. The resulting legislation is far from uniform and has become steadily more complex. But no matter how complex, badly framed, or impractical such legislation may appear to be, a responsible collecting institution must abide by it. The violation, real or apparent, of regulatory legislation by one branch of the University is likely to have adverse effects upon the legitimate interests of all other branches of the University who pursue activities within the countries in question; and a bad reputation, once gained, is difficult to improve.

What is needed is a firm, united stand, publicly taken, by leading institutional and private collectors against illicit commerce in these materials. We believe that Harvard has a generally good record in the policies that have been privately and independently developed by its several collecting agencies. But it is now highly desirable that our informal and private code be formalized and made public, and that Harvard join with other responsible institutions and private collectors in an effort to eliminate or at least diminish the power of the black market. Such an action will serve both the particular interests of various sectors of the University and the more general aims of teaching and research.

256

Regulatory legislation differs widely from country to country, and the different kinds of objects that are collected also differ widely in their method of production or appearance on the market, the channels through which they are normally procured, and the extent to which their origin and history can be reasonably documented. Certification is no guarantee; if the stakes are high enough, certificates can be bought or forged even more easily than art can be faked. On the other hand, objects from currently restricted areas may have been exported in the period before restrictions were imposed, or have come out through legal means, and they may be legitimately on the market. Because absolute criteria applicable to all cases are difficult or impossible to formulate, heavy reliance must be placed upon the knowledge and experience of the curatorial staff.

We believe that it is the business of the Curators of the several collections to master, as far as possible, these complexities in their individual fields of competence. Curators should be relied upon for judgment in such matters in their special fields, and they must assume responsibility for the decisions that they make. The integrity of Harvard's collecting policy must be firmly maintained. A Curator's basis for decision should be a matter capable of public record; whether it need actually be published will depend upon the circumstances surrounding each individual case. In doubtful cases and in unfamiliar circumstances Curators should have recourse to the advice of the General Counsel to the University, who may in turn call upon other Curators and officers of the University for assistance in reaching a decision. If a difference of opinion arises between branches of the University over a matter of acquisitions policy, and if agreement cannot be reached between the interested parties, a similar mechanism of advice and appeal should be available.

To a great extent the proposed rules reflect practices long observed by the collecting agencies of the University. It will be noted, however, that the rules are largely forward-looking. In view of the tangle of international legislation, the complications arising from trusteeship, the probability of conflicting claims, and the extreme difficulty or impossibility in many cases of establishing a clear and unbroken line of provenance for past acquisitions, something re-

257

sembling a statute of limitations must apply—as, in fact, it does among museum collections throughout the world. By taking a public stand along the lines we suggest, we hope that the University will play a significant role in the attempt to curb the abuses that have aroused so much public concern.

We therefore recommend that the President and Fellows adopt the following general principles to govern the University with respect to the acquisition (whether by gift, bequest, or purchase, or through the activities of scientific or archaeological expeditions) of works of art and antiquities:

1. The museum director, librarian, curator, or other University officer (hereinafter to be referred to as "Curator") responsible for making an acquisition or who will have custody of the acquisition should assure himself that the University can acquire valid title to the object in question. This means that the circumstances of the transaction and/or his knowledge of the object's provenance must be such as to give him adequate assurance that the seller or donor has valid title to convey.

2. In making a significant acquisition, the Curator should have reasonable assurance under the circumstances that the object has not, within a recent time, been exported from its country of origin (and/or the country where it was last legally owned) in violation of that country's laws.

3. In any event, the Curator should have reasonable assurance under the circumstances that the object was not exported after July 1, 1971, in violation of the laws of the country of origin and/or the country where it was last legally owned.

4. In cases of doubt in making the relevant determinations under paragraphs 1–3, the Curator should consult as widely as possible. Particular care should be taken to consult colleagues in other parts of the Univeristy whose collecting, research, or other activities may be affected by a decision to acquire an object. The Curator should also consult the General Counsel to the University where appropriate; and, where helpful, a special panel should be created to help pass on the questions raised.

5. The University will not acquire (by purchase, bequest, or gift) objects that do not meet the foregoing tests. If appropriate and

feasible, the same tests should be taken into account in determining whether to accept loans for exhibition or other purposes.

6. Curators will be responsible to the President and Fellows for the observance of these rules. All information obtained about the provenance of an acquisition must be preserved, and unless in the opinion of the relevant Curator and the General Counsel to the University special circumstances exist in a specific instance, all such information shall be available as a public record. Prospective vendors and donors should be informed of this policy.

7. If the University should in the future come into the possession of an object that can be demonstrated to have been exported in violation of the principles expressed in Rules 1–3 above, the University should, if legally free to do so, seek to return the object to the donor or vendor. Further, if with respect to such an object, a public museum or collection or agency of a foreign country seeks its return and demonstrates that it is a part of that country's national patrimony, the University should, if legally free to do so, take responsible steps to cooperate in the return of the object to that country.

3. THE FIELD MUSEUM OF NATURAL HISTORY STATEMENT ADOPTED JULY, 1972

1 (a) The Museum will not acquire any archaeological or ethnographic object that cannot be shown to the satisfaction of the Museum official or committee responsible for its acquisition to have been exported legally from its country of origin.

(b) Further, the Museum will refuse to acquire objects in any case where the responsible Museum official or committee has reasonable cause to believe that the circumstances of their recovery

259

involved the recent unscientific or intentional destruction of sites or monuments. These restrictions shall also apply to archaeological objects excavated in the United States.

(c) "Acquire" shall include acquisitions through purchase, gift or bequest. "Country of origin" means both "country of ultimate origin," when the objects in question have been recently transported across several international boundaries, and also "country of intermediate origin," when applied to objects anciently transported and then deposited in an archaeological or historical context.

(d) This Museum policy shall be taken into account in determining whether to accept loans for exhibition or other purposes.

2 This Museum policy shall apply especially to objects of appreciable market value. The pedigrees of such items will be subjected to particular scrutiny. Regardless of value, however, no archaeological or cultural object of any kind will be acquired unless the responsible Museum official or committee is satisfied as to the legality of its exportation and the circumstances of its recovery.

3 The Museum will hereafter acquire no questionable objects except those that can be demonstrated to have left their country of origin before the approved date of this document. The same date shall apply as to the acquisition of objects reasonably believed to have been illegally or unscientifically excavated within the United States. The responsible Museum official or committee shall be entitled, however, to utilize the principles contained in this Policy Statement in determining whether to acquire any object reasonably believed to have been improperly exported or recovered before that date.

4 The Museum has for many years refused to appraise archaeological objects. Extending this policy, the Museum shall hereafter refuse to authenticate any antiquity the acquisition of which by the vendor or owner does not meet the criteria listed in paragraphs 1 and 3. In this manner the Museum hopes to avoid encouraging, even indirectly, the trade in illicit or irresponsibly recovered antiquities.

5 In the future, if the Museum should inadvertently acquire an object that is thereafter determined by the responsible Museum official or committee to have been exported or recovered in violation

of this policy, the Museum shall promptly return the object to the transferor or, whenever appropriate, to the government of the country of origin or other proper owner thereof, as the case may be.

4. THE BROOKLYN MUSEUM POLICY ADOPTED DECEMBER, 1972

The Brooklyn Museum will not acquire or accept as a loan any work of art when it is either known or suspected that the work of art may be stolen property or may be in the United States illegally, *that is, contrary to the laws of this country*. When a work of art is in question, it is the responsibility of the curator to establish its provenance and, where indicated, to make all reasonable inquiries of the appropriate agencies of foreign governments to determine (a) that the Museum can obtain clear title and deed if a purchase is contemplated or (b) that a proposed lender has clear title and deed at the time the loan is made.

Where it is determined that a work of art offered to the Museum for purchase or loan is stolen property or is in the United States illegally, then the curator is responsible for reporting all of the pertinent facts to the Director at the earliest opportunity. The Director, at his discretion, will advise the appropriate law enforcement agencies.

Where any member of the Museum staff enters into an arrangement to purchase a work of art or to accept a loan of a work of art when there is doubt as to the legal status of the work, it is recognized that the member of staff may be becoming an accessory to a criminal act. Should this occur when the member of staff has failed to

261

take action as described above, then that member of staff will be considered to have committed both a breach of ethics and a breach of Museum policy.

(Author's Note: This statement was accepted by action of the Governing Committee at its regular meeting, December 12, 1972. The italicized language was added during the course of the Committee's discussion of the original draft statement submitted by the Director.)

APPENDIX D

1. RESOLUTION ADOPTED BY THE COUNCIL OF THE ARCHAEOLOGICAL INSTITUTE OF AMERICA, DECEMBER 27, 1970

RESOLVED, THAT:

The Archaeological Institute of America condemns the destruction of the historical and material record of the past by the plundering of archaeological sites both in the United States and abroad and by the illicit export and import of antiquities.

The Archaeological Institute of America supports wholeheartedly the UNESCO Draft Convention on the Means of Prohibiting and Preventing the Illicit Import, Export and Transfer of Ownership of Cultural Property, and urges ratification of the Draft Convention by the United States Government at the earliest practicable moment. It further urges its members, individually and through the local societies of the Institute, to make their support of the Draft Convention felt by communications to the appropriate Governmental authorities.

The Archaeological Institute of America calls upon its members, as well as educational institutions (universities and museums) in the United States and Canada, to refrain from purchasing and accepting donations of antiquities exported from their countries of origin in contravention to the terms of the UNESCO Draft Convention.

The Archaeological Institute of America urges that, in accordance with the provisions of the UNESCO Draft Convention, concerned countries take practical steps to facilitate the legitimate export, import and exchange of archaeological materials and antiquities.

The Archaeological Institute of America applauds the efforts of local authorities, both in the United States and abroad, to prevent the despoliation of archaeological sites and the illicit export and import of antiquities and archaeological materials, and pledges its support in such efforts.

2. REPORT OF THE AMERICAN ASSOCIATION OF MUSEUMS SPECIAL POLICY COMMITTEE MAY, 1971

The Special Policy Committee of the American Association of Museums has given careful consideration to the Draft Convention of UNESCO on the Means of Prohibiting and Preventing the Illicit Import, Export and Transfer of Ownership of Cultural Property.

We realize the importance of the preservation of the patrimony of each country, and we recognize the need to halt the wanton destruction of archaeological sites by illegal excavators in search of salable antiquities. We also realize our responsibilities to our museums whose function it is to collect, preserve, study and exhibit original works of art and antiquities.

Accordingly, on October 5, 1970, this Committee gave conditional approval to the UNESCO draft convention reserving the right to submit modifications at a later time before it is ratified by the United States Government.

Background

Cultural property can be divided broadly into two types. The first is the indigenous material produced in the country claiming control. This, of course, includes archaeological sites, ethnological works, objects of art and material of historic importance. The second type is composed of nonindigenous material which by happenstance is currently in a country. Many paintings and sculptures are housed in countries far removed from their place of origin. For instance, the Rosetta Stone and the Elgin marbles are in England, the Mona Lisa is in France, and the Pergamon Altar is in Berlin. These ownerships represent the fortunes of war, the chance of purchase, and the success of an expedition. While they are now considered to be national patrimony, they are not indigenous.

We are used to considering the United States as a rich nation and many of the other nations of the world as the "have nots." But in the field of cultural property, because of our comparatively recent founding, we must be considered a relative "have not" and many of the financially poor nations as culturally rich.

There is also the consideration of archaeological material, both from the standpoint of aesthetic values and from that of scientific documentation. Indigenous masterpieces are objects of national importance and they must be kept *in situ* or in the local museums. However, we believe that it is highly important to international understanding that the historic and cultural resources of nations be known beyond the boundaries of the nations that produced them. This is particularly important in the United States where there are people who are proud of their ancestry.

If illegal excavation and smuggling are to be eradicated, it is mandatory that the culturally rich nations set up legal methods of controlled exportation of duplicate material. This could be done by direct sale, exchange, or long term reciprocal loans. It is necessary that such arrangements be made simultaneously with the enforcement against illicit export. Only then will the vandal and the smuggler be stopped.

In regard to exportation of nonindigenous objects, most countries have export prohibitions on all major works. Objects are listed in a national register regardless of whether they are in a public or private collection. If a piece is to be sold and exported abroad, it must be approved by a governmental agency. In this area the United States is woefully vulnerable. Any piece of cultural property can be sold and exported freely from this country. Consequently, in recent years we have begun to experience a cultural drain as our works of art from private collections are being sold abroad in increasing numbers.

If now we are being asked to police the export of non-indigenous works from foreign countries, then we must enact similar prohibitions for the export of the cultural property from the United States. We must protect our patrimony, too, but this is more than a case of *quid pro quo*. We will need cultural property which can be exchanged with foreign governments or deposited on long term loan in return for their cultural works. Arrangements should be made for foreign sale of objects by review of a cultural property export board similar to the arrangements now in effect in Japan and England. The declared valuation for a sale would fix the price at which any United States institution would have the right of first purchase. If it were not exercised, the piece could be exported.

Recommendations

We urge individual and institutional members of the AAM to abstain from purchasing and accepting donations of antiquities exported from their country of origin in contravention to the terms of the UNESCO Draft Convention. This abstention is to apply only to antiquities from a country which has adopted the farsighted policy of making duplicate material available through legal channels, or has installed a procedure for granting export licenses to material which has been approved by a board of review. We feel that this policy of combining both the abstention of questionable acquisitions, and the requirement of the foreign government to make available duplicate material is the most effective method of achieving the objective of safeguarding archaeological sites and preserving national art treasures.

Joseph Veach Noble (Chairman), Director, Museum of the City of New York

Dr. William Bascom, Director, Robert H. Lowie Museum of Anthropology, University of California, Berkeley

Charles C. Cunningham, Director, The Art Institute of Chicago

Dr. Frederick J. Dockstader, Director, Museum of the American Indian

Dudley T. Easby, Chairman, Department of Primitive Art, The Metropolitan Museum of Art

Dr. Gordon S. Ekholm, Curator of Mexican Art (Pre-Columbian), The American Museum of Natural History

Dr. Sherman E. Lee, Director, The Cleveland Museum of Art

Dr. Froelich Rainey, Director, University Museum, University of Pennsylvania

3. RESOLUTION OF THE ASSOCIATION OF ART MUSEUM DIRECTORS ON ACQUISITION POLICY ADOPTED JANUARY 23, 1973

Be it resolved: That the Association of Art Museum Directors co-operate fully with foreign countries in their endeavors to prevent the illicit traffic in works of art.

The Association of Art Museum Directors believes that member museums can best implement such cooperation by refusing to acquire through purchase, gift or bequest objects of art imported into the United States or Canada in violation of the relevant laws obtaining in the countries of origin.

The directors, curators and governing bodies of member museums should, in determining the propriety of acquiring a given work of art, be governed by and act in accordance with the provisions adopted by states implementing the UNESCO Convention on the Means of Prohibiting and Preventing the Illicit Export, Import and Transfer of Ownership of Cultural Property as ratified by appropriate governmental authority.

In the event the governing board of a member museum believes it necessary to augment or further clarify the intent of this resolution and determine procedural methods for accomplishing the aim of this resolution, such a board should promulgate an appropriate acquisition policy statement commensurate with the by-laws and operational procedures of its institutions.

It is the recommendation of the members of this association that all nations establish effective export laws and develop proper controls over illegal export so that illicit traffic may be stopped at its sources. Wherever possible, within the limits of national law, encouragement should be given to a legitimate and honorable trade in works of art.

The United States and Canada are composed of peoples of many ethnic origins, people who take pride in their ethnic and cultural heritage. It is reasonable that these people desire to see these cultures represented in their local institutions. Therefore it is hoped that nations will release for acquisition, long term loan, or exchange duplicate material of high artistic quality for public display for the benefit of all people.

(Author's Note: The resolution was drafted by a special Committee on the Ethics of Acquisition chaired by Charles C. Cunningham, Chief Curator of the Sterling and Francine Clark Art Institute, Williamstown, formerly the Director of the Art Institute of Chicago; and Sherman E. Lee, Director of the Cleveland Museum of Art; Laurence Sickman, Director of the Nelson Gallery, Kansas City; and Daniel Robbins, Director of the Fogg Art Museum, Harvard University. The Association of Art Museum Directors is composed of approximately ninety directors of the major art museums in the United States and meets semiannually.)

APPENDIX E

1. UNITED STATES ANTIQUITIES LEGISLATION (1906)

An Act for the preservation of American antiquities.

Be it enacted by the Senate and House of Representatives of the United States of America in Congress assembled, That any person who shall appropriate, excavate, injure, or destroy any historic or prehistoric ruin or monument, or any object of antiquity, situated on lands owned or controlled by the Government of the United States, without the permission of the Secretary of the Department of the Government having jurisdiction over the lands on which said antiquities are situated, shall upon conviction, be fined in a sum of not more than five hundred dollars or be imprisoned for a period of not more than ninety days, or shall suffer both fine and imprisonment, in the discretion of the court.

SEC. 2. That the President of the United States is hereby authorized, in his discretion, to declare by public proclamation historic landmarks, historic and prehistoric structures, and other objects of historic or scientific interest that are situated upon the lands owned or controlled by the Government of the United States to be national monuments, and may reserve as a part thereof parcels of land, the limits of which in all cases shall be confined to the smallest area

269

compatible with the proper care and management of the objects to be protected: *Provided*, That when such objects are situated upon a tract covered by a bona fide unperfected claim or held in private ownership, the tract, or so much thereof as may be necessary for the proper care and management of the object, may be relinquished to the Government, and the Secretary of the Interior is hereby authorized to accept the relinquishment of such tracts in behalf of the Government of the United States.

SEC. 3. That permits for the examination of ruins, the excavation of archaeological sites, and the gathering of objects of antiquity upon the lands under their respective jurisdictions may be granted by the Secretaries of the Interior, Agriculture, and War to institutions which they may deem properly qualified to conduct such examination, excavation, or gathering, subject to such rules and regulations as they may prescribe: *Provided*, That the examinations, excavations, and gatherings are undertaken for the benefit of reputable museums, universities, colleges, or other recognized scientific or educational institutions, with a view to increasing the knowledge of such objects, and that the gatherings shall be made for permanent preservation in public museums.

SEC. 4. That the Secretaries of the Departments aforesaid shall make and publish from time to time uniform rules and regulations for the purpose of carrying out the provisions of this Act.

Approved, June 8, 1906 (34 Stat. L. 225).

2. TREATY OF COOPERATION BETWEEN THE UNITED STATES AND MEXICO PROVIDING FOR THE RECOVERY AND RETURN OF STOLEN ARCHAEOLOGICAL, HISTORICAL AND CULTURAL PROPERTIES ENTERED INTO FORCE MARCH, 1971

The United States of America and the United Mexican States, in a spirit of close cooperation and with the mutual desire to encourage the protection, study and appreciation of properties of archaeological, historical or cultural importance, and to provide for the recovery and return of such properties when stolen, have agreed as follows:

ARTICLE I

1. For the purposes of this Treaty, "archaeological, historical and cultural properties" are defined as

(a) art objects and artifacts of the pre-Columbian cultures of the United States of America and the United Mexican States of outstanding importance to the national patrimony, including stelae and architectural features such as relief and wall art;

(b) art objects and religious artifacts of the colonial periods of the United States of America and the United Mexican States of outstanding importance to the national patrimony;

(c) documents from official archives for the period up to 1920 that are of outstanding historical importance;

that are the property of federal, state, or municipal governments or their instrumentalities, including portions or fragments of such objects, artifacts, and archives.

2. The application of the foregoing definitions to a particular item shall be determined by agreement of the two governments, or failing agreement, by a panel of qualified experts whose appointment and procedures shall be prescribed by the two governments. The determinations of the two governments, or of the panel, shall be final.

271

ARTICLE II

1. The Parties undertake individually and, as appropriate, jointly

(a) to encourage the discovery, excavation, preservation, and study of archaeological sites and materials by qualified scientists and scholars of both countries;

(b) to deter illicit excavations of archaeological sites and the theft of archaeological, historical or cultural properties;

(c) to facilitate the circulation and exhibit in both countries of archaeological, historical and cultural properties in order to enhance the mutual understanding and appreciation of the artistic and cultural heritage of the two countries; and

(d) consistent with the laws and regulations assuring the conservation of national archaeological, historical and cultural properties, to permit legitimate international commerce in art objects.

2. Representatives of the two countries, including qualified scientists and scholars, shall meet from time to time to consider matters relating to the implementation of these undertakings.

ARTICLE III

1. Each Party agrees, at the request of the other Party, to employ the legal means at its disposal to recover and return from its territory stolen archaeological, historical and cultural properties that are removed after the date of entry into force of this Treaty from the territory of the requesting Party.

2. Requests for the recovery and return of designated archaeological, historical and cultural properties shall be made through diplomatic offices. The requesting Party shall furnish, at its expense, documentation and other evidence necessary to establish its claim to the archaeological, historical property.

3. If the requested Party cannot otherwise effect the recovery and return of a stolen archaeological, historical or cultural property located in its territory, the appropriate authority of the requested Party shall institute judicial proceedings to this end. For this purpose, the Attorney General of the United States of America is authorized to institute a civil action in the appropriate district court of the United States of America, and the Attorney General of the United Mexican States is authorized to institute proceedings in the

appropriate district court of the United Mexican States. Nothing in this Treaty shall be deemed to alter the domestic law of the Parties otherwise applicable to such proceedings.

ARTICLE IV

As soon as the requested Party obtains the necessary legal authorization to do so, it shall return the requested archaeological, historical, or cultural property to the persons designated by the requesting Party. All expenses incident to the return and delivery of an archaeological, historical or cultural property shall be borne by the requesting Party. No person or Party shall have any right to claim compensation from the returning Party for damage or loss to the archaeological, historical or cultural property in connection with the performance by the returning Party of its obligations under this Treaty.

ARTICLE V

Notwithstanding any statutory requirements inconsistent with this Treaty for the disposition of merchandise seized for violation of laws of the requested Party relating to the importation of merchandise, stolen archaeological, historical or cultural property which is the subject matter of this Treaty and has been seized, or seized and forfeited to the requested Party, shall be returned to the requesting Party in accordance with the provisions of this Treaty. The Parties shall not impose upon archaeological, historical or cultural property returned pursuant to this Treaty any charges or penalties arising from the application of their laws relating to the importation of merchandise.

3. LAW ON IMPORTATION OF PRE-COLUMBIAN
SCULPTURE AND MURALS (1972)

Mr. Mills of Arkansas, from the Committee on
Ways and Means, submitted the following

REPORT
(To accompany H.R. 9463)

(Author's Note: The authoritative analysis of this new legislation is contained in the following report submitted by Congressman Wilbur Mills, Chairman of the House Committee on Ways and Means.)

The Committee on Ways and Means, to whom was referred the bill (H.R. 9463) to prohibit the importation into the United States of pre-Columbian monumental and architectural sculpture, murals, and any fragment or part thereof, exported contrary to the laws of country of origin, and for other purposes, having considered the same, report favorably thereon with amendments and recommend that the bill as amended do pass. . . .

PURPOSE

The purpose of H.R. 9463, as reported, is to prohibit the importation into the United States of certain pre-Columbian monumental or architectural sculpture or murals if they are exported in violation of the laws of the country of origin, and to provide that any such sculpture or murals illegally imported into the United States be seized, forfeited, and thereafter either returned to the country of origin upon request therefor by such country, or otherwise disposed of in accordance with law.

GENERAL STATEMENT

H.R. 9463 was proposed by the Department of State to assist countries in Latin America which are experiencing serious depredation of archaeological sites of the pre-Columbian era. Your committee is informed that the ceremonial centers and architectural complexes of the ancient civilizations of Latin America are being pillaged and mutilated in order to meet the demands of a flourishing international market for pre-Columbian art objects. Frequently, art objects taken from these centers and complexes are broken into pieces and otherwise seriously damaged for the convenience of the looters who export the fragments from the country of origin for sale to collectors and cultural institutions.

Despite the efforts of most of the affected countries in Latin America to control the outflow of these culturally significant objects, the large number of sites, often in remote locations, and the high prices commanded by these objects in the international market, work against effective regulations. In addition, adequate resources are not available in some countries to prevent the pillage and exportation of these objects. Clandestine archaeological operations, which are encouraged by existing circumstances, destroy the scientific value of the objects and of the sites from which they are removed. While these problems are not unique to Latin America, your committee is informed that the situation in that area is particularly urgent.

Insofar as the United States is concerned, a number of illegally exported pre-Columbian treasures have appeared in this country. Also, it is not uncommon to see advertisements in art circulars for the sale of art objects coming from documented pre-Columbian Mayan sites. While legal remedies for the return of such objects are available in U.S. courts in some cases, these procedures can be extremely expensive and time consuming, and do not provide a meaningful deterrent to the pillage of pre-Columbian sites now taking place. A number of Latin American countries have requested the cooperation of the United States in stopping this pillage through the placing of controls on the importation of such objects not legally exported from those countries.

A panel of the American Society of International Law on International Movement of National Art Treasures has suggested to the Secretary of State that legislation be drafted which would prohibit the future importation into the United States of pre-Columbian monumental and architectural sculpture and murals exported without the consent of the exporting country. The legislation which was subsequently introduced as H.R. 9463, is supported by the panel of representatives of major collecting institutions and art dealers in this country as well as interested scientists and attorneys. Enactment of H.R. 9463 has also been recommended by the American Institute of Archaeology.

Your committee believes that the type of import limitations provided for in H.R. 9463, as reported, would be an effective means of assisting the interested countries in preserving their cultural heritage. In addition, such limitations will facilitate the work of American and foreign archaeologists.

PROVISIONS OF THE BILL

H.R. 9463, as reported, would prevent the importation into the United States of a narrow class of valuable archaeological objects exported contrary to the laws of the respective countries of origin. The objects to which the bill applies are pre-Columbian monumental or architectural sculpture or murals which are defined under section 5 (3) of the bill as any stone carving or wall art which (1) is a product of the pre-Columbian Indian culture of Mexico, Central America, South America, or the Caribbean Islands; (2) was an immobile monument or structure or was part of, or affixed to, any such monument or structure; and (3) is subject to export control by the country of origin. Under the first section of the bill, the Secretary of the Treasury, after consultation with the Secretary of State, is directed to promulgate, and from time to time revise, by regulation a list of stone carvings and wall art (which may be arranged by type or other suitable classification) which meet that definition.

Section 2 of the bill provides that a pre-Columbian sculpture or mural included on the list promulgated by the Secretary of the Treasury, or any part or fragment of such a listed object, may not be imported into the United States if it was exported from the country of origin (whether or not such exportation is to the United States) after the effective date of the regulation placing such sculpture or mural on the list unless the importer can produce a certificate issued by the government of the country of origin stating that the exportation was not in violation of the laws of that country.

An importer may enter a pre-Columbian sculpture or mural without such a certificate if he can produce (1) evidence establishing that the sculpture or mural or fragment thereof, was exported from the country of origin on or before the effective date of its listing, or (2) evidence that the sculpture or mural is not covered by the list. Section 2 of the bill further provides that an importer whose sculpture or mural has been seized at the time of entry has a period of 90 days, or such longer period as the Secretary of the Treasury may allow for good cause shown, to produce the certification or evidence necessary to establish his right to enter the sculpture or mural into the United States. During such period, the sculpture or mural will be retained in customs custody. Any sculpture or mural for which such documentation is not produced within the specified period is imported into the United States in violation of the bill.

Section 3 (a) of the bill provides for the seizure and forfeiture under the customs law of any sculpture or mural imported in violation of the bill. Seizures and forfeitures of such objects would be processed in the same manner for any other article imported contrary to law. Petitions may be filed under section 618 of the Tariff Act of 1930 (19 U.S.C. 1618) to mitigate any forfeiture where appropriate. Section 3(b) of the bill provides that any sculpture or mural which is forfeited shall be returned to the country of origin (which is defined in section 5(4) of the bill as the country where the sculpture or mural was first discovered) if that country bears all of the expenses incurred incident to such return and it complies with all other requirements relating to such return as may be prescribed by the Secretary of the Treasury. If a sculpture or mural is not returned to the country of origin, it will be disposed of in accordance with the laws which apply in the case of other articles forfeited for violation of the customs law.

Section 4 of the bill authorizes the Secretary of the Treasury to prescribe such rules and regulations as are necessary and appropriate to carry out the provisions of the act.

The Bureau of Customs has advised the committee that the application of such import controls to this limited class of objects is administratively feasible. Your committee believes that the enactment of this legislation should have the desired impact on the illicit traffic in pre-Columbian monumental and architectural art between Latin America and the United States.

(This legislation was adopted by the Congress and signed by the President in 1972.)

APPENDIX F

1. PRESIDENT NIXON'S MESSAGE OF
TRANSMITTAL OF CONVENTION
ON OWNERSHIP OF CULTURAL PROPERTY
(1972)

To the Senate of the United States:

With a view to receiving the advice and consent of the Senate to accession, I transmit herewith the Convention on the Prohibiting and Preventing the Illicit Import, Export and Transfer of Ownership of Cultural Property.

The illicit movement of national art treasures has become a matter of serious concern in the world community. Many countries have lost important cultural property through illegal exportation. The theft of art objects from museums, churches and collections is increasing. Rising prices for antiquities stimulate looting of archaeological sites, causing the destruction of irreplaceable resources for scientific and cultural studies. In addition, the appearance in the United States of important art treasures of suspicious origin gives rise to problems in our relations with other countries.

The Convention, adopted on November 14, 1970, by a vote of 77 to 1 with 8 abstentions at the Sixteenth General Conference of the United Nations Educational, Scientific and Cultural Organization, is a significant effort at multilateral cooperation to help preserve the cultural resources of mankind. Under the Convention, each state undertakes to protect its own cultural heritage and agrees to cooperate in a number of important but limited respects to help

279

protect the cultural heritage of other states. Perhaps the heart of the Convention from the standpoint of the United States is Article 9, which establishes an important new framework for international cooperation. Under this Article, the states parties undertake to participate in a concerted international effort to determine and to carry out the necessary corrective measures in cases in which a state's cultural patrimony is in jeopardy from pillage of archaeological or ethnological materials.

The Convention also requires states parties to prohibit the import of cultural property stolen from museums, public monuments or similar institutions and to take appropriate steps, upon request, to recover and return such cultural property. In addition, they pledge to take what measures they can, consistent with existing national legislation, to prevent museums and similar institutions within their territory from acquiring cultural property originating in another state party which has been illegally exported after entry into force of the Convention.

I am enclosing the report of the Secretary of State, which more fully explains the Convention and the reservation and understandings we recommend. Certain provisions of the Convention will require implementing legislation, which the Executive Branch will be prepared to discuss during the Senate's consideration of the Convention.

I believe international cooperation is required in order to preserve the priceless heritage of humanity, and I urge the Senate to give prompt advice and consent to the United States accession to this Convention, subject to the reservation and understandings recommended in the report of the Secretary of State.

Richard Nixon

The White House, February 2, 1972.

2. STATE DEPARTMENT SUMMARY
OF THE UNESCO CONVENTION

The Convention provides that the states parties recognize that the illicit import, export and transfer of ownership of cultural property is one of the main causes of the impoverishment of the cultural heritage of the countries of origin and pledge themselves to oppose these practices by a variety of specific measures. The Convention has no retroactive effect. Each state undertakes to protect its own cultural heritage through national services, as appropriate for each country, and to establish an export certificate for cultural property designated by each country as being of importance. The states parties are required to prohibit the import of cultural property stolen from museums, public monuments or similar institutions and to take appropriate steps, upon request, to recover and return such cultural property, provided that the state of origin is prepared to pay just compensation "to an innocent purchaser or to a person who has valid title to that property." Further, in cases of jeopardy to cultural patrimony by pillage of archaeological or ethnological materials, the states parties are to determine and apply controls on an *ad hoc* basis to specific materials.

The states parties to the Convention also undertake "to take the necessary measures, consistent with national legislation, to prevent museums and similar institutions within their territory from acquiring cultural property originating in another state party which has been illegally exported after entry into force of this Convention in the states concerned." The reference to "national legislation" was inserted in this paragraph to accommodate the problems of governments, such as the United States Government, which do not have legislation regulating the acquisition policy of private institutions. Thus, in the United States this provision would apply primarily to institutions controlled by the Federal Government. It is expected

281

that private institutions would develop their own code of ethics consistent with the spirit of this provision.

The Convention also includes other obligations of a general character that in most cases are subject to the existing legislation of each state party or to the discretion of each such state.

While the specific provisions of the main operative articles and the negotiating history of the Convention make clear that no retroactive effect is intended and that the provisions of the Convention are not intended to be self-executing, to avoid any ambiguity an understanding as follows would be appropriate: "The United States understands the provisions of the Convention to be neither self-executing nor retroactive."

ARTICLE BY ARTICLE ANALYSIS
(Excerpts)

Article 1

This Article defines "cultural property" for the purposes of the Convention. The text was inspired in part by a desire of some countries to conform the definition to the nomenclature of the 1950 Brussels Convention on Customs Cooperation. Additional categories of cultural property were added, and the whole was made subject to specific designation of cultural property by each state "as being of importance."

The operation of certain later articles depends upon the definition of "cultural property" in Article 1, as property designated by a state "as being of importance for archaeology, prehistory, history, literature, art or science." For example, Article 7(b) obliges a state party to bar the import and seek the return of "cultural property" stolen from certain institutions. Consequently, to enjoy the benefits of this provision, the United States will designate in its instrument of accession "as being of importance for archaeology, prehistory, history, literature, art or science" all cultural property encompassed by Article 1 of the Convention which has been or shall from time to time be accessioned to the collection of a museum or a religious or secular public monument or similiar institution in the United States. No further action would appear necessary to designate

United States cultural property more specifically at this time, but the right to do so would be clearly reserved. . . .

Article 3

This Article declares illicit the import, export or transfer of ownership of cultural property contrary to the provisions adopted under the Convention by the states parties. This Article was given varying interpretations by the states that participated in its negotiation. To insure against construction that might affect property rights, it would be advisable to adopt the following understanding: "The United States understands Article 3 not to modify property interests in cultural property under the laws of the States parties." . . .

Article 5

Article 5 concerns measures that states parties can take internally to insure the protection of their cultural heritage through the establishment of national services. Each state party is to determine in its discretion which of the measures contemplated in the Article are appropriate for it and to what extent. The fulfillment of the obligation of Article 5 should assure that the burdens of enforcing the substantive obligations of the Convention are fairly distributed among the parties to the Convention.

The "National Services" called for in Article 5 exist already to an extent in the United States. The National Park Service of the Department of the Interior is charged with the preservation of historic sites, monuments, antiquities and other objects on government reservations, and through grants-in-aid programs it assists the states in preservation planning, acquisition and development of historic properties. The Park Service maintains the National Register of Historic Places, and is assisted by the Advisory Council on Historic Preservation in protecting these registered properties from the effects of federally approved activities. The Library of Congress and the National Archives also have responsibilities for the protection of cultural property. Although not government agencies, the National Trust for Historic Preservation and the Smithsonian Institution are

283

chartered by Congress to perform national roles in the preservation and interpretation of historic properties and the national collections.

Article 6

Article 6 requires each state party to the Convention to prohibit the export of cultural property from its territory unless accompanied by an export certificate. It is recommended that the United States make a formal reservation to Article 6 as follows:

The United States reserves the right to determine whether or not to impose export controls over cultural property. While export controls may one day be deemed desirable, the United States should reserve the right to determine for itself whether or not it should impose such export controls.

Article 7

Under Article 7(a), a state party undertakes "to take the necessary measures, consistent with national legislation, to prevent museums and similar institutions within their territories from acquiring cultural property originating in another state party which has been illegally exported after entry into force of this Convention in the states concerned." The phrase "consistent with national legislation" was inserted at the suggestion of the United States. The United States Delegation to the UNESCO Sixteenth General Conference, which adopted the Convention, made a statement before voting that in its view Article 7(a) is a compromise provision which applies to institutions whose acquisition policy is subject to national control under domestic legislation, and that it does not require the enactment of new laws to establish national control over other institutions, but will exert powerful moral influence on all institutions. No delegation objected to the United States interpretation. It is suggested that an understanding along similar lines be made by the United States in acceding to the Convention, *viz.*, "The United States understands Article 7(a) to apply to institutions whose acquisition policy is subject to national control under existing domestic legislation and not to require the enactment of new legislation to establish national control over other institutions."

The term "illegally exported" in Article 7(a) should be interpreted only to refer to property exported in violation of Article 6.

Article 7(b) obligates states to prohibit the import of cultural property stolen from a museum or a religious or secular public monument or similar institution. The import prohibition would create a juridical basis for later actions to recover the cultural property involved. It is not expected that illicit cultural property ordinarily could be discovered by customs authorities at the frontier. In the United States and other countries judicial process frequently would be necessary to effect recovery. The procedures for recovery and return set forth in paragraph (ii) refer only to Article 7(b) (i) property. Article 7(b) would be implemented by appropriate legislation.

Article 7(b) does not affect existing remedies available in state or federal courts. The purpose is to provide a framework for special government cooperation. United States laws prohibit the knowing receipt and transportation of stolen property in interstate and foreign commerce. Stolen cultural property frequently can be recovered by normal police cooperation. Moreover, the true owner of stolen property could always bring an action in the appropriate court, and he might be able to recover the property without payment of compensation even if the holder were an innocent purchaser. Article 13(c) of the Convention specifically contemplates such actions. However, if the government is requested to bring a judicial action under Article 7(b) (ii) of the Convention to recover a foreign cultural property from one of its nationals, the requesting state must be prepared to pay "just compensation to an innocent purchaser or to a person who has valid title to that property."

This provision may require compensation in some cases of persons who would not be entitled to it under present American law, for example, the innocent purchaser of stolen property who does not acquire good title as against the true owner. Some countries, however, apparently insist that an "innocent purchaser" must be compensated. In order to ensure that existing remedies are preserved and that anomalies are minimized an understanding should be made as follows: "The United States understands that Article 7(b) is without prejudice to other remedies, civil or penal, available under the laws of the states parties for the recovery of stolen cultural property to the rightful owner without payment of compensation. The United States is further prepared to take the additional steps contemplated by Article 7(b) (ii) for the return of covered stolen property without payment of compensation, except to the extent required by the Constitution of the United States, for those states parties that agree to do the same for the United States institutions."

Article 7(b) is not tied by any reciprocity to Article 6, and a state party may claim its protection even if it has no export certificate system. At the Sixteenth General Conference of UNESCO, which adopted the Convention, the United States Delegate stated before voting that in his view application of Article 7(b), unlike 7(a), does not depend upon the existence of export controls in the state in which the property is stolen.

Article 8

This Article requires states to impose sanctions on persons responsible for infringing the export prohibitions established under Article 6(b) or the prohibition against importing stolen property found in Article 7(b). Article 6(b) will not be applicable to the United States unless and until it determines to apply export controls. With respect to Article 7(b), the laws of the United States, and presumably the laws of most states, prohibit theft and the receipt and transportation of stolen property. (See Title 18, United States Code, Sections 2314–15.) Further, Title 18 United States Code, Section 545 would apply to willful violations of Article 7(b) when that provision is implemented by statute.

Article 9

This Article contemplates the application of import or other controls on an *ad hoc* basis to specifically defined archaeological or ethnological materials in situations in which a state's cultural patrimony is in jeopardy from pillage of these materials. Appropriate controls would be determined and applied to specific materials by mutual agreement of the states parties most directly concerned. The Congress will be asked to enact legislation to establish an appropriate framework for United States participation in these negotiations and controls.

At the UNESCO Sixteenth General Conference, the United States Delegate said before voting that in his view the procedure in Article 9 for determination of concrete measures to deal with pillage of archaeological or ethnological materials will permit the states affected to determine by mutual agreement the measures that can be effective in each particular case to deal with the situation and to accept responsibility for carrying out those measures on a multilateral basis. Two examples of such situations are (1) the case in which the remains of a particular civilization are threatened with destruction or wholesale removal as may be true of certain pre-Columbian monuments, and (2) the case in which the international market for certain items has stimulated widespread illegal excavations destructive of important archaeological resources.

Interested states are to take provisional measures "to the extent feasible" in order to prevent irremediable injury to the cultural heritage of the state concerned.

Article 10

Paragraphs (a) and (b) require states to seek to combat illicit movement of cultural property through means of education. In addition, states are required by paragraph (a) to regulate antique dealers, as appropriate for each country. The language "as appropriate for each country" gives each state considerable discretion to determine what, if any, regulations and/or sanctions should be imposed and in what manner. Since such regulation is normally within the domain of the several States of the United States, and not the Federal Government, the following understanding is recommended:

The United States understands the words, "as appropriate for each country" in Article 10(a) as permitting each state party to determine the extent of regulation, if any, of antique dealers and declares that in the United States that determination would be made by the appropriate authorities of state and municipal governments.

Article 13

Article 13 deals in general terms with measures other than import controls to prevent illicit transfer of cultural property and to facilitate the restitution of such property. In the view of the Department of State, the language "consistent with the laws of each State," which applies to all the subparagraphs of the Article, insures that this Article does not require action by any state in conflict with or going beyond its existing laws.

Paragraph (a) is of relevance primarily to the exporting state.

Paragraph (b) contemplates the normal cooperation of law enforcement agencies and cultural services within the framework of existing law. Under United States procedures, the rightful owner of stolen property may be able to recover it through normal police action if issues and interests requiring litigation do not arise.

Paragraph (c) contemplating judicial actions for recovery of lost or stolen property conforms with United States law. The obligation of this Article is procedural, i.e., to provide a judicial remedy for the vindication of a property right if one exists. The action must be brought on behalf of the property owner; the right of a government to bring such an action would be determined by the law of the forum.

As paragraph (d) of Article 13 is worded, each state party must facilitate the recovery of certain cultural property exported illegally from another which has been declared by the latter to be "inalienable." The Chairman of the UNESCO Special Committee of Governmental Experts, in April 1970, said in his remarks on this Article that the obligation of subsection (d) would be satisfied if a state party opened its courts to admit action for recovery of lost and stolen articles under subsection (c) of Article 13. Presumably, the relevant law in the United States would recognize the validity of foreign legislation declaring certain cultural property within the jurisdiction of a foreign state to be inalienable. Illegal removal of such property without consent of the owner should be recognized as theft. This provision is not self-executing, however, and in the absence of federal legislation, the decision in each case would be governed by state law.

To avoid any appearance of a commitment broader than intended, the following understanding is proposed:

The United States understands Article 13(d) as applying to objects removed from the country of origin after the entry into force of this Convention for the states concerned, and, as stated by the Chairman of the Special Committee of Governmental Experts that prepared the text, and reported in paragraph 28 of the Report of that Committee, the means of recovery of cultural property under subparagraph (d) are the judicial actions referred to in subparagraph (c) of Article 13, and that such actions are controlled by the law of the requested State, the requesting State having to submit necessary proofs.

Conclusion

I believe that the illicit movement of cultural property is a serious problem that warrants action on the international plane. The UNESCO Convention represents a pragmatic approach that deserves our strong support. Not only is the United States sympathetic to this effort to help other countries stem the illegal outflow of their national art treasures, but in addition we should recognize that accession to this Convention is in our national interest. The destruction of irreplaceable remains of ancient civilizations is a loss to the cultural heritage of all mankind. And the appearance of important art treasures of suspicious origin in the United States gives rise to problems in our relations with other countries. Some countries have reacted to this problem in a fashion which unduly restricts the work of archaeologists within their territories as well as the legitimate trade of cultural property. In seeking to prevent the illegitimate trade in cultural property, the Convention should allay the anxieties of these countries and thus encourage the liberalization of laws governing the legitimate trade in such property. Moreover, the Convention should create a climate more conducive to the continued work of American archaeologists abroad. Further, Article 7 (b) is of direct benefit to the United States for it would require states to prohibit the import of, and take appropriate steps to recover and return, cultural property stolen from museums, religious or secular public monuments, or similar institutions.

The Convention is a balanced document. It represents an accommodation of the interests of the art importing and art exporting states and contains a realistic allocation of burdens. The Convention recognizes that the primary responsibility for the prevention of illegal export of cultural property rests on the individual states concerned. It recognizes, however, that a multilateral effort to deal with the problem is also required. Thus Article 9 provides a flexible framework for the development of future international cooperation in this area. If special cases should arise in which the multilateral actions contemplated by this Article are not adequate to prevent significant impairment of important archaeological materials or sites, the United States Government would remain free to consider what further measures of cooperation it might be able to undertake that could be effective in the circumstances. On the whole, the Convention is a significant effort to deal with a complex problem that does not easily yield to legal solutions. While it is a compromise text and contains several ambiguities, it should be possible to overcome these problems by the reservation and understandings I have suggested.

Concerned private groups have supported the Convention. A lawyers' committee of the American Society of International Law Panel on the International Movement of Art Treasures sent me a letter on October 21, 1970, enclosing its report and recommending that "the United States should approve it [the Convention] with certain explicit reservations and understandings." That general approach has also been supported by the Special Policy Committee of the American Association of Museums. On December 30, 1970, the Archaeological Institute of America passed a resolution by a vote of 103 to 8, with 7 abstentions, supporting the UNESCO Convention "wholeheartedly" and urging ratification by the United States "at the earliest practical moment." The Society for American Archaeology and the College Art Association have also adopted resolutions supporting the UNESCO Convention.

United States accession to this Convention at an early date is, in my opinion, in the interests of the United States, and, in addition, would indicate to other countries our honest desire to deal with the

problem of illicit international movement of national art treasures.
Respectfully submitted.

William P. Rogers
Secretary of State

3. CONVENTION ON THE MEANS OF PROHIBITING AND PREVENTING THE ILLICIT IMPORT, EXPORT AND TRANSFER OF OWNERSHIP OF CULTURAL PROPERTY (1970)

The General Conference of the United Nations Educational, Scientific and Cultural Organization, meeting in Paris from 12 October to 14 November 1970, at its sixteenth session,

Recalling the importance of the provisions contained in the Declaration of the Principles of International Cultural Co-operation, adopted by the General Conference at its fourteenth session,

Considering that the interchange of cultural property among nations for scientific, cultural and educational purposes increases the knowledge of the civilization of Man, enriches the cultural life of all peoples and inspires mutual respect and appreciation among nations,

Considering that cultural property constitutes one of the basic elements of civilization and national culture, and that its true value can be appreciated only in relation to the fullest possible information regarding its origin, history and traditional setting,

Considering that it is incumbent upon every State to protect the cultural property existing within its territory against the dangers of theft, clandestine excavation, and illicit export,

Considering that, to avert these dangers, it is essential for every

State to become increasingly alive to the moral obligations to respect its own cultural heritage and that of all nations,

Considering that, as cultural institutions, museums, libraries and archives should ensure that their collections are built up in accordance with universally recognized moral principles,

Considering that the illicit import, export and transfer of ownership of cultural property is an obstacle to that understanding between nations which is part of UNESCO's mission to promote by recommending to interested States, international conventions to this end,

Considering that the protection of cultural heritage can be effective only if organized both nationally and internationally among States working in close co-operation,

Considering that the UNESCO General Conference adopted a Recommendation to this effect in 1964,

Having before it further proposals on the means of prohibiting and preventing the illicit import, export and transfer of ownership of cultural property, a question which is on the agenda for the session as item 19,

Having decided, at its fifteenth session, that this question should be made the subject of an international convention,

Adopts this Convention on the fourteenth day of November 1970.

ARTICLE 1

For the purposes of this Convention, the term "cultural property" means property which, on religious or secular grounds, is specifically designated by each State as being of importance for archaeology, prehistory, history, literature, art or science and which belongs to the following categories:

(a) Rare collections and specimens of fauna, flora, minerals and anatomy, and objects of palaeontological interest;

(b) property relating to history, including the history of science and technology and military and social history, to the life of national leaders, thinkers, scientists and artists and to events of national importance;

(c) products of archaeological excavations (including regular and clandestine) or of archaeological discoveries;

(d) elements of artistic or historical monuments or archaeological sites which have been dismembered;

(e) antiquities more than one hundred years old, such as inscriptions, coins and engraved seals;

(f) objects of ethnological interest;

(g) property of artistic interest, such as:

(i) pictures, paintings and drawings produced entirely by hand on any support and in any material (excluding industrial designs and manufactured articles decorated by hand);

(ii) original works of statuary art and sculpture in any material;

(iii) original engravings, prints and lithographs;

(iv) original artistic assemblages and montages in any material;

(h) rare manuscripts and incunabula, old books, documents and publications of special interest (historical, artistic, scientific, literary, etc.) singly or in collections;

(i) postage, revenue and similar stamps, singly or in collections;

(j) archives, including sound, photographic and cinematographic archives;

(k) articles of furniture more than one hundred years old and old musical instruments.

ARTICLE 2

1. The States Parties to this Convention recognize that the illicit import, export and transfer of ownership of cultural heritage of the countries of origin of such property and that international cooperation constitutes one of the most efficient means of protecting each country's cultural property against all the dangers resulting therefrom.

2. To this end, the States Parties undertake to oppose such practices with the means at their disposal, and particularly by removing their causes, putting a stop to current practices, and by helping to make the necessary reparations.

ARTICLE 3

The import, export or transfer of ownership of cultural property effected contrary to the provisions adopted under this Convention by the States Parties thereto, shall be illicit.

ARTICLE 4

The States Parties to this Convention recognize that for the purpose of the Convention property which belongs to the following categories forms part of the cultural heritage of each State:

(a) Cultural property created by the individual or collective genius of nationals of the State concerned, and cultural property of importance to the State concerned created within the territory of that State by foreign nationals or stateless persons resident within such territory;

(b) cultural property found within the national territory;

(c) cultural property acquired by archaeological, ethnological or natural science missions, with the consent of the competent authorities of the country of origin of such property;

(d) cultural property which has been the subject of a freely agreed exchange;

(e) cultural property received as a gift or purchased legally with the consent of the competent authorities of the country of origin of such property.

ARTICLE 5

To ensure the protection of their cultural property against illicit import, export and transfer of ownership, the States Parties to this Convention undertake, as appropriate for each country, to set up within their territories one or more national services, where such services do not already exist, for the protection of the cultural heritage, with a qualified staff sufficient in number for the effective carrying out of the following functions:

(a) Contributing to the formation of draft laws and regulations designed to secure the protection of the cultural heritage and particularly prevention of the illicit import, export and transfer of ownership of important cultural property;

294

(b) establishing and keeping up to date, on the basis of a national inventory of protected property, a list of important public and private cultural property whose export would constitute an appreciable impoverishment of the national cultural heritage;

(c) promoting the development or the establishment of scientific and technical institutions (museums, libraries, archives, laboratories, workshops . . .) required to ensure the preservation and presentation of cultural property;

(d) organizing the supervision of archaeological excavations, ensuring the preservation "in situ" of certain cultural property, and protecting certain areas reserved for future archaeological research;

(e) establishing, for the benefit of those concerned (curators, collectors, antique dealers, etc.) rules in conformity with the ethical principles set forth in this Convention; and taking steps to ensure the observance of those rules;

(f) taking educational measures to stimulate and develop respect for the cultural heritage of all States, and spreading knowledge of the provisions of this Convention;

(g) seeing that appropriate publicity is given to the disappearance of any items of cultural property.

ARTICLE 6

The State Parties to this Convention undertake:

(a) To introduce an appropriate certificate in which the exporting State would specify that the export of the cultural property in question is authorized. The certificate should accompany all items of cultural property in accordance with the regulations;

(b) to prohibit the exportation of cultural property from their territory unless accompanied by the above-mentioned export certificate;

(c) to publicize this prohibition by appropriate means, particularly among persons likely to export or import cultural property;

ARTICLE 7

The States Parties to this Convention undertake:

(a) To take the necessary measures, consistent with national legislation, to prevent museums and similar institutions within their territories from acquiring cultural property originating in another State Party which has been illegally exported after entry into force of this Convention, in the States concerned. Whenever possible, to inform a State of origin Party to this Convention of an offer of such cultural property illegally removed from that State after the entry into force of this Convention in both States;

(b) (i) to prohibit the import of cultural property stolen from a museum or a religious or secular public monument or similar institution in another State Party to this Convention after the entry into force of this Convention for the States concerned, provided that such property is documented as appertaining to the inventory of that institution;

(ii) at the request of the State Party of origin, to take appropriate steps to recover and return any such cultural property imported after the entry into force of this Convention in both States concerned, provided, however, that the requesting State shall pay just compensation to an innocent purchaser or to a person who has valid title to that property. Requests for recovery and return shall be made through diplomatic offices. The requesting Party shall furnish, at its expense, the documentation and other evidence necessary to establish its claim for recovery and return. The Parties shall impose no customs duties or other charges upon cultural property returned pursuant to this Article. All expenses incident to the return and delivery of the cultural property shall be borne by the requesting Party.

ARTICLE 8

The States Parties to this Convention undertake to impose penalties or administrative sanctions on any person responsible for infringing the prohibitions referred to under Articles 6 (b) and 7 (b) above.

ARTICLE 9

Any State Party to this Convention whose cultural patrimony is in jeopardy from pillage of archaeological or ethnological materials may call upon other States Parties who are affected. The States Parties to this Convention undertake, in these circumstances, to participate in a concerned international effort to determine and to carry out the necessary concrete measures, including the control of exports and imports and international commerce in the specific materials concerned. Pending agreement each State concerned shall take provisional measures to the extent feasible to prevent irremediable injury to the cultural heritage of the requesting State.

ARTICLE 10

The States Parties to this Convention undertake:

(a) To restrict by education, information and vigilance, movement of cultural property illegally removed from any State Party to this Convention and, as appropriate for each country, oblige antique dealers, subject to penal or administrative sanctions, to maintain a register recording the origin of each item of cultural property, names and addresses of the supplier, description and price of each item sold and to inform the purchaser of the cultural property of the export prohibition to which such property may be subject;

(b) to endeavour by educational means to create and develop in the public mind a realization of the value of cultural property and the threat to the cultural heritage created by theft, clandestine excavations and illicit exports.

ARTICLE 11

The export and transfer of ownership of cultural property under compulsion arising directly or indirectly from the occupation of a country by a foreign power shall be regarded as illicit.

ARTICLE 12

The States Parties to this Convention shall respect the cultural heritage within the territories for the international relations of

297

which they are responsible, and shall take all appropriate measures to prohibit and prevent the illicit import, export and transfer of ownership of cultural property in such territories.

ARTICLE 13

The States Parties to this Convention also undertaken, consistent with the laws of each State:

(a) To prevent by all appropriate means transfers of ownership of cultural property likely to promote the illicit import or export of such property;

(b) to ensure that their competent services co-operate in facilitating the earliest possible restitution of illicitly exported cultural property to its rightful owner;

(c) to admit actions for recovery of lost or stolen items of cultural property brought by or on behalf of the rightful owners;

(d) to recognize the indefeasible right of each State Party to this Convention to classify and declare certain cultural property as inalienable which should therefore *ipso facto* not be exported, and to facilitate recovery of such property by the State concerned in cases where it has been exported.

ARTICLE 14

In order to prevent illicit export and to meet the obligations arising from the implementation of this Convention, each State Party to the Convention should, as far as it is able, provide the national services responsible for the protection of its cultural heritage, with an adequate budget and, if necessary, should set up a fund for this purpose.

ARTICLE 15

Nothing in this Convention shall prevent States Parties thereto from concluding special agreements among themselves or from continuing to implement agreements already concluded regarding the restitution of cultural property removed, whatever the reason, from its territory of origin, before the entry into force of this Convention for the States concerned.

ARTICLE 16

The States Parties to this Convention shall in their periodic reports submitted to the General Conference of the United Nations Educational, Scientific and Cultural Organization on dates and in a manner to be determined by it, give information on the legislative and administrative provisions which they have adopted and other action which they have taken for the application of this Convention, together with details of the experience acquired in this field.

ARTICLE 17

1. The States Parties to this Convention may call on the technical assistance of the United Nations Educational, Scientific and Cultural Organization, particularly as regards:

(a) Information and education;

(b) consultation and expert advice;

(c) co-ordination and good offices.

2. The United Nations Educational, Scientific and Cultural Organization may, on its own initiative conduct research and publish studies on matters relevant to the illicit movement of cultural property.

3. To this end, the United Nations Educational, Scientific and Cultural Organization may also call on the co-operation of any competent non-governmental organization.

4. The United Nations Educational, Scientific and Cultural Organization may, on its own initiative, make proposals to States Parties to this Convention for its implementation.

5. At the request of at least two States Parties to this Convention which are engaged in a dispute over its implementation, UNESCO may extend its good offices to reach a settlement between them.

ARTICLE 18

This Convention is drawn up in English, French, Russian and Spanish, the four texts being equally authoritative.

ARTICLE 19

1. This Convention shall be subject to ratification or acceptance by States members of the United Nations Educational, Scientific

and Cultural Organization in accordance with their respective constitutional procedures.

2. The instruments of ratification or acceptance shall be deposited with the Director-General of the United Nations Educational, Scientific and Cultural Organization.

ARTICLE 20

1. This Convention shall be open to accession by all States not members of the United Nations Educational, Scientific and Cultural Organization which are invited to accede to it by the Executive Board of the Organization.

2. Accession shall be effected by the deposit of an instrument of accession with the Director-General of the United Nations Educational, Scientific and Cultural Organization.

ARTICLE 21

The Convention shall enter into force three months after the date of the deposit of the third instrument of ratification, acceptance or accession, but only with respect to those States which have deposited their respective instruments on or before that date. It shall enter into force with respect to any other State three months after the deposit of its instrument of ratification, acceptance or accession.

ARTICLE 22

The States Parties to this Convention recognize that the Convention is applicable not only to their metropolitan territories but also to all territories for the international relations of which they are responsible; they undertake to consult, if necessary, the governments or other competent authorities of these territories on or before ratification, acceptance or accession with a view to securing the application of the Convention to those territories, and to notify the Director-General of the United Nations Educational, Scientific and Cultural Organization of the territories to which it is applied, the notification to take effect three months after the date of its receipt.

ARTICLE 23

1. Each State Party to this Convention may denounce the Convention on its own behalf or on behalf of any territory for whose international relations it is responsible.

2. The denunciation shall be notified by an instrument in writing, deposited with the Director-General of the United Nations Educational, Scientific and Cultural Organization.

3. The denunciation shall take effect twelve months after the receipt of the instrument of denunciation.

ARTICLE 24

The Director-General of the United Nations Educational, Scientific and Cultural Organization shall inform the States members of the Organization, the States not members of the Organization which are referred to in Article 20, as well as the United Nations, of the deposit of all the instruments of ratification, acceptance and accession provided for in Articles 19 and 20, and of the notifications and denunciations provided for in Articles 22 and 23 respectively.

ARTICLE 25

1. This Convention may be revised by the General Conference of the United Nations Educational, Scientific and Cultural Organization. Any such revision shall, however, bind only the States which shall become Parties to the revising convention.

2. If the General Conference should adopt a new convention revising this Convention in whole or in part, then, unless the new convention otherwise provides, this Convention shall cease to be open to ratification, acceptance or accession, as from the date on which the new revising convention enters into force.

APPENDIX G

THE NBC "TODAY" SHOW: THE VASE UNVEILED

(Author's Note: Metropolitan Director Thomas P. F. Hoving and Dietrich von Bothmer, curator, appeared on the nationally broadcast morning show following the announcement, on November 12, 1972, of the purchase of the Euphronios krater. Mr. Hoving's own words convey the tone and flavor of the Metropolitan's outlook during his tenure.)

FRANK MCGEE: This morning we'll get our chance to discover the source of Keats's enthusiasm because we have in our studio a great work of beauty, the Metropolitan Museum of Art's most recent important acquisition, a sixth-century B.C. Greek vase by the artist Euphronios, said to have cost the museum $1 million in cash and $300,000 in ancient Greek gold coins. It has been carefully, quite carefully, brought to our studio by Thomas Hoving, the director of the Metropolitan Museum, and Dr. Dietrich von Bothmer, the museum's curator of Greek and Roman art. Gentlemen, welcome and thank you for bringing the vase which I call vase [pronounced vāz] and which Barbara [Walters] called vase [pronounced väz]. It doesn't matter to the studio. Now, how did you get it, who did you buy it from and how much did it cost?

HOVING: Three of the questions the museum in its crafty way never answers, but I'll try to give you some information on it. The poor people have to know about this.

We got it from a dealer who was the agent for a person who has had this in the family collection since about the First World War and we don't talk about the name of these people because they have other things that we might want to buy in the future. You know, we might lose some of these things.

302

McGEE: That's part of your understanding with them then, I take it.

HOVING: People prefer to remain anonymous in this type of business.

And then as far as prices, the Metropolitan has a policy that we never divulge it. And all I can say is what has been reported about it is high. We got a far better deal on this great beauty than what has been reported.

McGEE: Somewhat less than a million dollars, then.

HOVING: All I can do with that is to smile smugly and say [laughter] . . .

McGEE: Well actually what is more important—there's one other aspect of this controversy I suppose we should take up. There has been some criticism as you know far better than I that the museum has recently disposed of some paintings that many people felt should not have been removed from the museum. This was done rather on the sly—if I may use that word. And then you take the money—that's not the same money, but money from the museum and purchase this vase on the sly. Is this the sort of thing that the museum must do? Why do you have to be so—if I'm using the right word—sly about it?

HOVING: I don't think it's quite the right word. What we've done is to take works of art from various departments in the museum and there are seventeen of them including the Paintings Department and weeded out those things that to us no longer look as important as they once did, within the overall collection, that they are not as great as other things that we have by the same man or that exist in the City of New York. And we'd take those and we'd exchange or trade or sell them for cash to buy things that are unique and magnificent and of which we have none.

And this great, great calyx krater which it is called because of its shape is by the—I would suppose one of the top two greatest Greek vase painters in existence—and it is the best piece known by him to be in the world and this is one of these moments in museum collecting that in my opinion is the perfect example and the perfect justification for trading out the stuff that we no longer want to

303

show and to put in their place things that indeed will be one of the top pieces in the entire museum which has three million works of art in it.

McGEE: Well, without disputing your appraisal and your judgment that this is a work of art at all I am given to understand, Dr. von Bothmer, that this vase is not referred to in any literature on Greek vases, that there was precious little if any consultation with other authorities in the field before you made the purchase. How did you establish its authenticity?

VON BOTHMER: By looking at it. Simply by looking at it. I've looked at many.

McGEE: And you're confident with his look, obviously, Mr. Hoving?

HOVING: Well, Dietrich von Bothmer has been involved in the business of Greek vase painting for forty-two years. He was trained by the great Sir John Beazley, who was the man who literally started this science of dating and naming painters of these vases. There must be tens of thousands in the world; I imagine you've seen pretty much all of them. . . .

VON BOTHMER: About two-thirds of them.

HOVING: About two-thirds of them. An expert like that can literally in an instant know.

McGEE: Without even seeming to imply that I question your credentials, I'm just curious to know how you can know. Can you tell me how you can know that this is the work of Euphronios and that it is his best.

VON BOTHMER: Well, we have a slight help, because he happened to sign his name.

McGEE: That does help, doesn't it?

VON BOTHMER: It helps. But even if he had not signed his name it would have been relatively easy to attribute it to Euphronios. It would have been more difficult to attribute the potting to Euxitheos. That would be a somewhat trickier question.

WALTERS: I've listened but I might have missed something. Did you get this from a person who is Greek and is in Greece? I wondered why they would let it out of the country.

Hoving: Well, two things are important. First, at this time— Dietrich, I'm sure you'd agree with this—in the sixth century B.C. and the fifth century B.C. the great potters of Greece were there in Greece but they exported. You find pieces of great Greek pottery from England made their way to Tripoli. So it was a big industry that sent these things around.

Secondly, we bought it from somebody who happened to be in the country of Switzerland, who was acting as the agent for somebody who was even in another country whose family's had it since around the First World War and that goes back a nice long time.

Walters: If I came into the museum and, if anyone, you wanted to tell me or to give me a little lesson in what it is—whatever it is that makes this so superb and what I should know to appreciate it. What should I see?

von Bothmer: Well, to begin with the shape. The calyx krater is perhaps one of the most elegant vase shapes there is. It had a long history. It was copied later in Roman times and exists even today, alas, in the shape of flower pots and other urns.

Walters: A jug.

von Bothmer: No, not a jug. A jug is always supporting. This happened to be a mixing bowl for wine and water. Now after you have appreciated the shape I shall recommend that you locate the superb drawing because here you have a line which had to be correct the moment the glaze touched the plate. There was no chance of correcting anything, no way of using an eraser or a sponge. It had to be done in one fell swoop.

Walters: Are these the original colors?

von Bothmer: They are not faded. Remember another thing— at the time the vase was painted it did not have the warm terra- cotta color. It was gray. Clay is gray until it is fired and the glaze that was applied to it was also gray. So it is almost like making a design in invisible ink, and you do not get the results until after the firing.

McGee: That clearly is very difficult.

von Bothmer: Yes.

McGee: Do I see a little chip?

305

VON BOTHMER: Well, this is more than, in shape this is more important than a chip. It happens to be an ancient repair.

McGEE: A repair?

VON BOTHMER: Yes. A crack developed in the vase. It didn't go all the way through and they valued it so highly that they decided to pull the crack together with a bronze staple.

WALTERS: As long as we can do it, Frank.

McGEE: We're going to take a station.

[Commercials]

McGEE: We're talking actually about this Greek vase with Thomas Hoving and Dr. Dietrich von Bothmer, and you were explaining, Dr. von Bothmer, that at one time a crack appeared in the vase.

VON BOTHMER: Yes, and it was immediately repaired and significantly enough it was repaired in such a manner so as to not cut across the drawing. You will observe only on the black rim and in the black portion above the shoulder of this athlete do you have the evidence of the bronze staple and what is now a groove or channel may have been filled with wax or some other material in antiquity.

HOVING: This means of course that in its day, maybe a hundred years after it had been made, it was considered to be so extraordinarily precious and beautiful, the drawing on it so perfect, that it was very carefully repaired.

WALTERS: I don't know how you got this to the studio today. Was it all wrapped up in things and stuff on a truck, or did you both carry it down?

HOVING: We have a whole crew of specialists who are standing just offstage there looking very intently at all of us and they brought it down and they're expert at this and they've had a number of years of training and know exactly how to do it. We don't like to do it very often, I'll tell you that. We don't do this every morning.

McGEE: I'm told very often the paintings on the back if there is such a thing as a back of a Greek vase are of secondary importance. Is that true in this case?

VON BOTHMER: Not secondary, simply a little less dramatic. After all the drama . . .

306

McGEE: May I interrupt? How does one tell the front from the back?

VON BOTHMER: Supposing you had no figures, I would tell by the ornament. The ornament on the front is a double lotus palmette and if you turn it to the back you will see that this rather elaborate chain has given way to a single row of palmettes, so that would be your ordinary difference between front and back.

McGEE: The less elaborate would be the back.

VON BOTHMER: Yes, the less elaborate and they call it the more summery.

WALTERS: What do you call this, by the way? What do you say? Do you say "vāz" or "väz"?

VON BOTHMER: Well in England I've said "väz," but here I say "vāz."

McGEE: But you were explaining about the pictures, the drawings on the back of this one.

VON BOTHMER: The drawing you see of the ornament will give you one clue and when you look at the subject and the difference is in the composition. Here you have the height of compositional art of the late archaic period. The most moving subject—the removal of the body of Sarpedon while the twin brothers sleep in death flanked by two Trojans with Hermes standing behind. A truly memorable picture.

WALTERS: Mr. Hoving, can I ask one question? One of the things Frank asked Mr. von Bothmer—how do you know? And you said because I know. The kind of confidence and autocracy for which you have been known in your career. There are people who feel that a museum director should communicate more with the public, that the public should be more involved. You have tended more in your career to say this is the way I think it should be and you just have to trust me, boys.

HOVING: Well, I'm a schizophrenic, I think you'd probably get that from most people. On the one hand I'm the advocate of getting art to the people and getting people to understand more about art.

WALTERS: You've been criticized for that, too.

HOVING: On the other hand, being in this business since 1959 and an expert in having backup from extraordinary experts like

Dietrich we feel that that part of it is the surgeon's part of the job and only our hands can do that.

WALTERS: Are people upset when they give you costly paintings and then you sell them?

HOVING: Not at all, because they give us permission to do so.

WALTERS: They do?

HOVING: Yeah. Often when they give it to us they say, by the way, if you want to get rid of this and get something better, do it, and we put their name on the new thing and on this beautiful thing the names of three donors of past times that used to be on things the public didn't see are now on this incomparable piece.

McGEE: Was there any tax consideration at all involved in the person from whom you purchased this?

HOVING: I would probably think not but it would be in his own country which happened to be in the country of Switzerland.

McGEE: It didn't cheat the American taxpayer out of any money?

HOVING: No, not at all, no. It's over a hundred years old, therefore there's no tax as it comes into this country. We're very careful now.

McGEE: Thank you again for being with us.

HOVING: Thanks very much.

McGEE: And bringing the vase. A station break.

NOTES

CHAPTER ONE

4 The postwar art boom . . . See Keen, 1971, pp. 17–32; Rush, 1961, pp. 1–6; Reitlinger, 1961, pp. 222–38.

4 The gallery's chief . . . See Brough, 1963, p. 145.

4 but auctions are public . . . See Keen, 1971, p. 24.

4 As early as . . . See Hodgins and Lesley, 1955.

5 Not long ago . . . See "Value of Works of Art," letter to London *Times*, October 25, 1971, and comments on October 27 and 30.

6 The theft of . . . See R. McFadden, 18 November 1972 and Interpol fliers.

8 After the fighting . . . See Haque, 1972, p. 2.

8–9 Parke-Bernet . . . See Lucie-Smith, 1973.

9 Press releases . . . See *The Green Collection of American Indian Art*, Parke-Bernet catalogue, 1971.

10 The headlines the next day . . . See Gratz, 1971, and unsigned article in *New York Times*, November 20, 1971.

10 Made a millennium . . . See Miguel Covarrubias, *The Eagle, The Jaguar and the Serpent* (New York, 1954: Knopf), pp. 214–15.

11 In a letter . . . Private communication to author, dated June 24, 1972.

13 a Colima dog . . . See Saarinen, 1958, p. 392.

14 These prints . . . See Keen, 1971, p. 32.

14 "Here is . . ." . . . Bloomingdale's flier in author's possession.

14 With an eye to . . . Kennard catalogue in author's possession.

17 Early in 1966 . . . All details from personal interviews.

20 The collection had its beginning . . . See Meyer, 1964.

21 When a small . . . All details from personal interviews.

23 "Before Cortés . . ." See Meyer "Hello, Columbus," 1970.

26 If one were . . . See Jorge Luján Muñoz, 1965.

27 The Brooklyn Museum's . . . See Knox, 6 June 1972.

27 In January . . . See Melton, 21 January, 28 January, 26 June 1969.

27 In an article . . . See Melton, 17 November 1968.

28 A more sophisticated . . . See College Art Association, 1971, pp. 11–12.

29 The Center display . . . See Meyer, 1971.

31 The first fruit . . . See Graham, 1967.

31 Mr. Graham prepared . . . See Graham, 1969.

32 Early in March . . . See Williams, "Death and Destruction," 1972.
32 A federal grand jury . . . All details from court papers.
34 This hope . . . See Graham, 1971.
34 an important . . . See Proskouriakoff, 1961.
35 One can thus understand . . . See Gent, 1971.
39 This led . . . See Coggins, 1969.
39 She went on . . . See Coggins, May 1971.
42 The nature of that subsidy . . . See Keen, 1971, pp. 26–28.

CHAPTER TWO

45 Before the Civil War . . . See Pach, 1948; Spaeth, 1969.
45 Fifty years ago . . . See R. Gimpel, 1966, p. 217.
47 At a founding . . . See Tomkins, 1970, p. 30.
48 When a journalist . . . See Burnham, 1969.
48 An early warning . . . See Henry James, *The American Scene* (New York: Horizon Press, 1967), pp. 191–92.
49 The point was . . . See F. H. Taylor, *Babel's Tower*, 1945, p. 8.
49 Before his decision . . . See Tomkins, 1970, p. 324.
49–50 An example is . . . See Noble, 1970.
50–51 In his book . . . See Bazin, 1967, pp. 263–64.
51 In a series . . . Private interview.
51–52 On February 27 . . . See Canaday, 27 February 1972.
52 A week later . . . See Hoving, 1972.
52 While alive . . . See Cunningham, 1973.
53 By what right . . . See Hess, 17 January 1973.
53 The tersest . . . See Hess, 26 January 1973.
53 The portraits are . . . See Elizabeth du Gué Trapier, *Velázquez* (New York: Hispanic Society of America, 1952), pp. 13–15.
54 At an early stage . . . See Canaday, 19 March 1972.
56 An educated . . . The estimate is by Machteld J. Mellink.
56 Rich in its past . . . See *Turkey*, OECD Economic Survey, (Paris, 1972).
56–57 Turks who are . . . Private interview.
57 In 1964 . . . See U.S. Agency for International Development, *Economic and Social Indicators: Turkey* (Ankara, 1971), p. 38.
57 He recently remarked . . . See R. Taylor, 12 April 1970.
57 There is an active . . . See Owen, December 1971.
58 His estimate . . . See Carley, 1970.
58 Tragedy it may be . . . Kumluca story based on private interviews.
60 A subsequent catalogue . . . See Dumbarton Oaks, 1967.
63 The Vermeules . . . See Emily and Cornelius Vermeule, 1970.
64 Dr. Cornelius Vermeule has elsewhere . . . See Hoyt, 1970.
65 The spirit of . . . See Greener, 1966, p. 158.
65 The initial report . . . See R. Taylor, 12 April 1970.

66 The *New York Times* . . . See *New York Times*, 27 August 1970.

67 An earlier instance was . . . See Smith, 1956, pp. 136–39; and Wilson, 1964, pp. 157–58.

68 James J. Rorimer . . . Private interview.

68 In reward for his war services . . . E. McFadden, 1971.

69 Miss McFadden said . . . See E. McFadden, 1971, p. 249.

70 As an Ankara . . . See Alfred Friendly, Jr., 1970.

71 It began . . . See Mellaart, 1959.

71 By Mellaart's account . . . See Pearson and Connor, 1968, pp. 34–35.

74 When he completed . . . See Bass, 1970.

75 At Harvard . . . See Williams, March 1972.

75 At the Field . . . See Bronson, 1972.

76 The Vermeules expressed . . . See *Antiquity*, 1971, pp. 314–16.

77 "The Money Is . . ." See *Times Literary Supplement*, 1971.

78 One of them was . . . See Wardwell, 1973.

CHAPTER THREE

80 Art acquisition is . . . See *Wall Street Journal*, June 17, 1969, p. 22.

81 "In its upper . . ." See Hughes, 1971.

82 One calculation is . . . See Lerici, 1969, p. 23.

82 the Colosseum was . . . See "Colosseum in Danger, Is Completely Closed," unsigned report, *New York Times*, 27 September 1972.

82 "The tower is very, very ill . . ." See Paul Hofmann, 20 November 1972.

82 Meanwhile, the Italian . . . See Murray, 1973.

82–83 A symptomatic episode . . . See Hale, 1972.

83 While taking . . . See O'Keefe, 1973.

83 A skilled *tombarolo* . . . See Hamblin, 1970, p. 73.

83 "We have no . . ." See Hamblin, 1970, p. 93.

84–85 In a 1958 speech . . . See Lerici, 1966.

85 He attempted an . . . See Lerici, 1969.

85 He wrote . . . *Ibid.*, p. 10.

85 In 1972, an austerity year . . . See Italian Art and Landscape Foundation, 1972, and Hughes, 5 June 1972.

85 a qualified . . . See Murray, 1973.

85–86 one of the leading . . . See unsigned article, "Lack of Funds Closes Art Restoration Center," *New York Times*, 3 November 1972.

86 At one point . . . See "People" item, *New York Times*, 5 October 1972.

86 At a museum conference . . . American Association of Museums annual meeting, New York, June, 1970; author present.

87 The episode opened . . . See Mellow, 1972.

87 Later, writing in . . . See von Bothmer, 1972.

87 The official story . . . See Mellow, 1972.

88 He was a boy . . . *Ibid.*

89 In February, 1972 . . . All details based on personal interviews.

90 In Zurich, the curator . . . See Mellow, 1972.

90 When the Dutch forger . . . See Kilbracken, 1967.

92 "Archaeology is not . . ." See Pearson and Connor, 1968, quoted as epigraph.

92 His discoveries . . . See Hamblin, 1970, p. 79.

92 The point was . . . See Dietrich von Bothmer, "Greek Vases from the Hearst Collection," Metropolitan Museum of Art *Bulletin*, March, 1957, p. 167.

94 in the Fall . . . See Association for Field Archaeology, 1972.

96 The author, Xavier . . . See ICOM, April 1970.

96 He also supported . . . See ICOM, January 1970.

96 it was announced . . . See von Bothmer, 1971.

99 With some enthusiasm . . . Personal interviews.

100 The krater had been . . . See Gage, 22 February 1973.

101 Once, Dr. von Bothmer . . . See von Bothmer, 1971.

102 The painting's authenticity . . . See Shearman, February 1970.

103 In St. Louis . . . See Connor, 1971.

103 In due course . . . See *Sunday Times* (London), 1971, by far the best account.

106 And yet Shearman . . . See Shearman, April 1970.

107 In a complementary initiative . . . See Arnason, 1972.

109–110 He said of himself . . . See Arnau, 1961, p. 223.

110 When Dossena learned . . . See Hamblin, 1970, pp. 144–50.

111 The products of various . . . See von Bothmer and Noble, 1961.

113 An opportunity for . . . See *Archaeometry*, 1971.

113 The most celebrated . . . See Shirey, 24 December 1972.

114 In an issue . . . See Metropolitan Museum of Art, 1968.

115 "at the same time . . ." See Brown, 1969.

115 Carl Blümel . . . See Blümel, 1969.

116 This circumstance led . . . See Swauger, 1971.

118 This has been evident . . . See Shirey, 29 January 1973.

118 "No hammers go down . . ." See *Time*, 1 January 1973.

119 Another way . . . See Robert Hughes, 1971.

119 when he was asked . . . See Eder, 1972.

121 This fantasy . . . See Meyer, *The Pleasures of Archaeology*, 1970, pp. 40–44.

CHAPTER FOUR

123 The matter was . . . See Shirey, 10 March 1973.

124 But as one Swiss . . . See *Time*, 26 February 1973.

124 A published . . . *Ibid.*

124 Speaking from . . . See Bernard Berenson, *Seeing and Knowing* (New York: Graphic Society, 1968), p. 52.

125 In February, 1967 . . . See Gray, 1972.

126 In the preface . . . *Ibid.*, p. 7.

127 Plainly the chicanery . . . Private interviews.

128 Cornelius Vermeule of the . . . See Vermeule, 1968, p. 5.

130 In 1951, Mr. Pomerance . . . See Alsop, 1966.

131 At the same time . . . See Brooklyn Museum, 1966.

131–132 Mr. Pomerance at no point . . . See Finch, 1971.

133 As the Egyptologist . . . See Barbara Mertz, *Temples, Tombs and Hieroglyphs* (New York: Coward McCann, 1964), p. 309.

134 As Miss Hamblin . . . See Hamblin, 1970, pp. 81 *et seq.*

135 Dr. Heath made . . . See Heath, 1971.

138 A country with . . . See Bruhns, 1972.

139 Until the 1950s . . . See Schanberg, 1971.

140 In a report on . . . See Asher, 1971.

140 Elsewhere in Asia . . . See Solheim, 1971.

142 While still a student . . . See Langlois, 1966, *passim.*

144 It is a trifle harder . . . See Eckman, 11 May 1973; Shirey, 12 May 1973.

150 An instance was . . . See "Museum Agent-Thief Spoils Loot, Kills Self," Mexico City *News*, 3 May 1972; and M. Campos Diaz y Sanchez, "Se Mató un Inspector del INBA Implicado en Saqueos Arqueológicos," *Excelsior*, 3 May 1972.

152 Still, there are . . . See Hamblin, 1970, pp. 116–28.

153 In 1968, three . . . See *Time*, 29 January 1973.

153 More recently, in May . . . See McAllister, 1972.

153 One is often . . . See Meyer, 1972.

156 In 1957, the Italian . . . See Hamblin, 1970, pp. 94–95.

157 Early in this . . . See Evans, 1968.

157 In Panama . . . *Ibid.*

159 His words, written in . . . See Spratling, 1967, p. 165.

161 In March, 1973 . . . See Shirey, 10 March 1973.

CHAPTER FIVE

171 In 1924, the British author . . . All details from Nicolson, 1949.

172 Thomas Bruce, the seventh Earl . . . See St. Clair, 1967, for full account.

173 The *firman* . . . See British Museum, 1965, p. 12.

173 Among those who . . . See Nicolson, 1949.

174 As he wrote . . . See Grant, 1966, p. 107.

175–176 Even before their display . . . See St. Clair, 1967, p. 175.

176 He was among the first . . . See Benjamin Robert Haydon, *Auto-biography and Journals* (New York: Coward McCann, 1950), pp. 77 *et seq.*

177 In the arguments . . . See Leslie A. Marchand, *Byron: A Biography* (New York: Knopf, 1957), p. 225.

179 In his book . . . See C. M. Woodhouse, *The Philhellenes* (London: Hodder and Stoughton, 1966), p. 25.

179 Georges Dontas, the director . . . See Dontas, 1968.

181 The Father of the Turks . . . See Lord Kinross, *Ataturk* (New York: Morrow, 1965), pp. 528–36.

182 As Amos Elon . . . See Amos Elon, *The Israelis* (New York: Holt, Rinehart & Winston, 1972), pp. 282 *et seq.*

184 Everywhere in Mexico . . . See Victor Alba, *The Mexicans* (London: Pall Mall Press, 1967), pp. 14–15.

184–185 But as the British . . . See J. H. Plumb, *The Death of the Past* (London: Macmillan, 1969), p. 91.

185 "Do I look . . ." See Woodhouse, *op. cit.*, p. 41.

187 In September, 1972 . . . See Andrew H. Malcolm, "Beer Can Collectors Hold Barter-Fest," *New York Times*, 26 September 1972.

187 One can intelligibly . . . See Rheims, 1961, p. 32.

188 How can one account . . . See Jensen, 1963, pp. 612–13.

191 The point was . . . See Walker, February 1972.

192 In 1967, Thomas . . . See McPhee, 1967.

192 When the Metropolitan . . . See Burnham, 1973, p. 178.

193 As Mr. Hoving . . . See McPhee, 1967.

193 As the writer . . . See Munro, 1973.

193 An early American critic . . . See Dana, 1917.

194 In a book entitled . . . See Ripley, 1969.

195 And in the focus . . . See "Vasari," 1972.

195 Few better expressions . . . See David L. Shirey, "Vase's Outline Stressed," *New York Times*, 19 February 1973.

196 Mr. Hoving asserted . . . See D. Davis, 1973.

196 There was almost . . . See D. Davis, 1973.

197 Recently Tom King . . . See King, 1971.

198 As an example . . . See Society for California Archaeology, 1970.

201 As Dr. McGimsey . . . See McGimsey, 1972.

202 The political problem . . . See Riddell, 1971.

203 In a letter to . . . See *Science*, 1972.

206 In Afghanistan . . . See Christie, 1967, pp. 92–98.

207 Mohenjo-Daro . . . See Blumenthal, 1971.

207 Angkor Wat . . . See Melville, 1971.

208 A last example . . . See Frédéric, 1968.

BIBLIOGRAPHY

Author's Note: Since this is the first bibliography of any scope on this subject, I have tried to be as inclusive as possible. Asterisks denote material of special interest. Only one abbreviation is employed—NYT for New York Times.

ADAM, NICOLAS. "The Treasure They Buried Again," *The Observer* (London), 12 November 1972.

ADAMS, ROBERT McCORMACK. "Archaeology and Cultural Diplomacy," *Foreign Service Journal*, June 1968, pp. 24, 49–50.

———. "Illicit International Traffic in Antiquities," *American Antiquity*, January, 1971, pp. ii–iii.

ALSOP, JOSEPH. "Kato Zakro," *The New Yorker*, 17 August 1966, pp. 32–95.

Antiquity. "The Pennsylvania Declaration," *Antiquity*, 1971, pp. 314–16. (Reply by the Vermeules)

Archaeometry. Aitken, M. J., P. R. S. Moorey, P. J. Ucko, "The authenticity of vessels and figurines in the Hacılar style," 1971, pp. 89–142.

———. I. P. R. S. Moorey, "The origins of the Oxford inquiry and the archeological background," 1971, pp. 89–92.

———. II. M. J. Aitken, "The thermoluminescent tests," 1971, pp. 93–109.

———. III. P. R. S. Moorey and P. J. Ucko, "List of objects tested," 1971, pp. 110–14.

———. IV. P. J. Ucko, "Stylistic analysis," 1971, pp. 115–27.

ARNASON, H. HARVARD. "Introducing the International Foundation for Art Research," *Museum News*, April, 1972, pp. 28–30.

ARNAU, FRANK. *Three Thousand Years of Deception in Art and Antiquities* (Oxford: Alden Press, 1961).

*ASHER, FREDERICK K. "Looting in India," paper presented at American Association for the Advancement of Science (AAAS) meeting,

Philadelphia, December, 1971.

ASSOCIATED PRESS. "Angkor Wat Reported Damaged by Cambodian Shells," *NYT*, 12 May 1970.

———. "Museums 'Tricked' by Fake 'Ancient Tomb Painting,'" Bridgeport *Post*, 1 August 1972.

ASSOCIATION FOR FIELD ARCHAEOLOGY. "The Million Dollar Pot," AFFA Newsletter, editorial, Fall, 1972, p. 1.

BARDES, HERBERT C. "Research Hurt by Krater Acquisition," *NYT*, 4 March 1973.

BASS, GEORGE F. "Troy and Ur: Gold Links Between Two Ancient Capitals," *Expedition*, Summer, 1966, pp. 26–39.

———. "A Hoard of Trojan and Sumerian Jewelry," *American Journal of Archeology*, 1970, pp. 335–41.

*BAZIN, GERMAIN. *The Museum Age* (New York: Universe Books, 1967).

BEHRMAN, DANIEL. "Saving the Past from the Present," *Réalités*, June, 1972, pp. 42–47.

*BEHRMAN, S. N. *Duveen* (New York: Random House, 1952).

———. *People in a Diary* (Boston: Little, Brown, 1972).

BENDER, MARILYN. "The Boom in Art for Corporate Use," *NYT*, 28 January 1973.

BÊRNERT, PHILIPPE. "Les Russes Jouaient trop les «Goldfinger» Sur les Bords du Nil," *L'Aurore*, 25 July 1972.

BLÜMEL, CARL. "Zur Echtheitsfrage des Antiken Bronzepferdes im Metropolitan Museum in New York," *Archäologischer Anzeiger*, 1969, pp. 208–16.

BLUMENTHAL, RALPH. "Water, Salt Threaten 4,000 Year Old City." *International Herald Tribune*, 1 January 1971.

*VON BOTHMER, DIETRICH. "Observations of a Curator of Greek and Roman Art," speech at the Florence Conference on Illicit Trade, November 1971.

———. "Greek Vase Painting: An Introduction," Metropolitan Museum of Art *Bulletin*, Fall, 1972, pp. 1–68.

*VON BOTHMER, DIETRICH, and JOSEPH V. NOBLE. "An Inquiry into the Forgery of the Etruscan Terracotta Warriors in the Metropolitan Museum of Art," *Metropolitan Museum of Art Papers*, No. 11, 1961.

BREW, JOHN O. "The Menace of the Bulldozers," *The UNESCO Courier*, January, 1965, pp. 33–36.

THE BRITISH MUSEUM. *An Historical Guide to the Sculptures of the*

Parthenon (revised), (England: The British Museum, 1965).

*BRONSON, BENNET. "The Campaign Against the Antiquities Trade," *Field Museum of Natural History Bulletin*, September, 1972, pp. 2–5.

THE BROOKLYN MUSEUM. *The Pomerance Collection of Ancient Art* (Brooklyn, 1966).

BROUGH, JAMES. *Auction!* (New York: Bobbs-Merrill, 1963).

BROWN, LEWIS S. "Two Small Bronze Horses," *Curator*, No. 4, 1969, pp. 263–92.

*BRUHNS, KAREN O. "The Methods of the Guaquería: Illicit Tomb Looting in Colombia," *Archaeology*, April, 1972, pp. 140–43.

BUCHWALD, ART. "Paolo, the Grave Robber," New York *Post*, 6 March 1973.

BULL, RICHARD C. "The Metamorphosis of One Collector," *Expedition*, Spring, 1965, pp. 38–47.

Burlington Magazine. "Sales from the Metropolitan," December, 1972, p. 817.

BURNHAM, SOPHY. "The Manhattan Arrangement of Art and Money," *New York*, 8 December 1969, pp. 35–45.

———. "The Art Squad," *Saturday Review of the Arts*, 2 December 1972, pp. 33–36.

———. *The Art Crowd* (New York: McKay, 1973).

CABANNE, PIERRE. *The Great Collectors* (New York: Farrar, Strauss, 1963.

*CANADAY, JOHN. "Very Quiet and Very Dangerous," *NYT*, 27 February, 1972.

*———. "Mr. Hoving's Evasions, Contradictions, and Camouflage," *NYT*, 12 March 1972.

*———. "A Few Last Words, Very Calm, about Selling the Public's Pictures," *NYT*, 19 March 1972.

———. "Metropolitan to Auction 12 Paintings," *NYT*, 29 September 1972.

———. "Metropolitan Sells Two Modern Masterpieces in an Unusual Move," *NYT*, 30 September 1972.

———. "Metropolitan Museum Sells Two More Masters," *NYT*, 3 October 1972.

———. "Mr. Hoving's Lemonade Stand," *NYT*, 15 October 1972.

———. "An Unhappy Anniversary," *NYT*, 18 February 1973.

———. "Ethics and Antiquities," *NYT*, 27 February 1973.

CAPLIN, LEE EVAN. "Art, Taxes and the Law," *Art Journal*, Fall, 1972, pp. 12–20.

CARDENAS, HÉCTOR. "Paradise Lost; Recovering Mexico's Heritage," *Museum News,* March, 1972, pp. 32–33.

CARDENAS, ROY B. "Hallazgo de gran trascendencia en la zona arqueológica Kohunlich," *Diario Novedades de Yucatán,* 17 May 1969.

CARETTONI, TULLIA ROMAGNOLI. "Ancora del Patrimonio Culturale," speech at Rome, 18 June 1971.

*CARLEY, WILLIAM M. "Archeological Objects Smuggled at Brisk Rate as their Prices Soar," *Wall Street Journal,* 2 June 1970.

———. "Some of the Looters of Archeological Sites Now Turn to Murder," *Wall Street Journal,* 30 November 1971.

CARMODY, DEIRDRE. "Dealers Busy as Japanese Take Interest in U.S. Art," *NYT,* 17 March 1973.

CARTER, PHILIP D. "Ruthless Pillage of Priceless Artifacts," Washington *Post,* 6 December 1971.

*CHIERICI, MAURIZIO. Three-part series on contraband art in Italy, *Oggi,* 18 January, 25 January, 1 February 1968.

CHRISTIE, TREVOR L. *Antiquities in Peril* (New York: J. B. Lippincott Company, 1967).

CHRISTOPHE, LOUIS A. "The Survival of Philae," *The UNESCO Courier,* December, 1968, pp. 48–55.

CODET, HENRI. *Essai sur le Collectionisme* (Paris, 1921).

COE, MICHAEL D. *The Maya Scribe and His World* (New York: Grolier Club, 1973).

*COGGINS, CLEMENCY. "Illicit Traffic of Pre-Columbian Antiquities," *Art Journal,* Fall, 1969, pp. 94–98.

*———. "The Maya Scandal: How Thieves Strip Sites of Past Cultures," *Smithsonian,* October, 1970, pp. 8–16.

———. "An Art Historian Speaks Out," *Auction,* January, 1971, p. 33.

*———. Untitled paper, Society of American Archeologists meeting, Norman, Oklahoma, May, 1971.

———. Untitled paper, American Association for the Advancement of Science meeting, Philadelphia, December, 1971.

———. "Archeology and the Art Market," *Science,* 21 January 1972, pp. 263–66.

*COLLEGE ART ASSOCIATION. "Illegal International Traffic in Works of Art," transcript of symposium at 59th Annual Meeting of College Art Association, Chicago, 29 January 1971.

CONNOR, JACK. "Perry Townsend Rathbone and His Curator of Deco-

rative Art Stand Accused by the Italian Authorities of Smuggling,"
Boston *Metro,* June, 1971, pp. 52–55.

CONROY, SARAH BOOTH. "Council to Mull Art Ethics," Washington
Post, 12 January 1971.

COONEY, JOHN D. "Assorted Errors in Art Collecting," *Expedition,*
Fall, 1963, pp. 20–27.

COUNCIL OF EUROPE. "European Convention on the Protection of the
Archeological Heritage," Strasbourg: Council of Europe, May, 1968.

CULTURAL AND SOCIAL CENTRE FOR THE ASIAN AND PACIFIC REGIONS.
Preservation of Cultural Heritage (Seoul, 1971).

CUNNINGHAM, CHARLES. "Metropolitan Museum's 'Deaccessing' and Exchanges," *NYT* (letter to editor), 31 January 1973.

DAIFUKU, HIROSHI. "S.O.S. Angkor," *The UNESCO Courier,* December, 1971, pp. 4–5.

DANA, JOHN COTTON. "The Gloom of the Museum," *New Museum Series*
No. 2, 1917.

DARNTON, JOHN. "Iroquois Meet About Unearthing of Bones by Eighteen Students Upstate," *NYT,* 6 August 1972.

DAVIS, DOUGLAS. "Hoving: Last of a Breed," *Newsweek,* 12 March 1973.

*DAVIS, HESTER A. "Is there a future for the past?" *Archaeology,* October, 1971, pp. 300–6.

*———. "The Crisis in American Archeology," *Science,* 21 January
1972, pp. 267–72.

DE BROGLIE, AXELLE, and LEVONTAL, PHILIPPE. "Alerte aux Vols,"
Connaissance des Arts, February, 1972, pp 60–71.

*DONTAS, GEORGES. "The Parthenon in Peril," *The UNESCO Courier,*
June, 1968, pp. 16–19, 34.

DRYSDALE, SUSAN. "On the Cost of Old Vases," *Christian Science Monitor,* 2 December 1972.

DUMBARTON OAKS, WASHINGTON. *Handbook of the Robert Woods Bliss
Collection of Pre-Columbia Art,* (New York: Spiral Press, 1963).

———. *Handbook of the Byzantine Collection* (New York: Spiral
Press, 1967).

———. *Supplement to the Handbook of the Robert Woods Bliss Collection of Pre-Columbian Art* (New York: Spiral Press, 1969).

ECKMAN, FERN MARJA. "More Met Mysteries: Lydian Loot?" New
York *Post,* 26 February 1973.

———. "Turkey: Met's Trove Stolen," New York *Post,* 10 May 1973.

319

———. "Stolen Statue of Shiva Bought by Simon," New York *Post*, 11 May 1973.

Economist. "The Antiquities Business," 28 March 1970, pp. 58–59.

———. "The Sack of Italy," 11 September 1971, p. 54.

EDER, RICHARD. "Poverty a Fact of Life in Europe's Museums," *NYT*, 30 May 1972.

*ESTEROW, MILTON. "Air Pollution Is Eroding World's Stone Art," *NYT*, 13 April 1964.

———. *The Art Stealers* (New York: Macmillan, 1966).

*EVANS, CLIFFORD. "Archeology and Diplomacy in Latin America," *Foreign Service Journal*, June, 1968, pp. 35–37, 50.

L'Express (Paris). "Pillage: Comment Les Trésors Disparaissent," 17–23 January 1972, pp. 58–59.

FARBER, M. A. "UNESCO to Set Up New Heritage Aid," *NYT*, 2 December 1972.

———. "Albany Bill Aims at Art Smuggling," *NYT*, 6 April 1973.

FARRELL, WILLIAM E. "State Bill Would Return Historic Wampum to Iroquois," *NYT*, 11 March 1971.

FERRETTI, FRED. "Just Who Owns the Dürer Portraits?" *Art News*, December, 1972, pp. 16–18.

Financial Times. "High Prices for Tribal Art," 3 September 1969.

FINCH, CHRISTOPHER. "The Archeophiles: Leon and Harriet Pomerance," *Auction*, January, 1971, pp. 35–38.

FLEMING, ROBERT. "The Incredible Temple Thieves," San Francisco *Chronicle*, 3 April 1969.

FORD, RICHARD I. "Pots, Politics, and Professionals," paper presented at AAAS Meeting, Philadelphia, December, 1971.

FORGEY, BENJAMIN. "Lord Byron Cried 'Rape . . . ,' " *Museum News*, June, 1970, pp. 21–25.

———. "U.S. Joins the Battle Against Those Who Steal the Past," *Art News*, December, 1972, pp. 20–21.

*FRÉDÉRIC, LOUIS. "The City of Ten Thousand Masterpieces," *The UNESCO Courier*, December, 1968, pp. 20–33.

FRIENDLY, ALFRED. "Boston's Golden Hoard Stirs a Tempest," *International Herald Tribune*, 10 February 1970.

———. "Mystery Collection at Boston Museum Disturbs Turkey," Washington *Post*, 10 March 1970.

*FRIENDLY, ALFRED, JR. "Turks Warn of Ban to Archaeologists if U.S. Won't Aid Smuggling Fight," *NYT*, 3 November 1970.

———. "Archaeologists, in Belgrade, Ask Nations to Curb Antiquities

Thefts," *NYT*, 18 September 1971.

*GAGE, NICHOLAS. "How the Metropolitan Acquired 'The Finest Greek Vase There Is,'" *NYT*, 19 February 1973.

*———. "Italy Is Investigating Source of Met Vase," *NYT*, 19 February 1973.

*———. "Never Saw Vase Intact, Beirut Dealer Says," *NYT*, 22 February 1973.

———. "Sporadic Art Dealer: Dikran A. Sarrafian," *NYT*, 23 February 1973.

*———. "Farmhand Tells of Finding Met's Vase in Italian Tomb," *NYT*, 25 February 1973.

———. "Italians Seek FBI Aid on a Greek Cup," *NYT*, 2 March 1973.

———. "Met Withholds Photo of Vase," *NYT*, 11 March 1973.

GASKILL, GORDON. "They Smuggle History," *The Illustrated London News*, 14 June 1969, pp. 26–29.

GAY, CARLO T. E. *Xochipala: The Beginnings of Olmec Art* (Princeton University Art Museum, 1972).

*GENT, GEORGE. "Manuscript Could Change Views on Mayan's Religion," *NYT*, 21 April 1971.

———. "Art Historians at CUNY Score Sale of Metropolitan Paintings," *NYT*, 18 October 1972.

GHEERBRANT, M. "The Art Traffickers," *Continent 2000*, November, 1971, pp. 56–57.

GIMPEL, JEAN. *The Cult of Art* (New York: Stein and Day, 1969).

GIMPEL, RENÉ. *Diary of an Art Dealer* (New York: Farrar, Straus & Giroux, 1966).

GLUECK, GRACE. "Top Art Auctions Boom, Though Economy Sags," *NYT*, 16 April 1971.

———. "Smuggled Raphael Is Sent Back to Italy from Boston," *NYT*, 11 September 1971.

———. "Boston Museum Aide Quits in Dispute," *NYT*, 21 December 1971.

———. "Museums Try a New Tack to Shelter Art Treasures from Air Borne Pollution, *NYT*, 3 April 1972

———. "Lehman Pavillion Will Cost $8-Million," *NYT*, 11 May 1972.

———. "Metropolitan to Seek More City Funds." *NYT*, 10 June 1972.

GOLLIN, JUNE. "The Metropolitan Museum—It's Worse Than You Think," *New York*, 15 January 1973, pp. 54–60

GORDON, JOHN B. "The UNESCO Convention on the Illicit Movement of Art," *Harvard International Law Journal*, Fall, 1971, pp. 537–56.

Bibliography

GOUDSMIT, S. A. "Not for the Art Trade," *Expedition*, Summer, 1972, pp. 13–16.

GRAHAM, IAN. "Across the Petén to the Ruins of Machaquila," *Expedition*, Winter, 1963, pp. 2–10.

———. "Tesoros Arqueológicas del Petén al Etranjero," *El Imparcial*, 17 July 1965.

*———. *Archeological Explorations in El Petén, Guatemala* (New Orleans: Tulane University, Middle American Research Institute, Publication 33, 1967).

*———. "Maya Language Project, Phase I," submitted to Advisory Committee of the Maya Language Project, Stella and Charles Guttman Foundation and Center for Inter-American Relations, 22 September 1969.

———. "The Lawless Jungle," *Manchester Guardian*, 3 October 1972.

*GRANT, JUDITH. *A Pillage of Art* (London: Robert Hale, 1966).

GRATZ, ROBERTA B. "Indian Art: Big Money," New York *Post*, 29 November 1971.

———. "Met Oils Star at a 5M Art Auction," New York *Post*, 26 October 1972.

GRAY, JAMES A. "Working to Preserve Mankind's Heritage," *NYT*, 13 June 1965.

GREENER, LESLIE. *The Discovery of Egypt* (London: Cassell, 1966).

GROSLIER, BERNARD P. "Borobudur," *The UNESCO Courier*, June, 1968, pp. 23–27.

*HALE, ANDREW. "The Help-Yourself Treasure Chests," *The Sunday Times* (London), 17 December 1972.

*HALE, ANDREW, and COLIN SIMPSON. "The Stolen Masterpieces," *The Sunday Times* (London), 12 September 1971.

HALL, ARDELIA R. "The Recovery of Cultural Objects Dispersed During World War II," *Department of State Bulletin*, 27 August 1951, pp. 337–40,'344–45.

*HAMBLIN, DORA JANE. *Pots and Robbers* (New York: Simon and Schuster, 1970).

*———. "The Billion-Dollar Illegal Art Traffic—How It Works and How to Stop It," *Smithsonian*, March, 1972, pp. 16–27.

HAMMOND, NORMAN. "Tests show forged Turkish prehistoric pottery in many world museums," *The Times* (London), 30 July 1971.

———. "Chinese faked art exposed," *The Times* (London), 28 July 1972.

*HAQUE, ENAMUL. "The Museums, Monuments, and the Archeological

Sites in Bangla Desh: the Situation after the War of Independence, 1971," *ICOM* (Paris), June, 1972.

HARVARD UNIVERSITY—PEABODY MUSEUM and CENTER FOR INTER-AMERICAN RELATIONS. *The Art of Maya Hieroglyphic Writing* (New York, 1971).

HAZZARD, SHIRLEY, and FRANCIS STEEGMULLER. "Suicide Italian Style," *NYT*, 8 January 1972.

*HEATH, DWIGHT B. "Gold, Graves, and Greed: Professional Grave-Robbing in Costa Rica," paper, 1971.

*———. "Economic Aspects of Commercial Archeology in Costa Rica," paper presented at the American Association for the Advancement of Science Meeting, Philadelphia, December, 1971.

*———. "In Quest of 'El Dorado': Some Sociological Aspects of Huaquerísmo (Pot-hunting) in Costa Rica," paper, 1971.

HESS, JOHN L. "Dealers Irked at Museum over Coin Sale in Zurich," *NYT*, 24 October 1972.

———. "Metropolitan Finds 'Odalisque' Not by Ingres," *NYT*, 17 January 1973.

———. "Lefkowitz Opens Inquiry into Art Sales by the Met," *NYT*, 26 January 1973.

*———. "A Second Work by Master of Vase Comes to Light," *NYT*, 24 February 1973.

———. "Not Easy to Piece Together," *NYT*, 25 February 1973.

*———. "Euphronios Cup Is Reportedly Offered for Sale to the Metropolitan," *NYT*, 25 February 1973.

———. "Every Day a New 'Kefluffle,'" *NYT*, 25 February 1973.

HODGINS, ERIC and PARKER LESLEY. "The Great International Art Market," *Fortune*, December, 1955, pp. 118–132, 150–169; and January, 1956, pp. 122–125, 130–136.

HOFFMANN, HERBERT. *Collecting Greek Antiquities* (New York: Clarkson Potter, 1971).

*HOFMANN, PAUL. "Italy to Press Charges over a Raphael," *NYT*, 23 March 1971.

———. "Cables Truss the Tower of Pisa," *NYT*, 20 November 1972.

*———. "Rome: Treasures Face Many Perils," *NYT*, 26 December 1972.

———. "Foul-Air Masks Ordered Near Venice," *NYT*, 7 January 1973.

———. "Rome Tells Four to Retain Counsel in Vase Inquiry," *NYT*, 24 February 1973.

*————. "In Italy, New Hope Stirs the Tomb Robbers," *NYT*, 5 March 1973.

VON HOLST, NIELS. *Creators, Collectors, and Connoisseurs* (New York: G. P. Putnam's Sons, 1967).

*HOPKIRK, PETER. "Turks Angered by Backdoor Sale of Antiquities," *The Times* (London), 6 December 1967.

————. "Treasure Hunters Take Antiquities," *The Times* (London), 27 October 1969.

————. "Pirates of the 'Lost Cities,' " *The Times* (London), 14 February 1970.

————. "Museum Acts on Smuggling," *The Times* (London), 20 April 1970.

————. "Dealer Says Boston Raphael Is Fake," *The Times* (London), 25 April 1970.

*————. "Turkish Warning on Relics," *The Times* (London), 14 July 1970.

*————. "Turks Claim Croesus Gold Is in U.S. Museum," *The Times* (London), 27 August 1970.

————. "U.S. Museum Attacked over Raphael," *The Times* (London), 6 March 1971.

————. "Fools Gold in Velvet-lined Showcases," *The Times* (London), 31 July 1971.

————. "Mycenaean Treasures Plundered from Tombs are Smuggled Out of Cyprus," *The Times* (London), 16 August 1971.

————. "Break-up of Pitt-Rivers Collection Sends African Art Treasures to Sales Room," *The Times* (London), 15 December 1972.

*HOVING, THOMAS. "Very Inaccurate and Very Dangerous," *NYT*, 5 March 1972.

HOWARD, PHILIP. "Amateurs Pillage Ancient Wrecks," *The Times* (London), 2 August 1971.

HOWE, MARVINE. "In a Columbian Village the People Talk of the Treasure," *NYT*, 13 May 1973.

HOWE, THOMAS C., JR. *Salt Mines and Castles: The Discovery and Restitution of Looted European Art* (New York: Bobbs-Merrill, 1946).

HOYT, MONTY. "Boston Museum Denies Gold-Smuggling Story," *Christian Science Monitor*, 7 February 1970.

*HUGHES, ROBERT. "Who Needs Masterpieces at Those Prices?" *Time*, 19 July 1971, pp. 52–53.

*————. "Can Italy Be Saved from Itself?" *Time,* 5 June 1972.

————. "Breach of Trust," *Time,* 16 October 1972, pp. 67–68.

HUXTABLE, ADA LOUISE. "The Decline (and Fall?) of Italy's Cultural Environment," *NYT,* 12 May 1972.

INSTITUTO NACIONAL DE ANTROPOLOGÍA E HISTORIA. "Kohunlich," INAH *Boletín,* September, 1969, pp. 1–6.

INTERNATIONAL COUNCIL OF MUSEUMS (ICOM). "Meeting of Experts to Study the Ethical Rules Governing Museum Acquisitions," Paris: ICOM, January, 1970.

————. Papers prepared for above Meeting of Experts, ICOM, Paris, 8–10 April 1970; Lorenzo, J. L., "Les Acquisitions Directes de Musées;" Rivière, G. H., "Museum Acquisitions;" de Salas, Xavier, "Indirect Museum Acquisitions: Through Middlemen;" ICOM Secretariat, "Museum Acquisitions: Present State of the Problem."

————. "Meeting of Experts to Study the Ethical Rules Governing Museum Acquisitions: Draft Conclusions," ICOM, Paris, April, 1970.

————. "Ethics of Acquisition," ICOM, Paris, 1971.

————. "Ethics of Museum Acquisition: ICOM Reports and Publications," UNESCO-ICOM Documentation Centre, September, 1972 (bibliography).

————. "Report on ICOM Activities for the Suppression of Illicit Traffic in Cultural Property," paper submitted to UNESCO for the Meeting of International Inter-Governmental and Non-Governmental Organizations, Brussels, 13–15 September 1972.

INTERNATIONAL FUND FOR MONUMENTS. *Venice in Peril* (New York: International Fund for Monuments, 1970).

ITALIAN ART AND LANDSCAPE FOUNDATION. *Art and Landscape of Italy: Too Late to Be Saved?* (Florence: Centro Di, Publishers, 1972).

JENSEN, JENS. "Collector's Mania," *Acta Psychiatrica Scandinavia,* Vol. 39, 1963, pp. 4–32.

JOHNSON, JERALD JAY. "Archeological Sites as Non-Renewable Resources," paper, Society for American Archeology, annual meeting, May, 1972.

JOHNSON, STOWERS. *Collector's Luck* (New York: Walker & Co., 1969).

EL KAH, JELBL. "Carthage Must Not Be Destroyed," *The UNESCO Courier,* December, 1970, pp. 4–8.

KASHMERI, ZUHAIR A. "The Rape of Culture," *The Sunday Standard* (New Delhi), 11 July 1971.

KEEN, GERALDINE. "Impressionist Pictures and the Stock Market," *The Times Saturday Review* (London), 25 November 1967.

*———. *The Sale of Works of Art* (London: Thomas Nelson, 1971).

KEEN, GERALDINE, PETER NICHOLS, and MICHAEL KNIPE. "Italians Have Second Thoughts on the Boston Raphael," *The Times* (London), 6 March 1971.

KEYS, DAVID. "Saving a Lost City," *Illustrated London News*, September, 1972.

KILBRACKEN, LORD. *Van Meegeren: Master Forger* (New York: Scribner's, 1967).

KING, THOMAS F. "A Conflict of Values in American Archeology," *American Antiquity*, July, 1971, pp. 255–62.

KJELLBERG, PIERRE. "Cequi menace les églises," *Connaissance des Arts*, July, 1971, pp. 68–79.

KNOX, SANKA. "Apse Takes New 'Tonic' at Cloisters," *NYT*, 10 July 1970.

———. "Art Conference Finds Ally in Lab," *NYT*, 14 July 1970.

———. "Museum Returns Mayan Monument," *NYT*, 6 June 1972.

———. "Metropolitan Museum to Auction Coins in Zurich," *NYT*, 23 September 1972.

———. "Eleven Paintings from Metropolitan Highlight Auction," *NYT*, 26 October 1972.

KOHLER, ELLEN L. "Ultimatum to Terracotta Forgers," *Expedition*, Winter, 1967, pp. 16–21.

KURZ, OTTO. *Fakes* (New Haven: Yale University Press, 1948).

LANGLOIS, WALTER G. *André Malraux: The Indochina Adventure* (New York: Praeger, 1966).

LEBLANC, RICHARD. "Thief-Proofing Our Art Museums," *The UNESCO Courier*, November, 1965, pp. 4–7, 10.

LEICHTY, ERLE. "A Remarkable Forger," *Expedition*, Spring, 1970, pp. 17–21.

*LERICI, CARLO MAURILLO. "How to Steal Antiquities," in C. W. Ceram, ed., *Hands on the Past* (New York: Knopf, 1966), pp. 18–26.

*———. *The Future of Italy's Archeological Wealth* (Rome, 1969).

*LEWIN, SEYMOUR Z. "The Preservation of Natural Stone, 1839–1965: An Annotated Bibliography," *Art and Archeology Technical Abstracts*, Vol. 6, 1966, pp. 135–277.

*———. "Preserving Decayed Stone Sculpture," *National Sculpture Review*, Winter, 1971–72, pp. 22–27.

326

*"LORD ELGIN." "The Traffic in National Treasure," *Auction*, January, 1971, pp. 26–32.

LUCIE-SMITH, EDWARD. "Bidding Big at Christie's and Sotheby's," *World*, 16 January 1973, pp. 16–19.

*LUJÁN MUÑOZ, JORGE. "Dos Estelas Mayas Sustraidas de Guatemala: Su Presencia en Nueva York," *Revista Universidad de San Carlos*, No. LXVII, 1965, pp. 125–38.

LUJÁN MUÑOZ, LUIS. "Nómina Provisional de sitios arqueológicos de la República de Guatemala," *Antropología e Historia*, June, 1968, pp. 3–12.

McALLISTER, JOHN. "Art Worth $1 Million Stolen, Guard Shot at City Museum," *Telegram* (Worcester, Mass.), 18 May 1972.

McFADDEN, ELIZABETH. *The Glitter and the Gold* (New York: Dial Press, 1971).

McFADDEN, ROBERT D. "Met's Sale of Art Condemned by Dealers," *NYT*, 2 October 1972.

———. "Most-Wanted Art Posted by Interpol," *NYT*, 18 November 1972.

*McGIMSEY, CHARLES R., III. *Public Archeology* (New York: Seminar Press, 1972).

MacINNES, COLIN. "Art for Plunder's Sake," *Times* (London), 3 February 1973.

McPHEE, JOHN. "A Roomful of Hovings," *The New Yorker*, 20 May 1967, pp. 49–137.

MAILFERT, ANDRÉ. *Au Pays des Antiquaires* (Paris: Flammarion, 1968).

MARCO, JOHN ALLEGRO. *The Shapira Affair* (London: W. H. Allen, 1965).

MARTIN, KARL HEINZ. "How Abu Simbel Will Be Saved," *The UNESCO Courier*, December, 1964, pp. 11–14.

*MELLAART, JAMES. "The Royal Treasure of Dorak," *Illustrated London News*, 28 November 1959, pp. 754–60.

———. "Turkish finds," letter by Mellaart to *The Times*, re Boston Museum of Fine Arts acquisition of "Turkish gold," *The Times* (London), 7 February 1970.

*MELLOW, JAMES R. "A New (6th Century B.C.) Greek Vase for New York," *NYT Magazine*, 12 November 1972, pp. 42, 43, 114–16.

MELTON, JIM. "Guatemala Sues for Statue's Return," Houston *Post*, 14 November 1968.

————. "Art Smuggling Probe Ends," Houston *Post,* 15 November 1968.

————. "Art Dealers Accused of Profit Pillage," Houston *Post,* 17 November 1968.

*————. "Buying, Selling Stolen Art Apparently Not Much of a Crime," Houston *Post,* 17 November 1968.

————. "Guatemala May Reclaim Art," Houston *Post,* 21 January 1969.

————. "Guatemalans May Regain Stone Relic," Houston *Post,* 28 January 1969.

————. "Guatemala Presses Return of Statue," Houston *Post,* 26 June 1969.

————. "Return Ordered of Guatemalan Artifact Kept Here," Houston *Post,* 31 December 1970.

*MELVILLE, RICHARD A. "Angkor: A Progress Report," *Asia,* Summer, 1971, pp. 20–52.

*METROPOLITAN MUSEUM OF ART. "Art Forgery," Metropolitan Museum of Art *Bulletin,* February, 1968, pp. 241–76.

————. *Before Cortés: Sculpture of Middle America* (1970).

————. *Masterpieces of Fifty Centuries* (New York: Dutton, 1970).

MEYER, KARL E. "Jewel Case for Pre-Columbian Gems," *Art News,* February, 1964, pp. 36–39, 57–58.

————. "Hello, Columbus," *Art News,* November, 1970, pp. 46–49, 78–79.

————. "Ship Relic Thefts Prompt Protests," Washington *Post,* 29 December 1970.

————. "Archeologists Decry Looting of Antiquities," Washington *Post,* 31 December 1970.

————. *The Pleasures of Archaeology* (New York: Atheneum, 1970).

————. "The Stubborn Maya Mystery," *International Herald Tribune,* 9 February 1971.

————. *The Maya Crisis: A Report on the Pillaging of Maya Sites in Mexico and Guatemala* (New York: Center for Inter-American Relations, 1972).

MICHAELIS, ADOLF. *Ancient Marbles in Great Britain* (Cambridge: University Press, 1882).

MITCHELL, LESLIE. "Two Are Indicted in Disappearance of Ancient Tablet," *Arkansas Gazette,* 16 May 1973.

MONTGOMERY, PAUL L. "Indians Get Partial Victory on Sacred Objects' Sale," *NYT,* 21 October 1972.

328

MORLEY, GRACE. "Museum and the Market for Museum Objects," *Journal of Indian Museums,* 1970, pp. i–viii.

MUNIR, METIN. "A Peasant's Fakes May Have Fooled Museums," *The Times* (London), 31 January 1971.

*MURRAY, WILLIAM. "The Ageless Ruins of Italy Are in Danger of Finally Dying," *NYT,* 25 February 1973.

MUSCARELLA, OSCAR WHITE. "Hacilar Ladies: Old and New," Metropolitan Museum of Art *Bulletin,* October-November, 1971, pp. 74–79.

MUSEUM OF FINE ARTS, BOSTON. *Centennial Acquisitions: Art Treasures for Tomorrow* (Boston: Museum of Fine Arts, 1970).

MUSEUM OF PRIMITIVE ART. *Pre-Columbian Art in New York: Selections from Private Collections* (New York, 1969).

Newsweek. "Bull Market," 17 May 1971.

————. "The Great Culture Ripoff," 16 October 1972.

————. "Picture Puzzle at the Met," 29 January 1973.

————. "The Cup Runneth Over," 5 March 1973.

NAFZIGER, JAMES A. R. "Regulation by the International Council of Museums: An Example of the Role of Non-Governmental Organizations in the Transnational Legal Process," *Denver Journal of International Law and Policy,* Fall, 1972, Volume 2, pp. 231–53.

NEWTON, DOUGLAS. "American Museums," letter to the editor, *The Times* (London), 18 March 1970. [Reply to Hopkirk, 14 February 1970.]

New York Times. "Four More Countries to Help in Stone Preservative Test," 27 February 1966.

————. "Cambodia Trying to Save Statues," 21 February 1970.

————. "Greek Denigrates Boston's 'Hoard,' " 26 February 1970.

————. "Iroquois Are Seeking Return of Wampum Belts Held by State Museum," 17 April 1970.

————. "Metropolitan Museum Queried by Turks on Smuggled Artifacts," 27 August 1970.

————. "U.S. Museums Are Tightening Security to Curb Thefts, 24 May 1972.

————. "Montreal Museum Looted of Art Worth $2 Million," 5 September 1972.

————. "Gifts for Sale at the Metropolitan," letters to the editor from: 1) Francis Steegmuller; 2) Anna Goddard Potter; 3) John M. Montias, 10 October 1972.

————. "Should Museum Sell Its Paintings," letters to the editor from:

Bibliography

1) Milton W. Brown, 2) John Rewald, Leo Steinberg; 2) Thomas S. Buechner, 20 October 1972.

———. "Roman Coins Sold by Metropolitan," 12 November 1972.

———. "Metropolitan Museum: Of Purchase, Sales and Attributions," letters to the editor from: 1) Margaret Thompson; 2) George Heard Hamilton, 24 February 1973.

NICOLSON, HAROLD. "The Byron Curse Echoes Again," *NYT Magazine*, 27 March 1949, pp. 12–13, 33–35.

NOBLE, JOSEPH VEACH. *The Techniques of Painted Attic Pottery* (New York: Watson-Guphill Publications, 1965).

———. "Museum Manifesto," *Museum News*, April 1970, pp. 17–20.

———. "A Plea for Sense in Regard to Trade in Antiquities," *Archaeology*, April, 1972, p. 144.

O'KEEFE, PATRICK. "Art for the Taking," *Atlantic*, January, 1973, pp. 95–98.

DE ONIS, JUAN. "U.S. and Mexico Sign Pact for Return of Stolen Art," *NYT*, 18 July 1970.

ORGANIZATION OF AMERICAN STATES. "Final Report of the Meeting on Identification, Protection, and Safeguarding of the Archaeological, Historical and Artistic Heritage, São Paulo, 23–27 October 1972," Washington: OAS.

*OWEN, DAVID I. "Picking Up the Pieces: the Salvage Excavation of a Looted Fifth Century B.C. Shipwreck in the Straits of Messina," *Expedition*, Fall, 1970, pp. 24–29.

———. "The Illegal Antiquities Trade in Turkey: A Personal View," paper presented to AAAS Panel, December, 1971.

———. "Excavating a Classical Shipwreck," *Archaeology*, April, 1971, pp. 118–29.

PACH, WALTER. *The Art Museum in America* (New York: Pantheon, 1948).

PAIGE, CAMPBELL. "Amateur Threat to Digs," *Manchester Guardian*, 6 July 1971.

PALMER, MEREDITH A. "Harvard Attacks Art Looting: Proposes Acquisition Policy," *Harvard Crimson*, 18 November 1971.

PARKE-BERNET GALLERIES, INC. *Pre-Columbian and North American Indian Art* (New York, 1966).

———. *Ethnographical Art: African · Oceanic · American Indian* (New York, 1970).

———. *The Green Collection of American Indian Art* (1971).

———. *Ethnographical and Pre-Columbian Art* (1971).

330

Bibliography

————. *Pre-Columbian Art* (New York, 1972).

PEARSON, KENNETH, and PATRICIA CONNOR. *The Dorak Affair* (New York: Atheneum, 1968).

PLENDESLEITH, HAROLD J. "The New Science of Art Conservation," *The UNESCO Courier*, January, 1965, pp. 7–10.

PROSKOURIAKOFF, TANIA. "The Lords of the Maya Realm," *Expedition*, Fall, 1961, pp. 14–21.

PULESTON, DENNIS E. "Sacred Harps for the Chosen Few: A Report on Destruction of MesoAmerican Antiquities for the Sale of Art," paper presented at AAAS Philadelphia Meeting, December, 1971.

REBETEZ, RENÉ. "Josué Sáenz: Entrevistado," *Heraldo de Mexico*, 2 October 1966.

REIF, RITA. "Market Booms in Oriental Art, Thanks to Nixon," *NYT*, 6 October 1972.

————. "To Collectors, Navajo Design Is Irresistible," *NYT*, 28 November 1972.

REINHOLD, ROBERT. "Looters Impede Scholars Studying Maya Mystery," *NYT*, 26 March 1973.

————. "Traffic in Looted Maya Art Is Diverse and Profitable," *NYT*, 27 March 1973.

————. "Elusive Glyphs Yielding to Modern Technique," *NYT*, 28 March 1973.

————. "Precious Heritage in Jeopardy," *NYT*, 1 April 1973.

REITH, ADOLF. *Archeological Fakes* (New York: Praeger, 1970).

*REITLINGER, GERALD. *The Economics of Taste: The Rise and Fall of the Picture Market* (New York: Holt, Rinehart & Winston, 1961).

*————. *The Economics of Taste: The Rise and Fall of the Objects d'Art Market since 1750* (New York: Holt, Rinehart & Winston, 1963).

RENSBERGER, BOYCE. "Prehistoric Sites Feared in Peril," *NYT*, 3 January 1972.

REUTERS. "Undersea Treasure Stolen," New York *Post*, 30 September 1971.

————. "An Art Sales Boom in Japan Attributed to Inflation Hedge," *NYT*, 28 May 1972.

*REWALD, JOHN. "Should Hoving be De-accessioned?" *Art in America*, January-February, 1973, pp. 25–30.

*RHEIMS, MAURICE. *The Strange Life of Objects* (New York: Atheneum, 1961).

331

RICHARD, PAUL. "The Met under Siege," Washington *Post*, 18 February 1973.

RIDDELL, FRANCIS A. "The Crisis in American Archeology and the State of California," paper, 1971.

RIGBY, DOUGLAS and ELIZABETH. *Lock, Stock and Barrel* (New York: Lippincott, 1944).

RIPLEY, DILLON. *The Sacred Grove: Essays on Museums* (New York: Simon and Schuster, 1969).

ROBBINS, JACK. "The Art of Catching Thieves," New York *Post*, 23 September 1972.

ROBERTSON, MERLE GREENE. "Monument Thievery," paper presented to the Society of American Archeology Meeting, Norman, Oklahoma, May, 1971.

*———. "Monument Thievery in Mesoamerica," *American Antiquity*, April, 1972, pp. 147–55.

ROSE, BARBARA. "Scandal at the Met?" *New York*, 13 November 1972, pp. 18–23.

ROWELL, HENRY T. "A Home for the Muses," *Archaeology*, April, 1966, pp. 76–83.

*RUSH, RICHARD H. *Art as an Investment* (New York: Bonanza Books, 1961).

*RUZ, ALBERTO LHUILLIER. "Destruction and Pillage of Mayan Archeological Zones," paper at the Round Table on the Protection of the National Cultural Heritage, Mexican Academy of Culture, Guadalajara, Jalisco, Mexico, December, 1968.

SAARINEN, ALINE B. *The Proud Possessors* (New York: Random House, 1958).

SACHS, SAMUEL. "Art Forges Ahead," *Auction*, January, 1972, pp. 24–27.

*ST. CLAIR, WILLIAM. *Lord Elgin and the Marbles* (London: Oxford University Press, 1967).

EL SAMI, ABDEL MONEIM. "Nubia, Victory of International Solidarity," *The UNESCO Courier*, August-September, 1971, pp. 60–63.

SAWYER, CHARLES H. "Museum Acquisition Policies," paper, American Association of Museums Annual Meeting, Quebec, May, 1947, *Museum News*, 15 April 1948, pp. 6–8.

*SCHANBERG, SYDNEY H. "New Delhi: Pillage in the Eyes of the Gods," *NYT*, 30 August 1971.

SCHEFFLER, WINI. "Real Artifacts Protected by Fakes," *The News*

(Mexico City), 4 February 1972.

SCHMIDT, WILLIAM. "Stolen Art in City Museum?" Detroit *Free Press*, 21 March 1971.

*Science. "Archeological Looting and Site Destruction," letters to the editor from: 1) Terrence Jay O'Neil; 2) Ruth Gruhn; 3) Lloyd M. Pierson; 4) Frederic Johnson; 28 April 1972, pp. 353–55.

Science Digest. "Archeological Looting on the Rise," April, 1972, p. 82.

SELIGMAN, GERMAIN. *Merchants of Art: 1880–1960* (New York: Appleton-Century-Crofts, 1961).

SEVERO, RICHARD. "The Bulldozers' Assault on the Past in Mexico," *NYT*, 7 April 1972.

———. "Experts Smuggling Ancient Mexican Art to a Profitable Market," *NYT*, 17 June 1972.

SHEARMAN, JOHN. "Raphael at the Court of Urbino," *Burlington Magazine*, February, 1970, pp. 72–78.

———. "The Boston Raphael: Art Historian Puts His Arguments for Authenticity," letter to *The Times* (London), 27 April 1970.

SHIREY, DAVID L. "Brooklyn Museum Feels Pinch, Too," *NYT*, 31 March 1971.

———. "Rome Moves to Prevent Decline of Colosseum," *NYT*, 4 October 1972.

*———. "Metropolitan Bronze Horse Proves to Be Ancient," *NYT*, 24 December 1972.

*———. "Japanese Step Up Quest for Art in U.S.," *NYT*, 29 January 1973.

*———. "Seller of Greek Vase Named by Curator," *NYT*, 21 February, 1973.

———. "Seller of Greek Vase Flew to See Hoving Last Week," *NYT*, 26 February 1973.

———. "FBI and Police Here Begin Inquiry on Met Vase," *NYT*, 27 February 1973.

———. "Hecht Backs Vase Sale; Will Avoid Italy Now," *NYT*, 28 February 1973.

*———. "Most Ancient Arts Smuggled, Curator Says," *NYT*, 2 March 1973.

———. "Greek Bronze for Sale for $3.5 Million," *NYT*, 10 March 1973.

———. "Norton Simon Bought Smuggled Idol," *NYT*, 12 May 1973.

SHUSTER, ALVIN. "The Bulldozers' Assault on the Past in England," *NYT*, 7 April 1972.

333

SIBLEY, JOHN. "Drive Aims to Halt Looting of Mayan Art," *NYT*, 15 November 1972.

SIMMON, KAY. "Italy's Tarquinia: What the Tomb Raiders Missed," *NYT*, 12 March 1972.

*SIMPSON, COLIN. "Clues on the Trial of a Smuggled Raphael," *The Sunday Times* (London), 7 February 1971.

SLOAN, SARAH. "La fabulosa Colección de los Sáenz," *Novedades* (Mexico City), 27 November 1969.

SMITH, JOSEPH LINDON. *Tombs, Temples, and Ancient Art* (Norman: University of Oklahoma Press, 1956).

*SNEYERS, RENÉ. "Stones Also Die," *The UNESCO Courier*, January, 1965, pp. 26–27, 30–32.

*SOCIETY FOR CALIFORNIA ARCHAEOLOGY. "Death of the Past," a report to the people of California by the Society for California Archeology, December, 1970.

SOLHEIM, WILHELM G., II. "Security Problems for Antiquities in Southeast Asia," paper presented at the AAAS Meeting, Philadelphia, December, 1971.

SPAETH, ELOISE. *American Art Museums* (New York: McGraw-Hill, 1969).

*SPECIAL LAWYERS COMMITTEE. *Report of the Special Lawyers Committee* of the American Society of International Law Panel on the International Movement of National Art Treasures, January, 1971.

SPRATLING, WILLIAM. *File on Spratling* (Boston: Little, Brown, 1967).

STARKWEATHER, A. W. "Return of Wampum Belts, Treaty Concern Indians," Watertown *Times*, 9 December 1971.

STOCK, H. and K. G. SIEGLER. "Moving a Temple as Big as a Cathedral," *The UNESCO Courier*, December, 1964, pp. 38–39.

SULLIVAN, WALTER. "Jungle Search Is Planned to Break Mayan Code," *NYT*, 4 October 1969.

———. " 'Looting the Past' Is a Top at Parley," *NYT*, 30 December 1971.

The Sunday Times (London). "Italians Accuse Boston Museum Chiefs: You Smuggled the Raphael," 7 February 1971.

SWAUGER, JAMES L. "In Praise of Forgers," *Carnegie Magazine*, February, 1971, pp. 49–52.

TAUBMAN, HOWARD. "Greater Protection of Asian Art Urged," *NYT*, 22 December 1971.

———. "Sculptures Put on Market Stir Concern for Angkor," *NYT*, 14 March 1972.

*TAYLOR, FRANCIS HENRY. *Babel's Tower: The Dilemma of the Modern Museum* (New York: Columbia University Press, 1945).

———. "The Rape of Europa," *Atlantic*, January, 1945, pp. 52–58.

———. *The Taste of Angels* (Boston: Little, Brown, 1948).

TAYLOR, JOHN RUSSELL, and BROOKE, BRIAN. *The Art Dealers* (New York: Scribner's, 1969).

TAYLOR, ROBERT. "Hub Museum Gold Real, Say Experts," Boston *Globe*, 19 March 1970.

*———. "Gold, Graves and Smugglers, Boston *Globe*, 12 April 1970.

———. "Rueppel's Acquisitions in Dallas Questioned," Boston *Globe*, 27 March 1973.

———. "New MFA Chief States Acquisition Policy," Boston *Globe*, 28 March 1973.

THOMAS, GEORGE B. "Demonstrating the Pot-hunter Factor: Uncontrolled, Selective Treasure-hunting, and Controlled Surface Collection Near Mitla, Oaxaca," paper, Society for American Archeology, annual meeting, Miami Beach, May, 1972.

THOMPSON, EDWARD HERBERT. *People of the Serpent* (New York: Capricorn Books, 1932).

Time. "Angkor Imperiled," 28 February 1972, p. 29.

———. "Japan's Picture Boom," 7 January 1973, p. 37.

———. "Who Painted What?" 29 January 1973, p. 72.

———. "The Met: Beleaguered but Defiant," 26 February 1973, pp. 43–45.

———. "The Ill-Bought Urn," 5 March 1973, pp. 52–54.

*———. "Hot from the Tomb: The Antiquities Racket," 26 March 1973, pp. 93–94.

The Times (London). "Checking Decay on the Acropolis," 18 June 1967.

———. "Metropolitan Museum Queried by Turks on Smuggled Artifacts," 27 August 1970.

———. "Turkish Peasant Arrested in Forged Antiquities Case," 5 August 1971.

The Times (London) *Literary Supplement.* "The Money Is the Message," 26 March 1971.

———. "Art and Mammon," 4 August 1972.

TOMKINS, CALVIN. *Merchants and Masterpieces* (New York: Dutton, 1970).

*TOWNER, WESLEY. *The Elegant Auctioneers* (New York: Hill and Wang, 1970).

TREASTER, JOSEPH B. "Hué Curator Fears for Art Treasures," *NYT*, 22 May 1972.

TREUE, WILHELM. *Art Plunder* (London: Methuen, 1960).

TREVOR-ROPER, HUGH. *The Plunder of the Arts in the Seventeenth Century* (London: Thames and Hudson, 1970).

TRIMBLE, MIKE. "Mayan Relic Is Recovered," *Arkansas Gazette*, 29 January 1972.

TROCHE, MICHEL. "L'Art Maya en France," *France Nouvelle*, 15 February 1967.

TUOHY, WILLIAM. "The Big Business of Bootlegging Antiquities," *International Herald Tribune*, 8 March 1972.

UNITED NATIONS EDUCATIONAL, SCIENTIFIC AND CULTURAL ORGANIZATION (UNESCO). "Recommendation Concerning the Preservation of Cultural Property Endangered by Public and Private Works," adopted by the General Conference at its 15th session, Paris, 19 November 1968.

————. *The Conservation of Cultural Property* (Paris: UNESCO, 1968).

————. "Index of National Legislations on the Protection of Cultural Heritage," Paris, UNESCO, February, 1969.

————. "International Regulations for the Protection of Monuments, Groups of Buildings and Sites," Paris, UNESCO, 21 February 1972.

U.S. DEPARTMENT OF STATE. "Report of the United States Delegation to the Special Committee of Governmental Experts to Examine the Draft Convention on the Means of Prohibiting and Preventing the Illicit Import, Export and Transfer of Ownership of Cultural Property," prepared by Mark B. Fledman, Ronald J. Bettauer, Paris, UNESCO House, 1970.

*U.S. GOVERNMENT. "Convention on Ownership of Cultural Property," Message from the President of the United States," 2 February 1972. [See Appendix]

U.S. SENATE. "Destruction of Artistic and Archeological Heritage," by Senator Harris, *Congressional Record*, 18 June 1970.

"VASARI." "On the Mona Lisa Complex," in "Vasari's Diary," *Art News*, December 1972, p. 18.

VERMEULE, CORNELIUS, III. "The Basel Dog: A Vindication," *American Journal of Archeology*, April, 1968, pp. 95–101.

*VERMEULE, EMILY, and CORNELIUS VERMEULE III. "Aegean Gold Hoard and the Court of Egypt," *Curator*, Winter, 1970, pp. 32–42. (Also in *Illustrated London News*, 21 March 1970, pp. 23–25.)

VRIONI, ALI. "Still Time to Save Venice," *The UNESCO Courier*, December, 1968, pp. 4–9.

WALKER, JOHN. "How I Didn't Get Mr. Gulbenkian's Art," *Horizon*, Summer, 1970, pp. 29–43.

*———. "Secrets of a Museum Director," *Atlantic*, February, 1972, pp. 73–84.

———. "Let's Trade the Van Dyck and the Rembrandt for the Giorgione: The Inside Story of the Mellon Art Collection," *Atlantic*, December, 1972, pp. 68–87.

WALTER, RICHARD. "Undersea Treasure Stolen," New York *Post*, 30 September, 1971.

———. "F.B.I. Move in Greek Art Row," *The Observer* (London), 25 February 1973.

———. "$1 Million Vase: Magistrate Goes to Looted Tomb," *The Observer* (London), 3 March 1973.

WARDWELL, ALLEN. "The Ethics of Acquisition: Another Museum Dilemma," unpublished paper, 1973.

WELLES, BENJAMIN. "U.S. Acts to Bar the Import of Treasures Plundered from Mayan and Other Sites," *NYT*, 30 May 1971.

———. "Bill May Help to Safeguard Mayan Art Works from Theft," *NYT*, 25 October 1972.

*WHITEHALL, WALTER MUIR. *Museum of Fine Arts Boston: A Centennial History* (Cambridge: University Press, 1970).

*WILLIAMS, STEPHEN. "Destruction in the Name of Art," *Harvard Today*, March, 1972, pp. 2–5.

———. "Death and Destruction in the Name of Art," reprint of above article plus "Appendix" by Peabody Museum (Harvard University), Rules for the Acquisition of Art Objects, 1972.

———. "Ripping Off the Past," *Saturday Review Science*, October, 1972, pp. 44–53.

WILSON, JOHN A. *Signs and Wonders upon Pharaoh* (Chicago: University of Chicago Press, 1964).

———. *Thousands of Years* (New York: Scribner's, 1972).

WOODHOUSE, C. M. *The Philhellenes* (London: Hodder and Stoughton, 1969).

WRAIGHT, ROBERT. *The Art Game* (London: Leslie Frewin, 1965).

*ZELLE, ANN. "Acquisitions: Saving Whose Heritage?" *Museum News*, April, 1971, pp. 19–26.

*———. "ICOM Ethics of Acquisitions: A Report to the Profession," *Museum News*, April, 1972, pp. 31–33.

INDEX

Acropolis, 179–80; *see also* Elgin Marbles
African art, 13, 23, 144*n*
Agnew, Geoffrey, 5
air pollution (and deterioration of art), 82, 121, 122, 180, 208
Akurgal, Ekrem, 182
Alamilla, George, 33*n*
Alba, Victor: *The Mexicans*, 184
Alpha, George (pseudonym of dealer), 15–16, 19, 40–41
Alsop, Joseph, 131, 168–69
American Association of Museums, 75*n*, 104*n*
American Indian sites and art, xiv, 8–11, 197–203
American Journal of Archaeology: Bass article, 74
American Numismatic Society: Metropolitan Museum coins, 91*n*, 94, 95
American Society of International Law: Panel on the International Movement of Art Treasures, 43, 166–67
Andrews, E. Willys, 39
Angkor Wat (Cambodia), 207–08
Antalya Museum (Turkey), 59
Antiquity: Bass article, 74
Vermeule article, 76
Apamea (Syria), 194*n*

Archaeological Institute of America, 75*n*
meeting (1972), 92, 93, 94, 95
Archaeological Museum (Heraklion, Crete), 131
Archaeological Museum (Istanbul), 59, 60
Archaeological Museum (Mainamati, Bangla Desh), 8
archaeologists, 37, 40, 70, 73, 74; *see also* specific individuals
Archaeometry, 113
Arroyo Pesquero (Mex.): Olmec site, 146–47
Art Dealers Association: Metropolitan Museum sales condemned by, 53
Artemis Fund, 160–61
Art Institute of Chicago, 51, 78–79
art inventory, 80, 101, 106
Italy, 101, 151–52
Museum Computer Network, 106–07
pre-Columbian sites (theft and destruction), 38–39
U.S.—National Register of archaeological sites, 202
art investment firms, 160–61
The Art Journal, 39
art market, 80–81, 81*n*
African art, 13, 144*n*

353

KARL E. MEYER

A third-generation journalist, Karl E. Meyer was born in Madison, Wisconsin, and attended the University of Wisconsin. At Princeton University he received a Ph.D. in politics and a Master of Public Affairs degree from the Woodrow Wilson School of Public and International Affairs. After teaching at Princeton, he joined the staff of the Washington *Post* in 1956.

Mr. Meyer was an editorial writer and chief of the London and New York bureaus during fifteen years on the Washington *Post*. He was among the handful of reporters who interviewed Fidel Castro in the Sierra Maestra during the Cuban Revolution. From 1961 to 1965 he was Washington correspondent of the *New Statesman*, and also covered the 1972 presidential campaign for that English weekly.

While on a reporting trip through Latin America in 1959, Mr. Meyer became interested in archaeology. This led to *The Pleasures of Archaeology* (1970). In the course of writing it, he became aware of the international illicit market in antiquities. In 1971, he resigned from the Washington *Post* to carry out a full-scale inquiry. Three installments of *The Plundered Past* appeared in *The New Yorker*. Mr. Meyer makes his home in Connecticut.